Biography, Identity and Schooling: Episodes in Educational Research

Biography, Identity and Schooling: Episodes in Educational Research

Ivor F. Goodson and Rob Walker

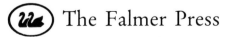 The Falmer Press

(A member of the Taylor & Francis Group)
London • New York • Philadelphia

UK   The Falmer Press, Rankine Road, Basingstoke, Hampshire, RG24 0PR

USA   The Falmer Press, Taylor & Francis Inc., 1900 Frost Road, Suite 101, Bristol, PA 19007

First published 1991

Library of Congress Cataloging-in-Publication Data—
Available on request

Library of Congress Cataloging-in-Publication Data

Goodson, Ivor.
     Biography, identity, and schooling : episodes in educational research / Ivor F. Goodson and Rob Walker.
     p.   cm.
     Includes bibliographical references and index.
     ISBN 1–85000–801–9 : ISBN 1–85000–802–7 (pbk.)
     1. Educational sociology—Great Britain. 2. Curriculum change—Great Britain. 3. Education—Research—Great Britain. 4. Teaching. I. Walker, Rob. II. Title.
LC191.8.G7G66   1990   90–41511
370'.7'8041—dc20   CIP

Jacket design by Caroline Archer

Typeset in 11/13 pt Garamond
by Graphicraft Typesetters Ltd. HK
Printed and bound in Great Britain by
Burgess Science Press
Basingstoke

Contents

Contents

Acknowledgments

To Clem Adelman who was part-author of an earlier version of Chapter 1; Barry MacDonald and Caroline Pick part-authors of Chapter 5; Saville Kushner who co-authored Chapter 13. Dennis Thiessen, Marshall Mangan and Valerie Rhea for reading and commenting on drafts and chapters.

Colleagues
Those at CARE, the University of Sussex, Deakin University and the University of Western Ontario who shared in the work, and those teachers who participated in the various research projects reported here. Also the following who, at various times sponsored our research: Ford Foundation, the Social Science Research Council (UK), the Social Science and Humanities Research Council (Canada), the National Science Foundation, the Nuffield Foundation, and the University Excellence Fund (Canada).

Acknowledgments

How does one deal with such a dismal field and meet even modest expectations to be interesting?

John Goodlad on *Curriculum* (in an address to a conference)

The field of curriculum is moribund ... [and] it has reached this unhappy state by inveterate, unexamined and mistaken reliance on theory.... Theory, by its very character, does not and cannot take account of all the matters which are crucial to questions of what, who and how to teach. [The important questions] are concerned with this student, in that school, on the south side of Columbus, with principal Jones during the present mayoralty of Ed. Tweed and in view of the probability of his re-election.

J.L. Schwab (1978)

While it may come decked out in political flags of various hues, or the latest in macrame or high tech parachute silk, classroom teaching will always be a conservative art ...

David McCrae (1988)

A complication of a different order arises from the fact that communities in general, perhaps especially American communities, have chosen to use the schools as repositories for certain ideals.... Among these ideals are those avowed moral principles which the majority of adults more or less disavow for themselves but want others to practice; they are ideals for the helpless, ideals for children and for teachers. There are other ideals which are nearly out of print, because people do not believe in them any more. Though most adults have left such ideals behind, they are not willing to discard them finally. The school must keep them alive. The school must serve as a museum of virtue.

Willard Waller (1932), *The Sociology of Teaching*

More important ... we must finally realize that the concept of rationality has no general scientific power (being ideological) to account for more or less powerful forms of cognition, the efficacy of shooling or anything else. Instead it must be seen for what it is, a taken-for-granted tenet in terms of which the world is seen by jpfs* and cognitive researchers alike. Under these circumstances it is difficult to defend claims for the universality of 'rational' models of good thinking as a scientific yardstick with which to evaluate situated cognitive activities. This may be put more strongly: constructing research in terms of mythological views of scientific thought insures blindness to questions of the structuring of everyday activities themselves.

* 'just plain-folks'

Jean Lave (1988)

On Academics:

He sensed that what distressed him was a gap which had opened up between thought and feeling, the remoteness, the impartiality of his friends to the subjects they were teaching or studying. Objectivity, he had to agree with them, was important obviously. But what was required he had declared ... was 'a passionate objectivity (whatever that might be)'.

J.G. Farrell, *The Singapore Grip*

The first forty years of life furnish the text while the remaining thirty supply the commentary; without the commentary we are unable to understand aright the true sense and coherence of the text, together with the moral it contains.

Arthur Schopenhauer

Preface

We both studied at the London School of Economics in the 1960s, at a time when the consensus among sociologists about what constituted sociological study was just beginning to face a methodological crisis that was partly of its own making. The previous decade had seen the emergence of a series of related studies which had revealed the effects of educational selection (the '11+') upon equity of provision. A major outcome from this research was the emergence of comprehensive secondary schooling as a key Labour party policy, a policy that was first implemented in the late 1950s and early 1960s, initially by Labour controlled authorities and then, following a central government directive in 1965, across the country.

The 'crisis' for sociology existed at a number of levels. On the one hand the previous generation of research had achieved its objective in terms of changing the organization of secondary schooling. Yet there was some sense of unease that all was not well in the comprehensive system. A number of small scale studies suggested that the key variables of social class and educational attainment remained critically associated even in the context of an 'open' system. However, it proved difficult to find ways of doing research which investigated the processes of schooling because the methodologies that were generally accepted lacked the ability to look inside schools and classrooms and to investigate curricula. Sociologists were mostly restricted, as one of us wrote at the time, 'to standing outside the school gates counting as children from different social class backgrounds came and went through different doors'.

In the early 1960s, while we were students of orthodox sociology, there were signs of alternative approaches emerging in the margins. Basil Bernstein's work at the Institute of Education, which recurs throughout this book as a touchstone, was the most important. Lawrence Stenhouse, through his work in curriculum, presented a more radical challenge, which rejected the claims of sociology, or even of social science in the new educational context. Stuart Hall, who showed how cultural analysis could be applied to the analysis of schooling, talked about the impact of the media on education and suggested that criminology could provide research methods (notably participant observation), which might be applied to the study of schooling: Harold Silver, who pointed to silences in the history of curriculum and began an assault on accepted positions in teacher education. There were other voices, but these four stood out for us in the early 1960s, perhaps in part because we studied with each of them at one time or another, because they knew each other, and because each was, at that time, part of an emerging phase of intellectual and cultural life.

The 1970s saw many of their ideas realized. Research in the sociology of education changed quite dramatically, accelerated by the publication of the first Open University courses in the late 1960s, racing through a succession of 'new frontiers' (a common term in book titles of the time). Symbolic interactionist studies were succeeded in turn by ethnomethodological, phenomenological, neo-marxist, structuralist, feminist, post-structuralist and post-modern analyses. Each year, it seemed, a new generation of students would emerge speaking a new language.

Just as the desert blooms before the drought, the 1980s saw a dramatic turn in political events and the fruits of this flowering turned bitter. Expansion in education turned to contraction, the curriculum development movement lost its oppositional voice and moved inside the bureaucracy to become the 'national curriculum', and sociology of education itself was substantially eroded as universities became more clearly focussed as training agencies for the state.

One of our shared memories of sociology in the early 1960s is the series of books known to us by their common cover design as the 'blue tombstones'. Indeed, it is said by some that Routledge and Kegan Paul's 'International Library of Sociology and Social Reconstruction' kept sociology alive in Britain through the two decades following World War II. We believe that, currently, in the specific sense in which we are concerned, sociology has reached an impasse and that there is a need to use books to re-enter the discourse of social reconstruction.

The world of publishing has changed, just as has the world of education, and some may see this book as purely nostalgic, the terminal ramblings of a lost generation. We are acutely conscious of our weakness in this regard (witness the record shelves at home), but our intention in looking back is to search for new ways of looking forward. We write at a time when educational research in Britain has virtually been captured by the drive towards the National Curriculum and vocationalism, when teacher education has become teacher training, and when universities have lost sense of any direction beyond the need to respond to their own managers. It may be true that we write from the margins about the past, but we do so without nostalgia. Our intention is to retrace footsteps, to pick up pieces we may have discarded in our haste, to search for hidden turns. By going back we hope to see where we have been, to relocate ourselves and plan future routes, projects and campaigns.

By providing evidence of an enduring search for alternative paradigms we have deliberately chosen a range of essays which reflect our collaborative quest over the past two decades. These essays therefore allow the reader to engage with the twists and turns, often contradictory and sometimes fruitless, through which any intellectual quest must proceed.

The mainstream paradigms from which we are in reaction are only critiqued in passing. Our starting point in the messy complexity of the classroom should indicate where our concerns lie, where the reaction began and where ultimately we should always return. But in the process we have sought to generate a model which not only embraces the immediate and partially apprehendable practice of the classroom but which provides some purchase on struggles over the 'parameters to practice'. In a sense, new initiatives in national curriculum in both England and Australia have made our argument for us — all too clearly we require a research paradigm which provides a social constructionist perspective at the level of both interactive realization and preactive definitions.

To capture such a complex conundrum as educational practice at the multiple levels at which it is conceived and produced requires that we connect ourselves not only to a long-run investigation of the 'surface realities' but also to the 'deep structures' of schooling. The common reaction against work from a previous decade in educational research is in itself a symptom of deeper malaise, an obsessive presentism which takes each new reform or initiatives as 'news without precedent'. Kliebard (1975) has argued rightly in our view, that in curriculum studies

> The urge to do good is so immediate, so direct and so overwhelming that there has been virtually no toleration of the kind of long-range research that has an immediate value to practioners. (p. 65)

Preface

This concern with immediacy leads educational researchers to conduct an endless search for the latest news. Presentism, is therefore allied to a very narrowly defined concept of 'usefulness'. As Bernstein (1974) has noted, with regard to sociology, 'the news of much contemporary socio- logy appears to be news about the conditions necessary for creating acceptable news' (p. 145).

In our view, much educational study is therefore constantly moving in the wrong direction. For educational research is more like anthropological fieldwork and theorizing: work is conducted over a long period and the researcher hurries backwards and forwards be- tween the field and his or her notebooks. The collaborative search is often for the enduring features of schooling and for the fundamental continuities which the prevalent concern with 'news' and 'numbers' does so much to obscure.

Episodes in Educational Research

The theme of this book is a simple one. It consists of a restatement of the central role that people[1] play in the educational process and in educational systems. Put like this it sounds a trivial idea, certainly not one worth book-length exposition, but we'd like to remind the reader that the word 'trivial' is itself a significant curriculum word. The 'trivium' was the central (perhaps the word 'core' is more appropriate) curriculum of medieval times. Literally it signified the 'three ways' of knowing: rhetoric, grammar and logic. It meant, in other words, not as it tends to mean now, 'that which is not worth knowing' but, on the contrary, 'that which you could take for granted would be known to an educated person'.

At a time when curriculum issues are increasingly treated as merely questions of political reach and administrative grasp, we make no apologies for restating the significance of persons in the educational process. We do so, not in a spirit of romanticism, but in order to counter the view that educational questions can be reduced to fit the scope of systems-thinking. The challenge for schools and school systems is not the implementation of centrally conceived policy, but the need to make policy respond to the educational potential of practice.

In this sense this book is less positivist in orientation than it might at first appear. It is true that we begin with studies of classroom interaction that have a strongly empirical character. We begin, too, with a respect for evidence, almost believing that recording the facts alone will itself make the world a better place. But even by the end of the first chapter a note of hesitation emerges. The fruits of empiricism turn out not to be signs of an emerging utopia, but the reduction of educational experience to the status of a commodity. As John Berger (1982) has written in a different context:

What sustained — [positivism as a practice] — was the belief that observable, quantifiable facts, recorded by scientists and experts, would one day offer man such a total knowledge about nature and society that he would be able to order them both. Precision would replace subjectivity, and all that was dark and hidden in the soul would be illuminated by empirical knowledge.

... Yet the positivist utopia was not achieved. And the world today is less controllable by experts who have mastered what they believe to be its mechanisms, than it was in the nineteenth century.

What *was* achieved was unprecedented scientific and technical progress and, eventually, the subordination of all other values to those of a world market which treats everything, including people and their labours and their lives and their deaths, as a commodity. The unachieved positivist utopia became, instead, the global system of late capitalism wherein all that exists becomes quantifiable — not simply because it *can be* reduced to a statistical fact, but also because it *has been* reduced to a commodity. (p. 99)

In the first chapter of this book we present an empirical study of teaching, and in what follows we try to escape from the truth of Berger's compelling rhetoric. We could have provided a more comprehensive view of current trends in educational research, but to do so would have been dishonest. If we, as persons, are to repossess the educational process we have to begin from self-recognition. Not, we hasten to add in the form of self-indulgent 'humanism', but out of self-respect and an urgent need for honesty. This book is personal, but we hope it is not, as a result, boring or even worse pedantic. The conventions of academic writing make little allowance either for honesty or for compelling reading, but we have tried.

We have brought together these essays written over the past twenty years because of their common preoccupations and assumptions. Though the reader will find that there are distinct shifts of style and changes of audience, they are held together by biography and history. As authors we belong to the same generation, we have had different but parallel experiences and, despite stylistic sleight of hand, have come to realize that what we have written is deeply autobiographical. This may not be immediately obvious to the reader, it certainly wasn't to the writers for a long period of time. Over the period of our collaboration we have only slowly worked to the surface the shared nature of our value position. We have 'watched' each other in professional practice but as we assembled this book we realized that more significantly we have 'watched' each other teach, live our lives, marry, bring up children, buy homes, choose schools, go into hospital, worry about ailing parents, support political parties and football teams, gossip about colleagues. At this stage (we are both 45) we have a sense of where we stand. At the moment, as we both experience settling in new countries, this sense of assessing where we stand is perhaps artificially heightened.

This may seem self-indulgent, but we have come to realize that with regard to our research, the value of our lives as lived is an integral part of the way we view our work, of the focus of that work, of the methodologies and perspectives chosen and deployed in the research studies reported here. Our focus on the personal nature of action and interaction is chosen not so as to concentrate on the individual act of 'history making' but rather as a grounded point of access into broader social contexts and structures. What is true for the writer is also true for the reader: at root we believe that what is personal is the most meaningful means of access into understandings of these wider domains — a sequence which holds where our concerns are methodological or, so to speak, pedagogical.

We sense too, that the present moment is significant in the context of educational change. The curriculum reform movement of the 1960s and 1970s has been replaced by more invasive, legislated, political and administrative actions. In orienting ourselves to changed conditions we need to assess how we came to be here and what we need to rescue from the wreckage.

The reader will find here a collection of essays that are about teaching, about research on teaching and about curriculum issues. They treat teaching and research as similar activities in that they share a concern with pedagogy, and in that they are both activities that are located within educational organizations and institutions.

There is a particular missing dimension in what we have written for we would like to have included policy and administration as a third element, with teaching and research, as a key theme in this collection. The perceptive reader will detect these concerns at some points in what we have written, but it is a theme that mostly remains hidden because, at the end of the day we felt that questions about teaching and curriculum were more pressing, more complex and more often neglected.

We begin with a sequence of studies that reveal how our position emerged. The chapter titled 'Classroom Identities' was first written as a seminar paper for a graduate student seminar series organized by Basil Bernstein at the London Institute of Education. The influence of Bernstein's work, which at the time was shifting from a research concern with sociolinguistic to curriculum questions, is clearly reflected in the style, language, conceptualization and approach of this paper, where we argue that there are inextricable connections between curriculum and pedagogy; between teaching and learning and between being a teacher and being a pupil, using language as an indicator of these connections.

The second chapter, 'Humour in the Classroom', builds on the first. We wrote it together on the basis of conversations about the first paper and the experience of recording on film a range of classroom pedagogical experiments in various schools in England, but particularly Countesthorpe in Leicestershire, (where Ivor was a humanities teacher), and Fairlop Girls' School in the London Borough of Redbridge, (where Rob spent a year as a research student). The style of analysis and presentation remain academic and even sociological, though it was clear to both of us that it was becoming more and more difficult to say what we wanted to say within such a framework. Both these chapters owe a debt to Clem Adelman who was a colleague of Rob's at the Centre for Science Education in London.

Chapter 3, 'Stations', marks a further development in this sequence of work. The same ideas are pursued, but the frame is a different one, borrowed less from sociology and being more directly influenced by the curriculum development movement, and particularly by ideas from the field of evaluation. It is significant that it was written at a time when Robert Stake was in England on study leave, and developing his notion of 'portrayal' as a legitimate activity of educational evaluation (Stake, 1972), and when Clem Adelman and John Elliott were working on the Ford Teaching Project. The style and presentation of this paper show all the signs of 'paradigm shift' — the search for forms that make it possible to say things that do not fit easily into existing frames.

Chapter 4 returns to some of the main themes that have emerged in this sequence of papers but attempts to address teachers and 'teaching' in a more direct manner. Ivor writes about confrontations in style and behaviour between teachers and students in a way that starts from the same typical patterns of classroom interaction, within which humour is again seen as a prominent theme.

Chapter 5, 'Other Rooms, Other Voices', marks a further shift, this time in audience. Instead of assuming an audience of researchers, an attempt is made here to talk directly, free of theory, jargon or prescription. The material was originally collected at a weekend conference for twenty science teachers and handed to a scriptwriter to develop as a radio play. Again, Stake's influence is apparent here, and that of Clem Adelman, Harold Silver, Hans Brugelman and Barry Macdonald who helped run the conference. Later, in Chapter 10, Ivor Goodson picks up the discussion of attempts to provide 'theory-free' accounts of practice and develops a more critical view.

The chapter that follows (Chapter 6), 'Social Research as a Deviant Activity', is a attempt to think through the implications of the shift in research methods and approaches marked here by the 'Stations' paper.

'Social Research as a Deviant Activity' marks an attempt to talk to sociologists, this time at one of the now defunct Westhill College Sociology of Education Conferences. In a conference that was concerned with deviancy, it attempted to look at the nature of research itself. Strongly influenced by the autobiographical writings of a number of social anthropologists it attempts to relate biography and autobiography and to stimulate a degree of reflection and reflexiveness among researchers. Researching deviancy, we claimed, it itself a deviant activity and we ought to examine out own motives and aspirations as well as those of our subjects.

Chapter 7, 'Making Sense and Losing Meaning', was written for a conference organized by Barry Macdonald and Rob Walker in Cambridge in 1979. Known among evaluators as 'Cambridge 2' this was one of a sequence of workshops, funded by the Nuffield Foundation, which developed ideas about the use of qualitative methods in educational evaluation. This paper was developed from conversations with Howard Becker and others during the conference. A report on the conference can be found in Adelman, Jenkins and Kemmis (1976) and a series of papers (including this one) in Simons (1980).

Chapter 8 introduces a further element into the story; the significance of history. To this point we have followed symbolic interactionist assumptions and have written about identities, interactions, events and experiences, as though their historical context was of little account. This chapter marks a significant development in the argument, attempting to place what we have said in terms, not just of personal history, but as a means of grasping historical features of a somewhat more structural kind. The difficulty all the time, is not one of reaching for structural theory, which, in some sense, is easy to do, but of locating structural points of reference in order to retain a sense of the integrity of persons — both researchers and researched.

In Chapters 9 and 10 Ivor Goodson draws on the ideas and

themes of this book in order to develop the need for theory in the curriculum field. These chapters set out much of our thinking in the context of mainstream thinking about curriculum, but it also points to some forward directions for research. One of these is the specification of an historical need; the need 'to know where existing curricula come from'. Another requirement is for a degree of specificity about schools, subjects, teachers and students. A third requirement is for kinds of theory that contain the space to consider individual human action.

In Chapter 12, however, we have tried to address these requirements more closely. This chapter which was jointly written with Saville Kushner, who played a major role in the study from which it is drawn, is extracted from the summary section of an evaluation report which attempts to 'theorize' about curriculum in ways that are specific to cases, and takes account of system level factors. The study as a whole also approaches structural features of the society through the biographies and experience of individuals. The kind of theory that emerges is 'local' and 'grounded' and its primary referents are to curriculum and change theories, rather than to educational sociology. It may be that we need to distinguish between the kinds and the purposes of theory and theorizing and further of substituting discussion of policy for thinking about theory. This is a point we pick up in the concluding chapter. In this final chapter our concern is to indicate some access points for the development of educational research and theory.

Note

1 Given our preface, it needs to be said that our view of 'the person' is social and cultural more than psychological (see, for instance Fletcher, 1975).

Chapter 1

Classroom Identities[1]

Rob Walker

During the 1960s and 1970s a large number of curriculum development projects and programs were established in countries throughout the world. In Britain one of the largest and most influential was the Nuffield Science Teaching Project, a wide ranging program which attempted both to modernize curriculum content and implement discovery approaches to science teaching. This chapter emerged from an early attempt to evaluate the classroom implications of the Nuffield Science Teaching Project.

An obvious way to do this was to observe a range of Nuffield science classes but initial and unsystematic observations of a number of science classes adopting Nuffield Science showed that the use of the terms 'Nuffield' and 'traditional' science teaching, while they were used extensively by curriculum developers and by teachers, did not seem to relate to what happened in the classroom. Some 'traditional' (or perhaps better, 'non-Nuffield') classes appeared to be working in ways that were similar to those apparently suggested by *Nuffield Guides*; such classes involved a large amount of experimental work, some of it conceived by the pupils, and on topics similar to those suggested in the guides. On the other hand, classes that professed to be 'doing Nuffield' sometimes appeared very conventional. Many of the curriculum development teams would joke about the 'Nuffield' teacher who taught the whole course by dictating notes to the class. (While the alternative exams devised to assess the Nuffield courses were designed to discourage this kind of adaptation there was some doubt about the extent to which the alternative exam papers really demanded different forms of classroom practice.)

As the Nuffield Science project/publications became more familiar to teachers, 'Nuffield' and 'non-Nuffield' classes became more and more difficult to distinguish and the categories more and more blurred, and curriculum development staff began to make informal distinctions between exemplary practice ('true' or 'real' Nuffield Science), and notional or nominal adoption of the projects (using the Nuffield materials but 'not really a Nuffield lesson').

It is important to emphasize that this observation, which some saw as a 'dilution of the Nuffield spirit' is not made here in a spirit of criticism. There is no doubt that important curriculum changes occurred as a result of Nuffield Science and indeed some might argue that the fact that Nuffield was not adopted in a 'pure' form accords more closely with the Project's ideals, than if it has been implemented uncritically and unadapted to local conditions and circumstances. I make the point simply to establish, in the context of classroom research, that the use of terms like 'Nuffield' and 'traditional', while they might usefully distinguish ideal types of science teaching or sets of ideas or assumptions or values held about science education, do not adequately distinguish the events to be observed in classrooms any more than terms like 'discovery methods', 'enquiry' or 'student-centred classes'.

The range of things you might encounter in any classroom to which one of these labels is attached are considerably greater than the differences each label indicates. Classroom events are not easily demarcated, labelled or described as the use of the labels seems to indicate. More specificity is required. It does not make much sense to say, 'This is a Nuffield Science lesson', but you can say it is a 'first year class following the Combined Science Project', or that 'It is a class using the Biology Guides as a basis for introductory genetics'. Even then you need a good bit more information before you can begin to build up a picture of what you might be likely to see if you were to observe the class at work. You need to know how the teacher has organized the tasks, what she/he is hoping to achieve in a particular lesson, what resources/materials/equipment are available and how they are used, how the lesson fits into the teacher's overall intentions for this class over a period of weeks or even longer. You might also want background information on the school, is it selective? Co-educational? Mixed race? And perhaps information on the teacher, what is her subject specialism, training, experience? When we once tried to list the kinds of questions that student teachers might want to ask before they went to observe lessons taught by teachers who were involved, one way or another, in the NSTP, we came up with a list several pages long (Walker and Adelman, 1975, pp. 13–16).

It seems perhaps a simple point to make, but the conditions that influence what goes on in the classroom are many and complex, no single variable is likely to distinguish adequately between different kinds of teaching. Classroom research has generated a large number of sophisticated observational methods but any evaluation that attempts to make use of these methods within a design that hinges on making a distinction between 'Nuffield' and 'non-Nuffield' classes is in danger of misusing the power of available research.

Neither is the definition of 'Nuffield' Science itself at all clear. I once spent several months assembling material in the hope of clarifying what the term stood for, but having collected the material I found it virtually impossible to use. I resorted, in the end, to a form of collage, a way of organizing the various definitions and descriptions that were available that was more like a musical score than a clear and unambiguous statement of an educational philosophy (Walker, 1973).

It is one thing to criticize commonsense evaluation models, but another to create an alternative. Given the brief (by the Project) of reporting on the changes in classroom roles implied by Nuffield Science, it seemed to me that what was needed was a better language for talking about what was happening in the classroom. A language that had some of the rigours of research but was accessible to, and usable by, teachers. I began by observing a range of classrooms, Nuffield and non-Nuffield, science and not-science in order to find words for talking about the variety of things I encountered.

A key distinction that emerged early on in this attempt to re-orientate my thinking was the distinction between what I called 'formal' and 'informal' classroom situations. These terms have since come to be used somewhat loosely, especially in the debates that followed publication of Neville Bennett's study (Bennett *et al.*, 1976), but I used them in a quite specific sense. Essentially, by 'formal' classroom situations I meant situations where there was, at any one time, only one speaker and every one else was a listener. Formal situations would therefore include the teacher lecturing to the class, class 'discussion', teacher questioning of pupils in the context of whole class teaching, and the whole class watching a demonstration experiment. I used the term 'informal' to describe situations where there was more than [one] speaker and where any individual (teacher or pupil) only had partial access to what was being said. Informal situations would therefore include various kinds of group and project work, 'circus' arrangements (as in Secondary Science for example), and many individualized learning schemes.

I have described these categories in more detail elsewhere (Walker, 1971, pp. 149–180; Walker and Adelman, 1975, pp. 38–71). I want to emphasize here that I am not offering this distinction as replacement for the terms 'Nuffield' and 'traditional' in the sense that I think all Nuffield classes are likely to be informal, and all traditional classes formal. Most classes will operate in *both* the formal and the informal mode within any one lesson, and over a sequence of lessons there may well be significant shifts in the use made of each type of activity. Nor do the terms imply any necessary overlap with enquiry, discovery or instructional modes. What I do claim is that the terms 'formal' and 'informal' distinguish types of interaction and activity that are qualitatively different. They are different in that they require different kinds of action and activity on the part of pupils and teachers. What is an appropriate action in an informal mode may well be inappropriate within a formal mode. The terms formal and informal do not simply distinguish different ways of organizing a class but relate to different kinds of social communication structures, which in turn, involve different roles and, perhaps, different kinds of learning.

The rest of this chapter attempts to follow this assertion through some of the empirical data that emerged from attempts to observe in classes which seemed to typify the distinctions between predominantly 'formal' and predominantly 'informal' forms of classroom organization.

The Meanings Communicated by Talk

At this point I want to shift the angle of approach. In the previous paragraph I asserted that there were important and significant qualitative differences between formal and informal forms of classroom organization. I want now to go back to the research that lay behind that assertion and to describe how it was I came to realize its importance.

One of the first classes I observed in detail was a low stream, fourth year group in a North London boys' secondary modern school. I was first directed to this class by a colleague, who before joining the Nuffield Secondary Science Project had been head of science at the school. What had intrigued him had been a teacher who taught this particular class for about half of the timetable. He taught not only science, but English, maths, social studies and RE. This was not the normal timetable arrangement for remedial classes (which were not specifically recognized as such) but the preference of the teacher, who felt that if he was to get anywhere with this class he had to teach them for more than the few periods a week allocated to science. Moreover, this arrangement had built up over a few years, so that by the fourth year, teacher and class knew each other extremely well. In a school that prided itself on its academic achievements (it was one of those secondary modern schools with exceptional 'O' level pass rates, especially in science), most of the school were happy for one teacher to take what was seen as a 'difficult' class off their hands. I was directed to this teacher because my colleague thought him an exceptional teacher. During a conversation about the nature of the 'Nuffield Approach' he had said to me, 'If you could only find out what makes him tick we would be in a much better position to know what we are doing'. Well I cannot claim that I ever succeeded in finding out what exactly what made this teacher so exceptional in the eyes of his colleagues, but I did start by looking closely at what actually happened in his lessons.

Here I want to consider one aspect of this teacher's classes, the use of humour. This related to the starting point I have just outlined in that an LEA (local education authority) adviser told me that what characterized the teacher (and some other teachers he thought of as 'good' or 'exceptional') was the quality of the relationships they had with those they taught. 'It is all about good relationships', he advised me, 'everything else follows from that'. While I did not want to foreclose on the possibility that good relationships were a consequence of effective teaching/learning rather than a necessary and sufficient prior cause, I had to admit that one of the things that dominated my observations was that this classroom was a pleasant place to be. It was ordered and hard working, and it was rare to hear a raised voice or any sign of anger or tension. There was also quite a lot of joking and laughter. I began to listen more closely to what it was that the class found amusing.

Example

> *Pupil A*: (Working through text exercises in English) Business is brisk when this is roaring ...? Trade.
> *Teacher*: Roaring trade — I don't quite know the origin of this. It may be —
> *Pupil B*: Lion tamer.
> *Teacger*: Lion tamer? (pause) Roaring trade (pause). Oh very witty, very witty.

This example is I think quite straightforward, an example of pure wit deriving from a play on words, almost a Christmas cracker joke. The teacher's response is interesting for he makes a performance out of it, seeming to delay the joke to draw it out, acknowledging the joke eventually by recourse to mock sarcasm. And this should not be thought of as diversion from the curriculum, in some ways it is closer to what the teacher is trying to teach than the exercise itself, for one of his major concerns is to encourage the boys' confidence in the use of the spoken word and to give them some sense of complexity and history of usage.

I referred to the first example as 'pure' wit, because the joke emerges intact from the transcript, but the humour was not always so transparently context free. Another example from the same lesson:

Teacher: What is a couplet? If it has got 'et' on the end, it means what?
Pupil A: A little.
Teacher: Little what?
Pupil A: Couple.
Teacher: A little couple, or a little pair. A little pair or couple of ... (Looking hard at C.) ... sentences or expressions (Pause) C., we know ... (laughter)

This illustrates what is a classic form of pupil joke, picking up in the teacher's usage inadvertent connotations, particularly those involving sexual innuendo. Like the first example it reveals the indeterminacy of meanings, for in what appears to be a straightforward, almost scripted exercise unintended meanings can be released by the use of quite subtle shifts and emphases.

One of the reasons both jokes are seen as funny is that they provide unexpected and bizarre shifts in meaning in what seems, superficially at least, to be a highly determinate series of utterances. It is as though the talk simultaneously carries a whole series of different levels of meaning which, most of the time, are dominated by relatively surface commonsense meanings intended by the speaker. In the perceptions of the listener however, it is possible to tune to other messages, carried by voice tone, phrasing or simply triggered by association. What is needed to make jokes like this work is some sharing of that process. The jokes function as sparks which short-circuit the insulation between commonsense intended meanings and other possibilities inherent in talk.

As most of know from our own experience, this is a process, which once released in a group can develop at a rapid rate, and most teachers learn ways to control it. This teacher tends to rely on being a step ahead of the game, and on turning the joke back in such a way that the joke itself becomes a joke; his joke. The first example I think illustrates this means of regaining control quite effectively, though it is important to remember (and this is a point we shall return to in the next chapter) that it is in one sense a dangerous game to play, for once having let jokes enter classroom discourse, the teacher can never quite be sure of total control over the process.

The two examples that follow also rely for their effect on the fact that it is impossible to communicate more than one meaning simultaneously. They differ from the two examples given already in that they are less transparent in transcript, the reader needing additional information that was available to those present at the time if they are to catch the full meaning of what was said.

Example

> *Teacher*:   Right, will you all sit down. Plumb, I can't tell if you are sitting or not. (laughter)

Example

> *Teacher*:   'Personification' is when you take something which hasn't got a body, or something visible (pause) something abstract and you sort of clothe it in flesh or being. You make a person out of it. In primary school when they have these sort of plays, like about the Good Fairy. They have someone who comes in and says 'I am the Fairy of Truth, and whoever follows me will do well'. And this person is the personification of truth. Then you get someone come in and say, 'I am wickedness. . . .' You remember these things? Alan, which one were you (pause) 'I am appetite?' (laughter)

These jokes rely to some extent for their effect on the fact that the participants know that Plumb is the smallest boy in the class and that Alan has a reputation for being the greediest. They are examples of the teacher assigning roles/identities to individuals, perhaps in part for control puposes. (See, for instance Louis Smith's account of how the role of 'court jester' emerged in one class, quoted in Chapter 2.)

All the jokes quoted so far were freely available to an observer, I could laugh too; but there were some jokes that were not so obvious. For example in one lesson the teacher was listening to the boys take turns to read out loud to the class short essays they had written for homework on the subject of 'Prisons'. After one boy had finished reading out his rather obviously skimped piece of work, the teacher sighed and said, somewhat crossly:

> *Teacher*:   Wilson, we'll have to put you away if you don't change your ways and do your homework. Is that all you have done?
> *Pupil*:   Strawberries, strawberries. (Laughter)

After the lesson I asked the teacher and some of the pupils why this was funny. They told me that one of the teacher's favourite expressions was that their work was 'like strawberries — good as far as it goes, but it doesn't last nearly long enough'. The reason I had not heard it before was that it was a remark the teacher had not used for a long time, but the pupils remembered it, and indeed part of what made the joke so amusing to them was that a pupil had seen just the right context in which to place it, as it were beating the teacher to the draw.

For those who see the essentials of teaching in the transmission of knowledge this incident might seem trivial and irrelevant, because in terms of institutional objectives it functions as a diversion and is peripheral to the main purpose of the lesson. I want, through the use of this quote, to dramatize and highlight an important aspect of classroom interaction that is often missed by those who use interaction data as the basis for research.

It is, I think, often assumed that the meanings communicated by talk are transparent. So long as we have encoded in our memories dictionary labels, then we can have as complete access to the meanings embedded in an interaction as those who are directly involved. As an approximation this may hold true when we look at many classrooms, because they are not stable enough settings for people to build up personal and private meanings, but in some classes this does happen. It happens in many primary school classes, and it happens in classes like the one I have been describing where teacher and pupils spent a lot of time together and know each other well. In such settings words do not simply have universal dictionary meanings that we learn from general cultural experience, they also have associations and particular, personal meanings not readily accessible to those outside the immediate experience of the group. (I use the word group, rather than class, deliberately for the group is in some sense united by the possession of shared memories.)

This is, of course, a fact well known to those sociologists who have studied groups that are rather more self-contained than school classes. So called 'deviant' groups in particular are often found to have developed a lexicon and a set of linguistic routines which separate 'insiders' from 'outsiders'. (For example, Becker, 1963; Polsky, 1971; Labov, 1973.) What is less often realized is that less exclusive groups to some extent mobilize the same process in a weaker form. For instance some teachers seem able to use the way they talk (and by this I mean the full range of attributes from voice quality to forms of expression) to create a sense of private domain, which functions to protect their pupils from the abrasive demands of the institution. These overtones can easily be missed by the observer or the analyst who looks at classroom interaction only in terms of the universal meanings freely available within the culture at large, and so misses much of the full richness of talk, which in some cases may be what makes it valuable and unique to its participants. It is remarkable just how much we can reconstruct on the basis of a few lines of transcript, but what is harder to grasp I would suggest are private and personal meanings stemming from shared memories and shared experiences — in short all those meanings that Bernstein describes as the domain of the 'restricted code'.

I would also suggest that the accumulation of these meanings is to a considerable extent, dependent on long-term immersion in what I have called 'formal' settings. The kinds of jokes I have described, which in turn are indicative of a particular set of ways of using language, are dependent on the establishment of an attentive and receptive audience, they really need the context of whole class teaching if they are to work their full effect.

Studying the Informal

One of the first problems that arose when this analysis was applied to a class that was predominantly 'informal' was that the data were virtually inaccessible. In the class I have just described I could sit in a spare desk and listen. In fact I spent about two terms in the class, visiting up to three lessons a week. I also collected a number of hours of tape recordings of lessons, and it is from some of these that the examples given above were extracted.

A little further on in this chapter I shall be using some comparable quotes extracted from an 'informal' setting, but first I should say a little about the context of the study.

The school is a purpose-built comprehensive junior high school in Leicestershire. The teacher I have chosen to look at here is in some ways comparable to the teacher whose class I have described already: A science teacher who also chooses to teach some of his science classes English and social studies. His reasons though are somewhat different, for the class is a mixed ability first year class and contact with one teacher was intended to help them bridge the gap between their experience of primary school and what they would be likely to encounter in the more specialized surroundings of the high school. It is therefore intended as a transitional arrangement to help bridge the organizational disjunctions in a three tier system.

Unlike the previous class, to sit in one of these classes was to gain only a partial picture of what was happening, for the teacher typically spent most of the lesson moving around the class spending considerable periods of time talking to individuals and small working groups. The only way to hear what the teacher was saying was either to follow (when you tended to become part of the interaction), or to listen at a distance by use of a radio microphone.

I chose the latter tactic, but then another problem emerged, for listening back to the tape it was difficult to reconstruct what had happened, the tape did not in itself locate where in the room the teacher was or identify to whom he was talking. It was not always clearly marked on the tape (by linguistic signals of one kind or another) when one encounter ended and another began. So parallel to the tape I ran a time lapse film which recorded what was happening at 2-second intervals. This film was synchronized to the tape by a pulse. In fact two cameras ran simultaneously, one following the teacher in a relatively narrow angle so as to pick up changes in posture, gesture and expression and another, with a fixed wide-angle view, located what was happening in the class as a whole (for technical details see Adelman and Walker, 1975). With currently available equipment it would be easier to use video tape recording but at this time the only video equipment available was large scale, intrusive, expensive and required technical staff to operate it.

It is important to emphasize that these developments in technique are not simply technical. The need for more contextual information in order to make sense of the audio tapes is itself an important indication of a qualitative shift in communication structures between formal and informal situations. In the formal situation the context is relatively fixed and easily reconstructed from the transcript. In the informal situation this is not always so. In the informal situation, the transcripts themselves read less like the scripts for plays. Indeed it is not always clear who is speaker and who is listening, and because the teacher is inevitable acting within a smaller circle of attention, the use of posture and gesture operate on a more subtle and less readily visible scale.

Earlier in this chapter, in discussing the evolution of pupil identities in the predominantly 'formal' class I gave considerable significance to the fact that the teacher and class together constituted an audience to whom most actions and statements were referred. Class visibility, I claimed, was a key to understanding the kinds of identities teacher and boys were able to make. In the informal class this is no longer the case: the dominant audience tends to be the friendship or work group, talk (whether involving the teacher or not) tends to become localized. This means that children cannot develop viable social identities through the creation of expectations amongst a large and attentive audience. They have, instead, to project themselves fairly continuously through face-to-face interaction, a process which requires rather different skills to those seen to be typical of the formal class.

It is clear now why I have tended to use the term 'identity' rather than the more commonly used term 'role'. For following a useful critique of the use of role theory by Ward Goodenough (1965), I feel it is important to separate the *social* from the *personal* aspects of 'role'. In the formal situation social identities are involved — that is to say parts are played even though they are not scripted, and expectations are created in an audience who in turn support the part. The different social identities taken by individuals interlock into something equivalent to the grammar of a language; the whole becomes an organic social structure which in some ways fits the metaphor of a stage play. In informal situations, however, it is predominantly *personal* facets of identity that are mobilized to sustain encounters. The boundaries (what Bernstein calls the 'frame') between life outside the classroom, and life inside, are weakly drawn and constantly negotiable.

In the first part of this chapter I looked at jokes as indicators of the kinds of relationships that were found in one formal class. Jokes are also found in informal classes, but they tend to be of a different character, and appear to play a different role in maintaining the fabric of classroom social structure. What characterizes the informal class, I shall argue, is not the joke, but the joking relationships. That is to say looking particularly at child-teacher interaction, what counts in the formal situation tends to be some skill in the use of wit, teacher and pupil engaging in a form of verbal duelling in front of the class. In the informal class however, what counts is the ability of the pupils to create and sustain distinctive identities by projecting themselves through a unique form of relationship not shared by others in the class.

In an attempt to illustrate this I want to look at the relationships two children have with the teacher in the informal situation I briefly described above. All the extracts I have quoted are taken from an integrated English/social studies lesson. (The figures in brackets indicated pauses in seconds.)

Karen

1   K: Colin, can you send that letter off please? (2.4 laugh)
    C: Watch it (3.2 um). That letter.
    K: Yes, that letter.

C: Tell you what Karen, I'll make certain it is sent off (2.4 um).

K: Miracles.

C: You know the science area?

K: Wonders'll never cease. Oh I'm not going over there.

C: Yes, know my room in the science room? (2.2)

K: Yes.

C: If you go over there — with that key you'll find my case on the floor.

Girls: Oh that's too lovely. Oh Colin.

C: Bring it over — your letter's in it.

2   C: You've just done what?

K: I've written it in my own words.

C: Oh well, providing you're making (0.2) it very brief.

K: Oh yes *now* you tell me.

C: You seem to have torn it up again — you're good at this aren't you. You're so *impatient* Karen (2.0) um.

3   C: — and you want a bloomin' envelope. You can't find it? It's in here. (5.6) Excuse me girls, could you conceivably let me — let me get to my (0.4) drawer. Thanks. Come on could you get out of the way (4.2) *Next time* you want to go there Karen —

K: Where?

C: — it's that one *there*. Alright?

K: Oh *you* said the second one on the left, and side on —

C: I meant the right hand side.

K: Ooh!

C: The second one down — alright? (1.2) Now the only thing you're going to need *next* is going to be the address isn't it?

K: You (0.6) you. Oh!

C: Relax — I was about to give you the address — OK?

K: I don't know why I waste my breath! (2.4)

Even without the intonation and phrasing it is clear that the talk here is of quite different quality to that quoted earlier. In may ways I feel it is more like everyday conversation, with Karen (the pupil) and Colin (the teacher) moving further away from the conventional roles of teacher and pupil than we saw illustrated in the other classroom.

One of the consequences of looser boundaries is to raise the indeterminacy of interaction sequences. In these quotes it is more difficult to predict what is likely to come next, not only for the reader, but for the participants too. In this situation it becomes difficult to do what we saw pupils doing earlier, that is building up an identity on the basis of an ability to induce a degree of tension (or humour) between was expected to be said, and what was actually said. The bounds that contain what is expected are here not tight enough to leave a margin for that kind of humour, and lacking an adequate audience pupils are not able to use that kind of means of establishing their identity within the class.

Instead we see, I would argue, Karen creating an identity for herself by insistently (if jokingly) playing on an identity she ascribes to Colin as likeable but inefficient. She uses her fluency to manage incidents, implying all the time a particular definition of the situation, which in turn implies an identity for the teacher. She therefore creates an identity for herself, not as a public figure in the class, but through her ability to use talk to establish and sustain a unique relationship with Colin; *her* identity is dependent on her image of him and her ability to make it stick in her encounters with him. It is, I might add, a kind of relationship that is only possible in relatively long-term and intensive relationships, and in this sense the reader might find more parallels in home or work relationships than in typical secondary school teacher-pupils relationships.

Karen is one of a group of girls who work together, and the whole group to some extent extend and amplify Karen's relationship with their teacher. Using Bernstein's term, it could be said that this relationship is constructed within the 'frame', for though it stretches the conventions of teacher-pupil relations, it does remain within them, at least as they are maintained in the context of this school and this class.

In contrast, Benny, the second pupil I want to consider has a relationship with the teacher premised on his constant ability to move outside the frame. Unlike Karen, Benny is something of a social isolate within the class. (*marks a strong rising intonation.)

Benny

1 C: Benny (0.8) I've heard too much of you for the past five minutes wandering around the room — what are you doing? (1.8)

B: Me? (0.2) I'm doing writing. (0.8)

C: I can *see* you're doing writing but *what* are you doing? (1.0)

2 C: Come on — what's this here?
   B: Bird.
   C: Well what bird is it?
   B: Ooh. (0.4)
   C: Well come on you put it here — what is it? (1.6)
   B: Giant Beak.
   C: No it's got a name Benny.
   B: No it's got a beak 'n' it.
   C: Yes, but what's its *name*?
   B: Well it's one of them i'n'it.

3 C: It's the Hornbill, good.
   B: Hornbill.
   C: Now make certain next time you know what it is. What's this one up here? (0.6) This big bird? (0.6)
   B: The Hornbill it?*
   C: *That's* the Hornbill. Now 'it' is the beginning of that sentence.

4 C: These are the things they eat are they?*
   B: Yes. (0.4)
   C: Right. What are they? What's *that*?
   B: Worm. (1.2)
   C: Caterpillar.
   B: Caterpillar (1.0) One of them — bugs that grow on trees. (2.2)
   C: Greenfly? (2.4) Is that what you mean? Is that what it's called?
   B: Yea. (0.0)
   C: Right.
   B: And that's er (2.2) What do you call it. What you 'ave for breakfast.
   B: Sometimes (1.6) Oranges. What 'you call 'em? (1.4) *Red* things.
   C: That you have for breakfast? (0.6)
   B: *Some*times.
   C: Oh — it is — it isn't a living thing this?*
   B: *No.*
   C: Strawberry.
   B: *Yes.* (1.0)

C: Do you have strawberries for breakfast?*
B: *Yea.*
C: Do you really?*

Compared to his conversations with Karen, when Colin talks to Benny his speech is slower and his intonation more measured. Where Karen hurries the conversation along, Benny's remarks are often so unexpected that they demand a considerable amount of remedying and filling-in on Colin's part if the encounter is to be sustained. Whatever the reasons for Benny's somewhat startling manner of talking (and there is some evidence to suggest to the teacher that they are in part due to unusual perceptual difficulties), their effect is to constantly place Colin in a position where he has to think carefully before he speaks. In part he does this because he is not quite sure what Benny is saying, but also because he does not want to obscure the situation further by saying things himself that might appear ambiguous. Colin expects not to understand Benny fully, so that when he talks to him he expects Benny to produce the puzzling and bizarre. This expectation and his response to it, of simplifying and carefully monitoring his own utterances, itself sets his relationship with Benny to some extent apart from other relationships he has with the class. In fact Benny can so undercut Colin's expectations that he is able, linguistically at least, to reverse roles, as at the end of the sequence I have quoted, where Benny has Colin groping for the word 'strawberry', in a way very similar to the way teachers conventionally make pupils guess at words.

Summary — Teacher's Classroom Identities

In this chapter I have looked at some of the difference between teacher and pupil roles/identities in a formal and in an informal classroom. I have used selected quotes from two lessons in order to illustrate these differences, though behind the analysis lies a good deal more material that I have looked at in some detail and with some care.

To summarize the distinction: the teacher in the formal situation is constantly 'on stage', having learnt those ways of becoming and remaining the centre of attraction for the class which best suit his/her own abilities and social skill. At the centre of this performance is the ability to 'control the class', which appears to involve both classroom organization and a strongly projected social identity, a social identity that may be markedly different to the personal identity of the teacher 'off stage'.

The teacher in an informal situation may be invisible to all but a few pupils for most of the lesson. Classroom control in such settings is more a matter of organization than of the presence of the teacher's authority (though this may well be more significant than appears to the observer). The identity of the teacher in the informal class is personal rather than positional, she/he seems to be much the same person outside the class as within it.

It is important to emphasize that this distinction does not simply describe kinds of classroom 'style' or 'personality' available as options to teachers. The distinction is one that relates different kinds of teaching to different kinds of classroom communication structure, and perhaps, in turn, to different forms of learned outcomes. In contemporary usage what is being examined here is, a structural feature that underlies what are currently referred to as different classroom 'genres'.

Coda

One particular implication to note is the consequence for the teacher of becoming part of the informal (in the more usual sense of the term) social structure of the class. Typically, teachers keep a certain degree of distance between themselves and their pupils. One of the functions of this distancing is to preserve a degree of 'fairness' or equality in the way individuals are treated. This is more difficult for the teacher in the informal setting, for friendship and work groups tend to become a more integral part of classroom organization, and work groups tend to become a more integral part of classroom organization, and the teacher may become more closely drawn into their intricacies. (Colin's interactions with Karen could be interpreted as a game in which he is trying to regain distance and she is trying to reduce it.)

It may be helpful at this point to refer to a little known study by John Withall (1956). Withall studied teacher-pupils interactions at an informal art class using a sequence of still photographs (taken at 15 second intervals) in order to count the number of interactions between the teacher and individual pupils in the class. The teacher incidentally emphasized developing the individual work of his pupils and felt he did a reasonable job in helping each pupil with their own work.

This first table shows the distribution of the teacher's contacts with individuals in the class:

Table 1   *Number of contacts per hour for each pupil — eight uncontrolled[+] sessions*

Pupils	Contacts per Hour	Pupils	Contacts per Hour
A	5.5	N	62.8
B	34.5[++]	O	4.7[+++]
C	17.7	P	29.3
D	9.6	Q	4.6
E	6.7[+++]	R	5.9
F	37.6	S	20.2
G	24.1	T	22.5
H	4.2	U	12.1
I	26.1	V	5.8
J	4.3[+++]	W	6.9
K	17.1	X	4.9
L	13.3	Y	1.9
M	9.4	Z	18.0
		Overall mean:	15.8

[+]   The teacher was unaware of the pattern of distribution of his contacts in the class.
[++]   Based on 445 minute total. Two class periods were missed; one of 75 minutes, the other of 35 minutes.
[+++]   Based on 525 minute total. One class period of 35 minutes was missed.

This table reveals a marked difference in the dispersal of teacher contacts amongst the class, and further, Withall notes those children who received most attention tended to be those with the highest IQ, who were themselves most popular amongst the class. In conversation with the teacher, John Withall reframed the research problem:

> The conscious attempt by the teacher to spread his attention more evenly within the class came about as a result of a discussion which the researcher had with him during one of their regular staff meetings. At this meeting we discussed the problem of some of the isolates in the class. We were impressed with difficulties facing these individuals some of whom, besides being rejected in everyday situations by their peers, seemed also to be 'neglected' by the teacher. It was agreed that both the 'fringers' and 'isolates' and the 'neglects' might be helped if the teacher began to evidence a greater interest in them and their work. The researcher and the class teacher agreed that up to this time little rapport seemed to have been established by the teacher with certain pupils, notably: Q, X, A, O, W, R, C and L. The teacher was greatly impressed with the findings we had made from an analysis of the classroom interaction and was only too anxious to do what he could to alter the situation

Table 2   *Number of contacts per hour for each pupil — eight controlled[+] sessions*

Pupils	Contacts per Hour	Pupils	Contacts per Hour
A	23.7	N	46.4
B	25.6	O	6.2
C	28.8	P	45.4
D	53.7	Q	44.4
E	11.2[+++]	R	12.3
F	72.6	S	18.2
G	Shop[+++]	T	13.9
H	1.6	U	22.4
I	Shop[+++]	V	13.1
J	7.0	W	4.8
K	12.0	X	29.8
L	35.3	Y	8.1
M	31.5	Z	27.6

Overall mean: 24.8

[+]   This term denotes the teacher's conscious attempt to distribute his attention more equitably among his pupils.
[++]   Based on one period of seventy-five minutes.
[+++] These two pupils worked during all three periods in the craft shop on a project and were not in the classroom.

that existed. He, therefore, undertook, deliberately, to work more closely with those eight whom we had specifically identified as well as the others in the room whom he may previously have tended to overlook. As a result of the teacher's efforts to redistribute his time so that the 'neglects' would get a greater share of his attention, we were able to collect data on several 'controlled' sessions. These data are presented in Table 2.

Comparing the frequency of teacher — pupil contacts before and after the teacher's attempt to control his interactions with individual children reveals a number of changes. First, Table 2 shows a marked increase in the overall rates of interaction, which presumably indicates the teacher making more, shorter contacts with individuals. (Table 2 shows an increase of 9 in the mean number of contacts per child per hour — or a 57 per cent increase overall, as compared with Table 1.) Second, some of these pupils 'lacking' contact in Table 1, gain by Table 2. For example, Q, described by Withall as 'a fringer in the peer group, rejected by the boys, with more of her share of pubescent problems, and the youngest in the class', increases her contact with the teacher considerably. On the other hand, H and Y remain 'neglected'. Third, while a teacher seems able to redirect his attention to other pupils, looked at overall, the distribution of contacts remains highly skewed to certain pupils at the neglect of others.

It would be wrong to generalize too far from this study, and unwarranted to assume that the class I described earlier was directly comparable. On the other hand there do seem to be some parallels between the problems faced by this teacher and the problems faced by Colin. In particular it would seem that in the informal class, friendship groups become an important organizational element, mainly through the differentiation and allocation of tasks, and the fact that contact with the teacher becomes a scarce resource. The teacher in the informal class does not encounter friendship groups, as the teacher in the formal class does, as a hidden agenda, but as part of the surface structure of the situation. In a sense the teacher is trapped in them, for they *are* the existing social structure through which she/he must work, and there is little that can be done to change them.

It follows that a major issue for the teacher may become the management and handling of pupil-pupil relationships in relation to work and task groups. For example, Karen in Colin's class is a member of a clique of girls who form the most cohesive friendship group in the class. Benny, on the other hand, is both an isolate and more isolated. In a formal situation perhaps their identities would be lost, at least superficially, in the similar roles they would need to take, and they would be treated more or less similarly by the teacher in that they would for most of the time act as audience with equal access to what was said.

In the informal situation their different identities come to the surface and are made more visible, in Bernstein's words, 'more of the child is made available for control'. This is reflected in some ways in the fact that Karen works with her group of friends, while Benny sits alone. Indeed one of Colin's constant problems is how to extricate himself from the demands made on him by Karen's group in order to get uninterrupted time with Benny. This means that his contacts with Karen's group tend to be brief, but frequent, and his relationship with them marked by teasing and joking, while his contacts with Benny are few, prolonged, conducted at a slower pace and more serious.

I do not make these observations critically, and it may be that when relationships between teacher and pupil become individualized the fact that each child gets access to rather different facets of the teacher is a good thing. I want simply to make the point that a consequence of adopting informal forms of classroom organization is to change the experience of teaching for each child in the class. The teacher sees the whole, but each child only sees a fragment, a particular fragment which might in some sense be seen as constraint on what is learnt. Individualization, taken to one extreme may be the ultimate in streaming.

It might be interesting to note that in a more recent study (reported in Walker and Wiedel, 1985) I have come across the case of a pupil who intuitively realizes this, and who had adopted a counter strategy. This study was part of an attempt to follow a first year class through all their lessons over a period of one year. The class was a mixed ability group in an Inner London comprehensive school and the main source of data was a large collection of photographs taken during regular lessons which were used as the starting point for interviewing teachers and pupils. In maths the class followed SMILE, an individualized maths programme based on the Kent Maths Project. In the photographs collected during one maths lesson the teacher noticed that she spent a lot of time sitting at her desk, and said how much she disliked this. 'When the lesson is going well I spend my time going around the class. When I am stuck at the desk and a queue of kids builds up, that's a sign things aren't running smoothly.' As she looked through a long sequence of pictures of the queue it was apparent that she felt increasingly frustrated by what was happening. In particular she said she felt 'trapped' at her desk by a girl who was particularly demanding in terms of wanting the teacher's attention. At the back of the queue appeared Jonathan, an able boy who she would have expected to be able to work through the material on his own. Indeed he is the kind of pupil that the project is designed to allow to work at his own level and pace, and not have to wait for the rest of the class to catch up. With every picture the teacher said: 'No! This is terrible. Jonathan is still there. I haven't seen him! Look he's missed his turn again!' At one point Jonathan stands behind the teacher, his head on one side. 'Look! Look at that ! He's still there, and he looks so bored! And I still haven't noticed him!'

When I asked Jonathan what was happening in the pictures I got rather a different story. 'You see I got bored just working on my own. There's just one thing to do all the time. I really like to do more than one thing at a time, and I have found that if I stand at the front I can be doing my own work, looking at what other people are doing as well. Every so often I sit down and write a bit more. Then I go and look at the kinds of problems that the others are taking to the teacher. I think I learn more seeing the things the others get wrong than I do by getting my own work right!' I asked him about the picture where his teacher said he looked so bored. 'No', he said, 'I wasn't bored, I was trying to see over the page to what was on the other side. That's why I've got my head on one side.'

Again I want to emphasize that I am not trying to be critical of informal, or independent, or individualized forms of classroom organization. My intention is to point out that such classes are not just alternative organizational forms, but that these in turn have quite important consequences for those who teach and learn within them. They are not different ways of accomplishing similar ends. They are simply different, and perhaps more so than we sometimes realize.

It is important too not to overstate the case. In most schools children and teachers have access to a variety of different kinds of teaching. It is quite rare to find cases where people remain within one form for long periods of time, and so looked at overall the categories are less powerful than they might at first seem. Nevertheless, my claim is that an analytic approach which begins by looking at differences between classroom communication structure ('formal' and 'informal', for instance), or even begins by looking at something as apparently superficial as humour, has more power than an analysis which begins from *a priori* distinctions between global concepts (like 'Nuffield' and 'traditional' Science). In short, in evaluating curriculum innovations, pedagogy is at least as significant as curriculum.

Note

This is a revised version of a paper published as Walker, R. and Adelman, C. (1976) 'Strawberries', in Stubbs, M. and Delamont, S. (Eds) *Explorations in Classroom Research*, London, Wiley.

Chapter 2

Humour in the Classroom

Ivor Goodson and Rob Walker

In this chapter we want to take up a theme from the previous chapter and develop it further. The theme concerns the relationship between certain forms of classroom humour and predominant communication structures within the classroom.

We argued in the previous chapter that the telling of 'jokes' as a basis of classroom humour, depended on the establishment of a knowledgeable audience, which in turn was a product of those classes where communication was focussed and centralized, or in the terminology we used 'formal'. This form of humour may be contrasted with 'joking *relationships*', in which the humour derives from 'comic' rather than 'funny' sources, and we suggested such humour tends to be characteristic of classrooms in which close, and to some degree, private, relationships develop between teacher and pupil. Such relationships tend to be associated with classroom social structures that are, in turn, characterized by a diffused sense of audience focus and communication patterns of a dispersed kind; structures we described as 'informal'.

This tentative line of analysis which we depicted as pedagogical rather than curricular, has been developed by referring to 'ideal types'; models established on the basis of close examination of relevant, but perhaps atypical instances. In continuing to develop this analysis it is appropriate to continue this method of selectively using data to illustrate and illuminate the model. No attempt will be made here to survey classrooms, and while we might want to claim that the analysis is generalizable, no assessment of the typicality of the model, is presented.

It is important too, to remember that the starting point for this analysis was concern with a practical problem, namely, what are the consequences for the teacher attempting to make some of the changes in classroom role implied by a number of curriculum development projects? In this context the emphasis is on humour as a useful indicator of deeper aspects of roles and relationships.

An Initial Formulation

The analysis may initially be formulated in diagrammatic form:

Situational structure:	Formal	Informal
Identities (Roles):	Joker	Joking relationship
Form of humour:	Jokes	Comic

The distinction between formal and informal situational structures is characterized by the nature of the communication pattern. In formal situations everyone in the class plays the role of an audience, or (in the case of silent work) a potential audience, for those who are speaking (and the established rule of thumb is that for two-thirds of the time someone will be speaking, and for two-thirds of that time the speaker will be the teacher). Informal situations are characterized by teachers who spend most of their time speaking only to individuals or to small groups, and where the rest of class is predominantly engaged in some activity other than listening to the teacher.

It will be clear that these are not categories of classrooms, though they do precisely demarcate different forms of classroom organization. In most classrooms you are likely to find both forms of organization used at various times, but this does not affect the argument in the sense that the claim we are making is that each form of organization makes different role demands on the teacher and on the pupils, and that when the form changes, roles too are changed.

Jokes and the Comic

Humour is a slippery subject, and its nature and mechanisms are notoriously difficult to analyze. In part this is because much humour derives from contributions and paradoxes inherent in the structure of language: humour thrives on misunderstanding and inappropriate usage. Trying to be serious about humour is an area particularly fraught with dangers; a metaphorical banana skin; for the attempt to be serious quickly becomes a joke in itself and about itself. Humour is not a static quality that can be built into an utterance or a statement to a calculated degree, but is more like a free and fast-flowing source of energy whose movement is difficult to predict and control.

Of all the meanings language and speech may be used to convey, humour is among the most fragile and subtle. When his jokes failed to get a response from his audience, one public speaker was known to repeat them, slowly and carefully, until the audience began to laugh. After some twenty minutes the audience was usually laughing to the point of collapse, even though the script was unchanged from their first cool response. The nature of humour is complex, in part because it resides, not just in the logic of what is said but in the performance of the teller, in the relationship between the teller and the audience and in the immediate context and atmosphere of the instance.

We have used the term 'humour' to describe a wide set of meanings, and the term 'joke' in a narrower sense. 'Jokes' are perhaps best defined as humour that survives reduction to a script. You can buy books of jokes, or put them into Christmas crackers, but humour in the wider sense is often difficult to record. Of course only some of the humour of the joke survives in the script, much of it has to be recreated in the telling, but a glance at professional humourists, on television for example, shows clearly that some forms of humour depend on scripted jokes, but that others depend on situations and on performances. This is particularly true of what is sometimes called 'situation comedy', where there may be very few jokes in the punch-line sense. The source of humour in this case lies in the ambiguities and tensions that arise within the situation as the narrative develops. The term 'joke' seems inappropriate for much of this humour, and the term 'comic' more accurate. Humour of the comic kind arises from the creation of comic relationships in the unfolding of the story, it is a structural feature of particular sequences and sets of human actions in the context of a narrative. As is well established in theatre, comedy and tragedy are closely interrelated: the tragic stalks the comic as its mirror image.

The distinction between 'jokes' and the 'comic' is crucial to the analysis we have outlined, and it is important to follow it beyond theatre into everyday life. Joking is essentially a product of formal situations, for it demands the existence of an audience. There is in Garfinkel's term an 'indexicality' between joking and certain forms of human communication. The telling of a joke both marks and reinforces certain kinds of relationships between people, and certain kinds of joking are characteristic of particular forms of relationships. There is, for example, a humour of the workplace, of which the following account is a good example:

> The miner's 'language' however strange it appears to the outsider is an inevitable part of him. The language of the miner

regardless of what dialects it embraces, is an intricate and inseparable part of his whole culture. It is directly related to his community, his work and the way he handles it, his trade union struggle and movements, his songs and stories. It is one political whole, each facet dovetails into the other.

The mine necessitates a different attitude of mind, a different temperament to that on the surface; necessarily it gives rise to the culture and language which are peculiar to that environment. A man who could not 'switch off' his surface self and change his nature when he went underground would not last long in the mine. The pit is a barbaric world, a world of filthy smells and stagnant air, of gases ever lurking in the roofs and floors, of small cramped places, of falling rocks, of gushing water and stranded pools, of thick clouds of dust and stifling heat. Sharp objects dart downwards from the roof to tear at the head and back; the floor buckles and rolls and the feet are never sure. Into such a world, shaking with weight and deafened by machinery, men with a solitary beam of light to aid them, fight out an existence. A man must become hardened to this hellish cavern; he is in a permanent state of aggression and the temper stimulates hard work; cruel things happen to men underground, and as in war, men must steel their minds against the thought of them. All day long the miners are being prodded and struck by supports and rock; the blood is at boiling-point; if it wasn't for the jokes which come non-stop we would all be fighting in a few minutes.

Certain of the miners' jokes may appear hard or cruel, but without the ability to make light of accidents nobody could keep sane underground. The obvious intention of jokes such as these is to laugh off the danger and try and make light of things which would stop other folks in their tracks.

A lot of mining humour is good-natured verbal combat with as much cut and thrust as could be found anywhere in court room or on stage. In Yorkshire this is called 'piliking'. Yorkshire miners love to 'pilik' or take the mickey out of each other; the sooner a man loses his temper the better; the crowed enjoys it and heaps on the ridicule. 'Piliking' goes on all day — a continuous stream of more or less violent banter — and keeps the men's spirits high and their minds alert.

> And so it goes on, non-stop, all day, the things one laughs
> about underground would seem silly to write about in the cold
> light of day. The way the 'patter' is delivered matters more
> than the words; the men revel in their dialects and pump the
> words out with the force of a tommy gun; the expressions men
> pull when telling a yarn, the twitch and movements of their
> hands, can reduce the audience to an hysterical heap and keep
> them smiling through the dust and grime. (Douglas, 1973)

Jokes are also used to create social ease between those who are divided
by power or status, and in situations where roles are in close contact
but where persons wish to retain privacy. So while the description
given of miners' humour might be extended to surgical teams and to
combat troops, joking may also be characteristic of salesmen and street
traders, classrooms and committees.

Rose Coser (1960), studying the social patterning of humour
during staff meetings in a mental hospital, found that 'those who were
of higher status positions more frequently took the initiative to use
humour; more significant still, the target of a witticism, if he was
present, was never in a higher authority position than the initiator'
(pp. 81–6). Clearly this would seem to have some relevance to the
classroom, especially that organized on formal lines. Coser goes on a
suggest that humour in the meetings she studied is predicated on a
significant structural ambiguity, for while 'humour serves to reduce
the social distance between persons occupying different position in the
social structure ... [thereby] ... bridging the fissures that tend to be a
consequence of the status system, and of division of labour', it also
serves other functions; humour, especially wit of the kind that appears
to be most prevalent in the meetings Coser observed, is often of an
aggressive nature. Arguing from a functionalist position, she sees this
as fundamentally threatening to the stability of institutions, and argues
that this explains the tendency for humour to follow the distribution
of power.

The very nature of the comic is different, for its meanings are not
freely available to those who happen to be present in the situation. The
humour of the comic divides those who know from those who do not,
and in this sense it is more fundamentally subversive than the kind of
witticism that Coser sees as normally directed at those in lower status
positions. Even comic presentations in the mass media (The Goons,
Monty Python, ...) depend for their humour on some people being
excluded. The audience always has to be initiated into the genre.
Where the joke offers ease between strangers, the comic offers identity

through the sharing of culture. It is in the nature of the comic that its humour is excluded from those who do not share a particular vocabulary of actions, events and memories. Jokes have a start and an end and their telling can be located as a particular, often ceremonial event in the course of an interaction; but the comic is seamless and irrepressible, having no respect for boundary or for social convention. Joke telling may be the social currency between those of differing social status but the comic thrives between equals in the face of authority. As a general rule teachers tell jokes to the class, but pupils mobilize the comic elements of their situation amongst themselves.

Humour and Power

Observation of social situations where one person has formal or effective power over others (teacher-pupil, boss-worker, officer-private, white-black, police officer-suspect, parent-child and perhaps TV interviewer-politician and husband-wife) reveals that humour frequently serves the delicate function of signifying the boundaries that mark limits of control. The humour thus hinges on rapid calculations that need to be made about the extent of control in the situation at particular moments of time. At one end of a continuum, when the distribution of power is strongly asymmetric, then the amount of humour up the power gradient is likely to be minimally expressed. Coser noted how few witticisms were of this kind, but there are forms of humour that are carried extra-verbally or non-verbally through slight exaggerations of posture, gesture, proximity of speaker to hearer, intonation or by highly extended metaphors. Those who experience long-term immersion in relatively powerless roles often develop subcultures in which the expression of humour is an important element. Oppression seems a fertile ground of humour.

Antonin Obrdlik, a Czech sociologist, caught up in the Nazi invasion of his country in the late 1930s attempted to chart the rise of what he called 'gallows humour', a form of humour that seemed to flourish in the initial phase of oppression. Summarizing his account he wrote:

> Humour in general, and gallows humour more specifically, is a social phenomenon the importance of which, under certain circumstances, may be tremendous. It originates in the process of social interaction and bears marks of the particular group by which it was and created and accepted. Its social character is

revealed by the fact that it changes its content — and sometimes also the form in which it is presented — in accordance
with the character of the group and the social events to which
it reacts. The specificity of the gallows-type lies in that it is
always intentional in the very real sense of the word. Not
humour-for-humour, but humour with a definite purpose —
that is to ridicule with irony, invectives, and sarcasm in order
to become a means of effective social control. (1942, pp. 715–6)

The humour that emerges in asymmetric relationships derives
from the recognition that the control of the powerful over the powerless is never total, and in the gap that remains humour may thrive.
Jules Henry's (1960) notion of the 'polyphasic' nature of human communication is significant here for, he argues, people always communicate more than they intend. Messages are never unidimensional or
unambiguous, and within even the most ritualized action lies the
potential for communicating an enormous range of possible meanings.
Consider, for example, Ray Birdwhistell's (1971) description of a
military salute:

During World War II, I became at first bemused, and later
intrigued, by the repertoire of meanings which could be drawn
upon by an experienced United States Army private and transmitted in accompaniment to a hand salute. The salute, a con-
ventionalized movement of the right hand to the vicinity of the
anterior portion of the cap or hat, could, without occasioning a
court martial, be performed in a manner which could satisfy,
please or enrage the most demanding officer. By shifts in
stance, facial expression, the velocity or duration of the movement of salutation, and even in the selection of inappropriate
contexts for the act, the soldier could dignify, ridicule, demand,
seduce, insult, or promote the recipient of the salute. By often
almost imperceptible variations in the performance of the act,
he could comment upon the bravery or cowardice of his enemy
or ally, could signal his attitude toward army life or give a brief
history of the virtuosity of the lady from whom he had recently arisen. I once watched a sergeant give a 3-second brilliant
criticism of English cooking in an elaborate inverted salute to a
beef-and-kidney pie. (pp. 79–90)

Consider also the humour of the rural American black observed
by a white researcher in the South during the 1930s:

Everyone has noticed at one time or another an aggressive element in jokes; for example, jokes about dictators inevitably arise once other forms of aggression are suppressed. The joke, of course, conceals its aggressive intent behind the facade of the little story, and often times it takes a bit of analysis to make it clear. In sarcasm, on the contrary, the aggressive element is plain. Negroes do not omit jokes from their arsenal of reprisal against white people. White informants frequently comment on the unaccountable manner in which Negroes laugh. Very often when whites suddenly come upon Negroes laughing and the Negro refuses to explain, it is not because he cannot give a reason or that he is a mere idiot laughing at nothing, but rather that the joke is on the white man and an explanation would be tactless.

There is a story of a white man who overheard a Negro in the field singing something that sounded a first like a mumble. He would sing for a bit and laugh to himself. Finally the white man made out the words of the song: 'Lazy white man sits on the fence, don't do nothing all day long'. The Negro had his little joke, and also his little revenge.

Negro humour often has a delicate suppressed quality, perhaps because of the danger of allowing the aggressive component to come through clearly. A Negro informant told the following story: A Negro named George went into a white store to buy a hat. The clerk said, 'Well, Bill, what will you have?' The Negro guessed he would have nothing. At the next store, 'Well, son, what will you have?' He said nothing. And so on, through a list of names such as 'uncle', 'Mose', etc. Finally he came to a store where the clerk said, 'Well, George, what will you have?' 'A hat', he answered, and bought it. This is also an example of the stubborn self-respect that this Negro could 'fix it with himself' to accept being called his first name only if the white man got it right. This story deserves a bit of thinking over; the least that can be said about it is that the fragile joke is on the white man. Negro humour is often so delicate that it is hard to locate, and one comes off with the battled general feeling that the whites have been lampooned without knowing quite how. (Dollard, 1939, p. 309)

These examples all have relevance to pupil humour, which is not something looked at closely in the previous chapter. The implication is that we need to add another layer to the analysis proposed at the beginning of this chapter, a layer which distinguishes between inside and outside the classroom, for both teachers and pupils. It is important to note, however, that the terms 'inside' and 'outside' are metaphorical rather than geographic, for though it is hidden beneath the surface of visible interaction, such humour often crosses the threshold of the classroom door.

The diagram set out at the beginning of this chapter may now be elaborated as follows:

Situation	Situational Structure	Interaction	Role	Form of Humour
Inside Classroom	Formal	P-T	Joker	Jokes
		T-P	Joker	Jokes
		P-P	Joking Relationship	Comic
	Informal	T-P	Joking Relationship	Comic
		P-P	Joking Relationship	Comic
Outside Classroom *(TEACHER)*	Formal (e.g., staff meeting)	T-T	Joking Relationship	Comic
		Senior T-Junior T	Joker	Jokes
		JT-ST	Joker	Jokes
	Informal (e.g., staffroom)	T-T	Joking Relationship	Comic
Outside Classroom *(PUPIL)*	Informal	P-P	Joking Relationship	Comic

When Power is Asymmetric but Negotiated

Reference to situations of an oppressive nature is, to a degree, misleading. Typically in the classroom, though power is asymmetrically divided between teacher and pupils, the division is not so extreme as to leave no room for negotiation. Indeed a good deal of time may be taken up in some classes negotiating and re-establishing the boundaries and limits of control. As one teacher in the science department of a hectic inner city comprehensive put it:

Control? I feel I'm like the Sheriff in a Western. Yes, I have control over the classes I teach. There is never a riot or even the threat of one. It's not that, that worries me. It's the continuous sense of tension. The control you have as a teacher has to be precarious because there's only me and twenty or more of them. Like the Sheriff, I never know when I'm going to get ambushed in the street. I have nightmares about it sometimes.

A good deal of the teacher's control derives from what this teacher calls 'bluff', and what sociologists might describe as the ability of a teacher to establish a definition of the situation in the minds of pupils. It derives from the teacher's ability to establish norms and conventions of behaviour and action. Humour may therefore frequently be thought of as a threat to a fragile and carefully protected and negotiated position, for humour may threaten to corrode the ignorance that forms the basis of *status quo*:

> Humour and sex may be equally dangerous to authority. Either may deflect the most determined wielder of power from his course. Ruthlessly dedicated organizations like armies and monasteries have tended to be single sex and solemn. The experienced schoolteacher recognizes the potential threat of humour and sex and suppresses manifestations of both. He knows that either leads quickly to the taking of liberties. (Musgrove, 1971, p. 46)

But as is often the case in discussion of the role and functions of humour, this is only half the story. The other half is that humour may act as a point of access to a relationship between teacher and class. Consider, for example, this extract from an interview with a young science teacher:

> *Question*: Can you think of an incident in class which made you come out feeling really good and that you had established something?
>
> *Answer*: Yes, first year of teaching, which was four years ago, at a comprehensive of 1500. I had a very difficult third-year group and I'd spent about six weeks getting absolutely nowhere managing just about to contain them in a small terrapin building miles from the rest of the school. We were doing chemistry and I had a bottle of red lead absolutely full and I stood at the front and banged again, absolutely no response so I banged slightly harder and the bottom of the bottle fell out. Red lead is a bright orange powder which covered me from head to foot. I was wearing cream at the time. There was just me and a cloud of red lead: it was the first time I got absolute silence. All the kids

> reacted beautifully, they howled with laughter and then all
> rushed to the front and tried to brush me down and just
> brushed the stuff in. I then fell off the rostrum because I was
> laughing so much and after that I have no problems with the
> kids at all because they were impressed that I could laugh at
> myself. I think that was probably the most exhilarating because
> there was complete spontaneity from the whole class. They
> were little buggers even so afterwards but at least we had
> established some kind of communication and it's something
> they've always remembered. I can meet them down the street
> and they will say 'Remember that day you disappeared in a
> cloud of red lead?'

Because humour has this two-edged quality most teachers attempt
to draw tight boundaries around the occasions when humour is permissible. Some will allow humour outside the classroom, but not inside. Others, like this primary school teacher confine humour to breaks
in the lesson:

> As a teacher, I'm really a song-and-dance man. In the way I
> teach I always try to ring the changes. The way I look at it,
> you can't work them hard all day, 9:30 a.m. to 3:30 p.m. So I
> give them a test. Then I'll clown around for a while; make a
> fool of myself to show them I don't think work's the only
> thing in life. After that they can do English or write an essay,
> that kind of thing. Then I'll take them into the gym. All the
> time I try to keep the pace going. You know, on-with-the-
> next-Act. As a junior school teacher you're stuck with them all
> day, and them with you. It's only fair on both of you to create
> as much variety as you can. . . .

In this class it was clear that humour played an important functional part. It was a class with a strong competitive edge, but high
morale. The prevalence of humour disguised a brittle social ethos which
stressed high individual achievement (the school was in an area where
the 11-plus exam had only recently been phased out). Humour acted as
a safety valve, and as a ceremonial means for reasserting the corporate-
ness of the class, and its shared experience in the face of powerful
centrifugal tendencies.

The combination of strong teacher control and a stress on individual pupil achievement often leads to the establishment of the pupil
role of 'court jester' (to borrow Louis Smith's term). Smith describes
the part played by Sam, court jester in Mr Geoffrey's eighth grade class:

Within a month, Sam had developed a special role of court
jester. He shuffled about the classroom in a Jackie Gleason
style. Physically he was heavy set and wore his hair uncut, and
his beltless bluejeans hung low on his hips. On occasion, he
gamboled tardily into class with a smile and big 'Hi, Mr
Geoffrey'. Once, after loudly volunteering an answer to a
question, he responded to 'Raise your hand, Sam' with both
arms waving vigorously. In a tense situation he had a ready
quip; he freely entered and exited in a banter of tete-a-tete
relationship with Mr Geoffrey. As an illustration we present an
episode from the afternoon of September 18. Geoffrey has just
been involved in a skirmish with Pete and Allison. The activity
shifts from spelling, where Sam had begun being playful, to
history. 2:45 — Geoffrey starts on history. He has Sam find
Jerusalem, the exact point where the lesson ended before. Sam,
with a flourish, finds it (several had helped him before lunch).
Geoffrey, in his perennial one-up game with Sam, then draws
down a map of the world (in contrast to the previous map of
Europe and the Mediterranean) and re-asks 'Where is Jerusalem?' Sam counters, with a twinkle, 'Can I peek?' (on the
original map underneath). Geoffrey, solemnly and with a
twinkle in his eye, says 'Yes'. Sam picks up a corner of the map
and peeks. After a moment he finds and asks for corroboration,
'Is it right?' Geoffrey indicates 'Yes'.

Here was a boy who behaved very differently from most of the
other children. The role in this instance was quite functional,
for it brought fun and lightness into the class and provided
Geoffrey with a challenge and an occasion for his own quick
humour. But in many instances such a role can be detrimental
to group purposes. Three weeks after the beginning of school
we were puzzled about Sam's evolution. When we went back
and carefully analyzed the notes, we were surprised to find
what had happened.

An important fact is that Sam is a pupil who failed seventh
grade last year with Mr Geoffrey. He did little or no work. On
the first day this year Sam had been teased sympathetically
about possible tardiness and being at Rhody's Confectionery
before school. Next, he had been given book number 13 and
was involved in teasing about superstitions. Thirdly, he was
called on to help Molly spell 'chalk'. Fourth, he volunteered to
help in the supply room and was teased with the others about

running off to play baseball. And fifth, he was pinpointed humorously regarding the fire drill. He had been extended five invitations, far more than any others (only Sandy and Bill were singled out with any frequency and they alternately took special roles). Day by day such interaction accumulated into a role and a related belief system.

The second day contained several more instances of Mr Geoffrey's public attention to Sam. One of these seemed particularly significant; it occurred during the spelling lesson as the papers were being corrected. Each pupil was entitled to one chance to respond. The teacher had made this clear with references such as, 'You've had one' to both Allison and Kent. Mr Geoffrey gave to Sam, the word 'tardy' and received the retort, 'I've had one'. He, Mr Geoffrey, then commented, 'I'm giving you this one special'.

Sam also has a degree of skill in repartee. Few of the pupils could respond with the 'wise humour' appropriate to the context. In addition, he responded well to termination cues from Mr Geoffrey. Banter contains these fundamental attributes.

We should comment further about the teacher's role in this instance. We had not realized, until we checked the names of the pupils who had been given opportunities to answer and compared them with the names of the children called on after Sam's second turn, that the next four pupils called upon had also given one answer before. In the space of a few minutes, Sam's role had been extended, and the teacher had built another subtle aspect of the pupil belief system regarding his own role — he was fair and equitable. Additional insight is provided from comments made by Mr Geoffrey:

'Teaching at Washington School can have a deadening effect on a normal, live, somewhat eager individual. To work day after day with pupils who aspirations and abilities are so typical of the culturally disadvantaged child — aspirations and abilities that need no description in these comments — is to court frustration and defeatism. Even what appeared in the beginning to be sensational after a while becomes commonplace.

The teacher in question suffered as much as any other in the environment. As a relief, he sought some humour and life in the children with whom he worked. Sometimes this could be found — as it was in Sam, Sandy, even Elma. Not to capitalize on this would have been a waste of natural resources.

Sam and a few others made it possible to inject joking and bantering into the classroom. It made it possible to smile. It made possible teaching in a personal and, I would hope, kind way. The teacher could treat some pupils as individuals (non-educational sense) rather than as a mob of dirty, sullen children. Some pupils, such as Sam, *responded*. One of the most discouraging aspects of teaching in a slum school is the lack of response from pupils. The teacher works, and at the end of the day leaves tired and irritable. This feeling comes from the continual effort to get these students to respond — in any acceptable way. To have them respond in humour, within bounds, is a most acceptable way. At least they are *alive*.

I do not deny that the consequences may be subject to question, I really don't think the teacher thought much of the consequences. I believe he thought more of finding life in a body than in what way the body, once awakened, would behave.

This, of course, leads to the question of teacher personality. When faced with frustration and failure other teachers may follow different courses to get through the days'. (Smith and Geoffrey, 1968, pp. 54–8)

In Geoffrey's comments emerge the image of a teacher for whom classroom humour is significant because it brings humanity into schooling. As Philip Jackson (1968) has pointed out (also in the context of the American elementary school), teachers do have a dual allegiance, as he puts it, 'to the preservation of both the institution and the individuals who inhabit it' (p. 144). Looked at rationally, schools make pervasive and extensive demands on the children in their care, but they also *care*. Humour may be one means for both softening the demands of an abrasive institution, and offering a degree of escape from it.

Joking Relationships

In the previous chapter, we attempted to distinguish between 'jokes' which are defined as being context-free; and 'joking relationships' in which the relationship between the speaker and hearer is an integral part of the joke. The 'strawberries' joke, while its meaning lay buried in the history of the class memories, is nevertheless a context-free joke, whereas the relationship between Colin and Karen depends for its humour on knowing the people concerned. Arriving at Smith's account of the court jester is to arrive at the boundary between the two, for though the court jester role, as Smith and Geoffrey describe it, is a product of the formal classroom, it is also a role that fits the definition of the joking relationship (a term incidentally borrowed from social anthropology, for the origins of which see Radcliffe-Brown, 1953). The distinction that has to be reiterated is that one considers the nature of the audience. Smith and Geoffrey's account of the court jester is of a role that is played to a class audience, whereas the roles played by Karen and Benny described in the previous chapter are more private, more personal, aspects of personal identity rather than of social identity, but this is a theme that will recur in the next chapter.

Summary: Connecting Hypotheses

This chapter has been concerned with an attempt at analysis of classroom humour, rather than return to the diagram we want to recast it as a set of hypotheses.

1 Classrooms exhibit different forms of humour, the forms indicating differences in situational structure. Formal situations generate jokes: informal situations engender comedy.
2 This distinction involves different forms of teacher-pupil relationships. The formal classroom situation creates roles as jokers. The informal situation tends to create joking relationships between teacher and pupil.
3 Joking relationships between pupils thrive in predominantly formal situations, but tend to be expressed primarily outside the classroom and are often inaccessible to teachers.
4 Joking relationships between teachers may well thrive in schools where formal classrooms predominate, they are mainly expressed outside the classroom and are inaccessible to pupils.
5 Jokes between teachers and pupils frequently function to negotiate the framing of educational knowledge (in Bernstein's sense). Teacher's jokes are often bids for social control; pupil jokes (to the teacher), are frequently challenges to that control.

6   Jokes are situation sensitive and function to negotiate the boundary between personal identity and social identity, often celebrating the primacy of social identity. Thus they may ease the awkward articulation of roles, or alternatively may be seen as invasions of privacy or misreadings of the nature of situations. Jokes may make more of the person available for control and so increase vulnerability, or may decrease the threat of the institution by softening the abrasiveness of institutional demands.

7   The comic, expressed within joking relationships, is sensitive to personal identity, celebrating the primacy of the person over the demands of the institution.

8   Jokes, especially witticisms, are symptomatic of asymmetry in the distribution of power within relationships.

9   Comedy is the humour of equals. Though the fiction of equality may become the source of humour.

10 Oppression creates equality amongst the oppressed, so providing the source of comic invention.

11 The main source of change in the humour of the oppressed is the leakage of meaning to the oppressor. A common counter-response is the inversion of meanings and values.

Note

This is a revised version of a paper first published in Hammersley, M. and Woods, P. (Eds) (1976) *School Experience*, London, Routledge and Kegan Paul.

Chapter 3

Stations: Episodes in a Teacher's Life

Rob Walker and Ivor Goodson

In this chapter we continue to develop the theme of the significance of humour as an indicator of pedagogic variations, but the level and style of the argument shifts. We look outside the classroom rather than within, and we move further from the presentational style of symbolic interactionism towards that which Bob Stake (1972) characterized as the method of 'portrayal'.

We retain a concern with some of the questions raised by the curriculum reform movement: questions this time about decision-making, planning and evaluation. 'Stations' was written as a report during the course of a project which attempted to address a number of questions about the implementation and adoption of curriculum reforms. Called 'SAFARI' ('Success and Failure and Recent Innovations') the project had a twin study, the Ford Teaching Project, which explored the notion of classroom action research in education. 'SAFARI' attempted to address some of the wider issues of school-based reform, then emerged as a response to centrally-funded curriculum programs. These two notions, action research and school-based reform are key themes in this book. For the moment, however, we return to 1974 and this report from the field.

What do you think the effect of the Beatles was on the history of Britain?

I don't know about the history. The people who are in control and in power and the class system and the whole bullshit bourgeois scene is exactly the same except that there is a lot of middle-class kids with long hair walking around London in trendy clothes and Kenneth Tynan's making a fortune out of the word 'fuck'. But apart from that, nothing happened here except that we all dressed up. The same bastards are in control, the same people are runnin' everything, it's exactly the same. They hyped the kids and the generation.

We've grown up a little, all of us, and there has been a change and we are a bit freer and all that, but it's the same game, nothing's really changed. They're doing exactly the same things, selling arms to South Africa, killing blacks on the street, people are living in fucking poverty with rats crawling over them, it's the same. It just makes you puke. And I woke up to that, too. The dream is over. It's just the same only I'm thirty and a lot of people have got long hair, that's all.

Nothing happened except that we grew up; we did our thing just like they were telling us. Most of the so-called 'Now Generation' are getting jobs and all of that. We're a minority because of something or other. (John Lennon quoted by Wenner, 1970)

Stations

A point at which one stands to take a view.

A person's position in the world; a state of life as determined by outward circumstances or conditions.

Position in the social scale, as higher or lower.

A stopping place on a journey; a place of temporary abode in a course of immigration.

A place where men are stationed and apparatus set up for some particular kind of industrial work, scientific research or the like.

Each number of holy places visited by pilgrims in succession...

To place or pose (a sentinel).

In botany, to have a certain position of growth.

A visit of a Roman Catholic priest and his curate to the house of a parishioner on a week day to give the opportunity for confession.

An act of pageant or mystery play.

The stationary point, crisis or height, or a disease.

In surveying — each of the selected points at which observations are taken.

In biology — the kind of place in which an animal or plant is fitted to live, the nature or essential characteristics of its habitat.

The location to which an official is appointed for the exercise of his functions.

A place where railway trains regularly stop for taking and setting down passengers ...

from *The Oxford Dictionary*

Points of Departure

*The Location to which an Official is Appointed for the
Exercise of his Functions ...*

SAFARI (Success and Failure and Recent Innovation) was a research project attempting to assess the consequences of curriculum reform, and in particular to evaluate the range of effects in the educational system of centralized curriculum development projects. Rob Walker was a research officer with the project, a researcher with problems but with a growing sense of possibilities.

Journal entry — December 17, 1973

I have been working on the SAFARI project six months and am finding it difficult to get to grips with the issues. I feel I should be studying the details of schools and classrooms, observing curriculum projects in action. But somehow it is difficult to find a research design that connects detailed studies of the real world of schools and classrooms to the concerns outlined in the brief. The gap between the world of developers and the world of the school seems a difficult one to fill.

Part of the difficulty stems from the fact that the proposal is highly individualistic, written by Barry MacDonald out of his experiences in evaluating the Humanities Curriculum Project. Basically SAFARI is conceived as an evaluation exercise focusing of a number of completed curriculum development projects but building on Barry's evaluation of HCP.

I have no direct experience of working in curriculum development or in evaluation; my intuition is that on the educational scene as a whole such projects are marginally important. I feel that in any research we do we must be careful not to reify the very idea of the curriculum project, making it seem more important than it is. If we really want to know about the successes and failures of projects why not study schools which have used none of the projects and ask why? Why don't we look at schools that have really succeeded in innovating, had run ahead of the projects, and ask how?

Barry finds this difficult to accept, he sees evaluation as evaluation of a *program*, and sees me pursuing a pure research line that threatens to become at best diffuse and at worst arid and academic.

Our ways are beginning to diverge. Barry is increasingly getting involved in another project which employs him half-time. I am beginning to extract ideas from the research I feel comfortable with, and to set off in my own direction. We talk around the problems at length, mostly on trains and at railway stations.

'A Holy Place Visited by a Pilgrim ...'

As Barry and I talked around the problem and began to build on the ideas we shared (which were ideas about methods and techniques in what he called evaluation and I called research), I began to formulate a justification for studying Elm Wood School under the auspices of SAFARI.[1] The idea I had was elusive, a difficult one to put into operational terms.

December 17, 1973

> Travelling cross-country from Norwich and between stations. On my way to visit Elm Wood School, a school with a national reputation in educational circles. On the surface a visit to a friend, at the back of my mind the thought that I might pursue the research in a new direction and attempt to look at a school that has succeeded in innovating, but which feels it owes little to particular curriculum development projects. My feeling is that if I could accomplish this, then the connections with the project brief would become clear. I find it difficult to make my case in the abstract but feel an example would make it for me. A sub-question is whether, in a two-day visit I can create an

'ethnography' of a school that might meet the growing need in evaluation circles for such studies.

In terms of curriculum theory, there are other questions. In previous weeks as I have listened to people talking about their experiences as members of curriculum development teams what struck me most forcibly was the excitement and exhilaration they felt. For many it was a culminating point in their professional careers where different views and interests came together in a genuinely creative manner. The more I listened to people recounting their experiences as team members, trial school teachers or project officers, I began making connections with other events that occurred concurrently. Events in education like the tidal wave of books published by Penguin Education, the first appearance of Open University courses, the accounts that emerged from particular schools — Risinghill, Summerhill, Countesthorpe ..., the Free School movement, changes in teacher education like microteaching and role play. The more I have thought about it the more I feel all those things seemed to fit into a common pattern. They seem to be part of the same fragment of culture: bits from the same jigsaw. The theme is one that connects cultural change and personal (and professional) motivation.

I keep thinking of an analogy of Levi-Strauss, that if you want to know the pattern of the jigsaw, perhaps you should look for the characteristics of the saw itself, *what is the formula might describe the cam that produces the pattern?* Is the underlying pattern a wave of cultural optimism, the source of which lies far from its genesis?

Casting my thoughts wider: Is there a connection between the events I had located in Education and other events in the wider culture? I find myself thinking of the people I know who had been active in curriculum reform, particularly at school level, and asking myself how far their professional lives had been influenced by their life styles. It sounds absurd at first sight but I began to think perhaps there are connections between what had happened in Youth Culture (John Lennon and George Best) and what has happened in schools.

Two alternatives present themselves. One is that each of these events reflects different facets of widespread cultural change. The other is that the change is less real than imagined: Schools have only changed superficially in order to retain their power — they had conceded personal style (long hair, pop music and football) but retained social control and kept their authority. It is possible both alternatives are partly true.

These were the ideas that I was thinking around on the long cold journey across the fens. In what follows I cannot pretend to have found answers, but I hope I have succeeded in elaborating the questions.

Ron Fisher

'A Person's Position in the World; A State of Life as Determined by Outward Circumstances or Conditions ...'

The thing everyone comments on is that Ron is a 'laugh'. In the way people tell you this it is clear that it is a two-edged quality, the pupils appear to like him ('If ever I was in any trouble he'd be the only teacher I could talk to.' 'He's the only teacher I don't feel a bit uneasy about calling him by his Christian name.'), but every so often the two-edged quality comes through — 'he *always* takes the piss out of you'.

Ron is a joker and he knows it and plays on it. To him joking is serious:

I'm certainly amenable to jokes — accessible to jokes, and accessible to people thereby. I think that's the important thing. I think you need a point of access with people. That's what most people lack. They don't lack the capacity to *make* a relationship. They lack the capacity to get into it.

One of the stories Ron tells about himself is about a parents' evening when one of the dads came up to him and said 'Our Jim always talks about you, and I can see why'. Then, almost as an aside, 'Here, have you heard the one about...'. In one way the story is misleading for it isn't that Ron constantly tells jokes, like salesmen are reputed to do. What he does seem able to do is release the comic element in any situation.

It follows that Ron does not necessarily enter his classes to a burst of applause, and conduct his lessons through gales of laughter (though we have come across one or two teachers who are able to do this). More often the humour reveals itself through the ridiculous, through underplayed status, or mock authority.

Ron is aware that a dominant theme that underlies his joking relationships with pupils is shared antipathy towards authority:

> It's something of the irreverence of it, basically you're not laughing at each other; you're getting together and laughing at someone else. That's why when you said it's not really what the teacher *does* (that makes it funny), I think there's an element of that in it. In other words it's like the kid and you getting together and you are laughing. Even if it's not particularly funny, it's you and them against the school. Against the institution, against something. Maybe it's you and them against other teachers or other kids, but you've entered into a joking thing, and that in itself is sufficient ... it gives you a certain strength, a certain isolating intimacy.

Joking creates personal relationships between teacher and pupil, but just because the relationship is personal some pupils are excluded:

> The more I think about it, I think that jokes are very exclusive. There's no doubt that they cut people out, but they also cut you in, they put you into something definite. They define the limits really. It's you and them against the rest. I think when you're into an irreverent joking situation, the attraction of it is its sheer irreverence to begin with.

From the evidence we have given so far it might seem that Ron's actions reveal an anti-teacher, someone who wants to escape from the authority implicit in the role. This point formed a central focus in one of our conversations, but before we got onto this we first established that Ron was aware of two classic uses of jokes by teachers who act more conventionally within their roles. One is the joke as a means of control:

> ... there is a joke as definitely a way of controlling the situation, by almost the kid being scared of the sort of joke you are going to make; because jokes can be very punchy. Kids can be very sensitive about things, and if you joke about them, obviously you can put them down, control them by that sort of joke, and if they are scared by that.... Whatever their weak point is, if you know it you can joke about it.

The other is the joke as a means of escape from embarrassing situations or confrontations:

> I think that sometimes one makes jokes because you're in a tight situation.... Like this morning, I had an essay to mark

and I said I'd lost it partly as a joke to relieve the pressure on myself.

Ron admits to using both, especially the latter. However, far from selling out on his obligations, he sees his joking as an indication of control in the classroom:

> My main reflection on reading through [the transcript of an interview] is what an utter ego-maniac I seem. The only re-deeming feature is that I do seem half aware of it. I think it might link up with the fact that only teachers who place jokes at the centre of their studies at Elm Wood School are all in a similar bag — big egos (big heads?), self-confident and so often dominant in many ways. I do think you need a strong sense of being in control, and of things going well for you before you would be willing to give jokes a central place in your teaching.

This is the point Ron makes more clearly when he describes how he starts off with a new class. One of the conventional wisdoms of teaching is that you should 'never smile before Christmas', or 'start tough and ease up later'. We see this as meaning that the teacher should establish the formal, institutionally prescribed and required re-lationships, before trying to enter a personal relationship with pupils. 'Never smile before Christmas' clearly implies that jokes are part of the process of letting yourself become a person in the eyes of the pupils.

> I never start with jokes actually with any group, because I think that jokes are quite an intimate thing. I don't start with jokes. I begin to *see* jokes quite early on, but I always start dead-pan, always. First lesson is dead-pan, and always I would say there are thresholds I would cross before jokes come in. Like I will never make a joke before the threshold ... it's the classic authoritarian stance in a way. I want the class to know that I can make things stick before I joke.

Ron's use of jokes as a means of initiating an encounter seems, in part, to be the other facet of the 'control' coin. For just as jokes can give access to areas of other people in a personally destructive sense, such as extensions of an institutional relationship beyond its formal bounds, they can also lead to something constructive. Jokes only have potential in this sense; they are not keys that of themselves unlock relationships. Several pupils have described to us cases of teachers who seemed informal, because they were always joking, but who in fact were using jokes to keep them within a tightly prescribed status. In this way the teachers were able to give the surface appearance of 'intimacy' without taking any of the risks of more fundamental change.

Ron echoes the point:

> I mean the real trouble with ... was not that he jokes, but that he was weak and he couldn't make things stick, and he was using jokes as a way out of that. Now that's a disastrous and pitiful way out, if the joke is a retreat, as it is, the joke is often a retreat....

Ron's self-deprecatory joking might in itself seem at first sight, a form of retreat, but this is an interpretation he strongly rejects.

> I am always aware that I am the teacher ... and that my fundamental job there is to be a teacher. I think it would be patently false to say I was a mate, and that's all, because I'm not. I'm a mate, I'll joke, but in the end I'm trying to get them to do something, and they know that. There are mates that try to get you to do other things, but I am the mate that is there to be a teacher, and that in the end does impose boundaries, but they just don't intrude in relationships.

Ron's expressed strong commitment to teaching and simultaneous rejection of much that passes for conventional teacher behaviour seems to pose a paradox, but it is not felt as a paradox by Ron, he resolves it this way:

> I would say I would be concerned for them to know, for all sorts of reasons at the beginning, that I am the teacher, and I am not pissing around in that role, and that role does matter to me, and it matters to them, and I do take it seriously. But as a person I am willing to accept almost anything, given that you do accept that I am a teacher. Ultimately what I am trying to do with you, somebody I like, is to teach you. In other words we are not going to be going nowhere every day. We are going to be you and me, but we are going to try and get somewhere. I don't see that as a contradiction at all if it doesn't intrude into the relationship.

Often teachers do feel that contradictions between themselves as teachers and themselves as persons. Hence the teacher who is friendly in the playground or in the corridor but who freezes in the classroom, or the teacher who allows a relaxed atmosphere in some parts of the lesson but who knows when to be serious. We detect nothing of this in

Ron and nor do those who know him better than we do. He seems the same in almost any situation.

It would be doing Ron an injustice to present him as a clown who acted on his own impulse and who had no rationale for acting in the way he did. In justifying his joking relationship with the fifth year leavers group we described earlier, Ron related his joking to the values of working-class adolescent boys. Here his own history as a working-class adolescent is no doubt important:

> There's a high fantasy level, a high joke input; far more jokes among working-class kids than there are among others, so jokes are really important to them. It's very much part of the lifestyle. For many working-class kids, to be in learning situation is somehow suspicious — if you are seen to be learning you are in a rather suspicious, tense relationship with your lifestyle. Now if this is true, that the learning situation is an alienating, tense thing for him, the each time he finds himself in this alienating situation he will want to back out, won't he? It seems to me that once he can see himself as a kid at a desk *learning* — once he can define that relationship, he's buggered. That is an alienating relationship that he does not want to be part of. He's too conscious that if your mates find you learning, that's hell. So you've got to cut it out. The central stage has got to be all the while that you're joking, that it's still a bit of a joke what you're doing.

Implementing New Curricula

It might seem we have drifted a good way from our point of departure, which was a concern for the implementation of new curricula in high schools. Our aim in portraying Ron's teaching is to present a background to an important idea that is his rather than ours.

Ron teaches in a highly progressive school and within the school is certainly one of the least conventional teachers. Yet he rejects most of what normally passes as innovation in education.

Q: How do you see the host of Schools Council projects?
Ron: It's just a huge charade, an absolutely meaningless charade.
Q: If anywhere has caught the impact of the blast I would have thought Elm Wood School had?
Ron: Yes, I'm right at the centre of this World History project

but it's absolutely irrelevance, total charade. The very fact that most projects and the Schools Council defines curriculum as something 'developed by teachers' implies the whole thing is just a charade. It must be if that is your starting point.... I've not seen anybody anywhere, even in the most liberal documents, who has any conception of the curriculum at all except as a total teacher monopoly. Nowhere is the possibility of any other kind of curriculum even considered. The whole Schools Council philosophy is that teachers evolve the curriculum, work it out beforehand and then take it from there and impose it on them, or at least present it in front of them.

Ron's conception of the curriculum is one in which content is inextricably linked with teaching relationships. He sees 'the curriculum' as something which can only be talked about as an ideal concept, the reality is what happens between teacher and pupil. He offers a definition:

The curriculum is in retrospect what has happened between you. That's all the curriculum is ever. It's just a retrospective evaluation of what has happened between you and a pupil. It's not good just preparing something in a vacuum and throwing it to the wolves. You've got to do it there, on the spot or you don't do it at all. That's where it matters, your curriculum. In that room, in front of those kids. That's where curriculum stands, in the interchange between you, or falls ...

Not surprisingly Ron rejects materials production approaches to curriculum development which he sees as designed to be basically 'teacher proof'.

Q: I suppose you could still argue that Schools Council projects have succeeded in replacing one curriculum by another.
Ron: That seems to me to be irrelevant if you are not in any sense changing any of the relationships on which the curriculum is based. I'm sure you can change one kind of package for another but all the packages are the same if they don't involve the kids.
Q: So that crucial thing is the relationship between teacher and pupils?
Ron: Of course it is. If the kid is not involved in the negotiation at all how the hell can you expect to devise anything that is of interest to him? You end up going into the classroom with your little bundle that it's been predicted they'll like and they just

crap on it like they always crap on it because it's something you're presenting as a *fait accompli*. Once again you turn around and say, 'What can I do next? Let's try Latin'. It's nonsensical.

We mentioned before that Ron rarely engages in whole-class teaching. Most of the time his pupils work on projects. The atmosphere in Ron's room is distinctive, there is a lack of busyness, little hurrying on of pupils, little pressure to write rather than talk. Ron sees joking relationships as quite important in building up this atmosphere:

It's the general atmosphere that is notable here. I think this would come out if you came for a day and compared the atmosphere in our team, and the one in the other team. In the first team jokes are a central fact of existence, perhaps the most manifest symptom of the relationships the teachers envisage. Here the kids seem open, happy, and dare I say it, industrious. They mostly seem to have things to do. In the other team there seems to be all the features of latent confrontation that you get in a more traditional classroom. Many kids are visibly bored, and there seems to be an air of hostility when the teacher approaches — all the time the teachers seem to be on their guard, watching their dignity, keeping their distance. Perhaps above all the use of, and more importantly accessibility to, jokes, signal to the kid that there is a person who is not going to impose the normal role demands that teachers make.

Not imposing the demands that teachers usually make is important to Ron because he feels that is what alienates most of school from the working-class adolescent. He describes school as he thinks it is seen by his pupils:

Things that you take seriously are the fun things. That's where you put your fucking energy, that where the centre of gravity is. After school normally, when you go down to the boozer or you go and play football, or when it's break time. Your life is lived exclusively for the time outside the classroom. The time inside the classroom is a penalty to be paid, just like working in a factory. And so you truant as much as you can when you are at school, because that's a few holidays before you end up in the factory. Obviously the things you do in school are a waste of time. You see generation after generation of people fail. When you go to school you fail, so you don't want to know about it, or any of the things you are supposed to do there. The only thing you want to know about are the things that don't seem related — so the things that are very important to you are the things like football or pop, and things outside the classroom.

In order to survive as a teacher in a school that places its emphasis on pupil-direction and self-motivation he finds himself disguising learning by making it a joke:

The other point is deferred gratification. The project you're doing has got to have a high laugh input, so every interval there has to be a laugh. And the only way you'll get commitment is by setting up as an irreverent, non-deferential situation as you can. It's a learning situation none the less, but it doesn't seem to the kid to be. It seems to him to be something which is a bit of a laugh, where you've got the teacher on his own, and he's sticking things in, but he's still a bit of a joke. You're having a laugh, it's a good time and maybe you're learning, but no-body's rumbled it so you're OK.

He extends the point by trying to describe himself as he likes to be seen by his pupils, and in doing so shows how he feels different to other teachers and indicates the significance of joking in his distinctive role:

So if you suddenly see somebody over there who's not doing what he's supposed to be doing. He's a teacher, but he's got kids around him and they're laughing. In general it's not a classic learning situation. There's nothing self-conscious about it. Kids don't come earnestly for information or anything. Maybe therefore he becomes very important to you, because in this desert of school time, you waste less time. In other words it finally becomes positive to you, you can get into relation-ships which are not what you had in other classrooms.

Collecting Thought before Making a Change of Tack

We have pursued Ron's joking because it seems a distinctive feature of his teaching that marks him off from many other teachers we have observed in informal classes. Although this pursuit might seem trivial in relation to our research aspirations we have found ourselves return-ing to significant themes. One has been the indivisibility of curriculum and pedagogy when looking at actual classroom practice rather than at debates at a philosophical level. Another theme has been the difficulty of making pedagogic change in comparison to the relative ease with which curriculum can be changed. A third theme has been necessity of changing teacher roles quite significantly if self-motivating teaching methods are to be effectively used with working-class pupils.

A Change of Tack: Elm Wood School

The account we have given of Ron Fisher's teaching needs to be situated in an account of the school. We are not able to give a full account of the school but what follows is a diary of a visit to the school starting in midday one day and continuing to late the following morning. Again the focus is on Ron Fisher but the context of the case is wider.

> '*A Place Where Men are stationed . . . for some Particular Kind of Work . . . Research or the Like.*'

Elm Wood is a secondary school with a national and international reputation as an innovating school. A trial school for a number of curriculum projects (Project Technology, General Studies, World History and various maths and science schemes), it has also been something of a mecca for educationists and researchers. It is the sort of school that did not merely become a project trial school, but which ran ahead of most projects, cannibalizing their ideas and materials and sometimes creating for the projects new visions of what might be possible.

Although several of the staff have at one time or another worked on curriculum development project teams, there was (and is) a strong feeling in the school that the role of central development projects is limited by their lack of contact with everyday problems of teaching and running a school. For the most part in its relations with project teams the school refused to be submissive, and projects (like the Humanities Curriculum Project), which made strong demands were passed by:

> We were too bloody arrogant to even try Stenhouse's project. I think we did buy one of the packs — yes, we got 'Education', but I don't think we ever really used it — at least not in the way it was intended to be used by the project team. Their view

of the neutral chairman was still too much of a teacher for us I think.

In its early days (it was opened in 1970 as a new school) Elm Wood School had many of the social and cultural characteristics of a curriculum project of the same period. There was a climate, not just a mood, of optimism and excitement, teachers worked enormously hard without complaint. There was a feeling that the school had cut through orthodoxy and convention and was touching the pulse of the educational process — a feeling of confidence and success.

Inevitably the school made enemies. A vocal group of parents mounted a campaign against the school which caught the attention of the local press. At the height of the campaign there was a fire in the school's administration area. The cause was later identified as an electrical fault in a piece of office equipment, but the news of the fire was inevitably associated with the stories of vandalism which fed the protest group.

The campaign reached out from County Hall to the Ministry. The local MP pressed for an enquiry and, finally, the Secretary of State announced an inspection by government officials.

I visited the school just before Christmas 1973, a week following the HMI's visit, and tried to see it through Ron's eyes. What follows is an account of one afternoon, an evening and the following morning in my life and his.

'Selected Points at which Observations are Taken ...'

December 17, 1973

I last visited the school in June 1973, just before the notorious fire, with Phil Robinson, a colleague in the University Education Department where I was teaching. It was his first visit to Elm Wood School and a year later I asked him to recall his first impressions:

> I went to Elm Wood School rather like a child going into Disneyland for the first time. That's not meant to be a disparaging remark, but I had that sense of awe and wonderment that here was a thing called 'school' that had the label 'school' attached to it, and it had children performing in the sorts of roles that schools tend to push children into. Yet at the same time they weren't, they seemed to have more control, more say, more responsibility for themselves.

The impression that remains with me is one of space, openness, I suppose in a sense the space and openness are there not only in the physical building but also in the human relationships, I think the best way of trying to remember the day is to try and talk my way through it as it actually was.

I remember arriving, walking round the outside of that circular building and going into a corridor to get to the administration so Ron would know we had arrived. We sat in a waiting room which was dark, possibly windowless — I would even go so far as to say that the paint on the walls was traditional school yellow.

Ron arrived, it must have been about break and we went for coffee, I know I had a feeling of envy in that coffee place, envy because of the ease of the relationships that were between the staff and the kids.

It seemed to me that human being actually mattered, that status wasn't important, that who you were as a person really counted. How far this was Elm Wood School or how far this was Ron Fisher I can't really say, I know that I felt he had the sort of relationship with kids that I admire, he got a respect and yet an informality with them.

We went back in the afternoon and spent quite a long time sitting in a room where we'd had coffee in the morning, and we sat at a table, facing the door leading onto a corridor which led to the administration buildings. On our right was a group of kids sitting at a table, chatting humorously amongst themselves. I can't remember why they were there, and as break came kids walked into the room and out again.

This is what amazes me about so many schools. The clanging bells and the whistles and the mass rush of kids from school into playground and from the playground into the school and even from lesson to lesson. This I didn't sense at Elm Wood at all — there was a much more gentle flow of work activity to leisure activity and back to work activity. I can't remember any bells, and how did kids know that the end of break or coffee had come and it was time to go back to their lessons? I know we were sitting there before, during and after that time and the kids came and went and I'm sure there was no sound at all.

Elm Wood School is different, built differently, it's organizational principles are different, in terms of time, space, the way in which knowledge is divided up and transmitted. I suspect there is far more dialogue than one way transmission. For a person going there for the first time, I had the feeling of being mesmerized by this sort of difference, yet at the same time it was a school.

I went last term to a college of education and in one of the groups that I watched was a guy from Elm Wood, he'd left the year before, so he must have been in the sixth form there whilst we were there. He had a missionary zeal about him for Elm Wood, for responsibility, for democracy. He was a lad who contributed very, very well to the discussion that was going on, in a college where the prevailing ethic in his particular group was one that said 'streaming is right, grammar schools are proper'. If I'm a working-class kid who's made it then this legitimizes even more the existence of grammar schools, if I can do it, everybody can do it.

But he was raising critical questions about hierarchies, status, authority, responsibility, self responsibility as well as responsibility for the community. I know I thought, listening to him, that if he is what a school like Elm Wood produces, and again I have no knowledge at all of how typical he was — then three cheers, amen and everything else for a place like Elm Wood. Here was a lad who was prepared to think, to argue, to reason, not in a bolshy bloody-minded way but in a very deeply socially concerned way.

If you read reports like the Jencks Report you can get a bit depressed about what schools do — perhaps schools can't do very much in any case; but if they can, and if that lad was a function of it he was a very powerful testament to whatever processes are going on in there.

My memories of the visit were similar. I had visited the school several times before but felt than that the school had succeeded in innovating to a point where it was changed. A feeling of non-reversibility; of success.

This time my first impressions were quite different. The school was surrounded by a sea of mud (the damage caused by the fire, still not repaired, had blocked the main corridor so students had to walk around the buildings to gain access). Windows that had been broken in

June were either unrepaired or had been broken again. It was cold and raining.

I found it difficult to find Ron. Teachers I asked said, 'You'll be lucky', 'Now you're asking', and 'He's probably at home'. The last hypothesis proved accurate. I found Ron in his flat over the village grocer's shop just a few hundred yards from the school.

Ron shares the flat with two (?) other teachers. His room is fairly chaotic. An enormous hi-fi system (much admired by his pupils who are often found using it). A collector's collection of rock records (no jazz) of which ten or eleven LPs seemed in more or less constant use. Magazines piled up around the room, the most used of which was *Let it Rock* which contained several of Ron's articles. Books on local industrial history (Ron was a joint author of one), on Russia and a scattering of sociology (Bernstein's *Class, Codes and Control*, Nell Keddie). Most of the floor space was taken up by an old mattress, the rest by socks, a tennis racquet, gym shoes (once white?), a big trunk, assorted letters (one applying for the post of 'geography teacher'). On the fading wallpaper a Beatles poster and a school report made out in Ron's name and signed by a pupil ('Could do better if he tried harder').

Ron got serious about education almost by accident. He was doing a PhD in history but abandoned this and took the postgraduate certificate at the London Institute before coming to Elm Wood. He came there because the woman he was living with moved with her job. The relationship crashed and this seems to have dominated his first two years at the school; a time when everyone else was feverishly involved in educational experiment. As the debates about education went on round him Ron rapidly acquired a reputation as a maverick, bright but unpredictable.

We talk about Ron's joking relationship with his pupils. He seems to relate to them mainly (some of the other teachers would say totally) through joking. For him joking is emblematic. He carries it around the school with him like other teachers wear long hair or Levis. It is the constant style he imposes on almost every encounter.

Ron feels that joking gives him a relationship with pupils that is both highly personal and educationally valuable. He feels strongly that the informal ethos of the school has been used by teachers as a way of abdicating from teaching. He feels many of them no longer attempt to teach anything but have simply become submerged in peer group culture.

For him joking isn't just a personal style but a way of short-circuiting the insulation between the culture of the teacher and the culture of the child, a gap which dominates his thinking about education.

'To Place, or Pose, Sentinel . . .'

That evening Ron's girl friend Pat wants him to go with her to a party, but he arranges for me to meet Jean, the deputy head's wife who once taught in the school and now works in curriculum development.

I meet Jean in the pub where she is talking to a group of teachers from the school. It's not a fixed group, there is a parents' evening in the school and people enter and leave as the evening passes. I find it awkward sitting in the pub with this close knit group I don't belong to. Partly it's me not wanting to dominate the conversation, partly I'm aware that I'm an outsider without access to the shared experiences that form the basis of the conversation. I concentrate on trying to listen in to catch the mood and tenor of conversations but I'm aware that they perceive me as uncomfortable.

Also going on in the pub is the local fishing club's annual meeting. All the wives formally dressed to see their husbands presented with silver trophies. Some time after 10:00 p.m. word goes round that the pub has an extension to 11:30 p.m. A long evening. I find myself constantly between two conversational groups, or out on the fringe where I can't hear half the conversation, but as time goes on I begin to pick up fragments about the way they see Ron. Jean is strongly critical of him. She says his claims to a unique relationship with the kids doesn't hold up. Liz (the remedial teacher) has equally good relationships and is just as much a joker (this fits with what I've seen of Liz in school).

We go on to talk about the school. I mention how it seems to be to have changed since my last visit, how the enthusiasm seems to have gone, the buildings look battered and the teachers seem tired. (On reflection it also seems to have become highly introspective — there is no longer that voracious appetite for knowledge from outside which once characterized the teachers at the school. Once they read the latest from Bernstein, now it's *Jonathan Seagull*.)

Jean says, yes the buildings are a little worn, but what do I expect of a school now three years old and heavily *used*. She feels that the first two years of the school, which I characterized as 'exciting' was really a period in which there was 'a lot of thrashing around', and now she sees 'more solid groundwork'. She says she sees things, in Peter's English lessons, for example, which she doesn't see in other schools she visits in her work as a curriculum developer. One nearby school which has a reputation rather similar to that of Elm Wood she describes as 'very traditional by comparison. They haven't really closed the gap between teachers and kids like they have at Elm Wood'.

John challenges Jean's strong attack on Ron. He admits he is unrealiable but feels you have to apply different criteria in assessing hin as a teacher. Ron 'has a different style to most of us, and you have to admit he does get through to some of the most difficult kids'. Jean doesn't accept this; she says the lower sixth are always complaining about him. When I ask if she thinks they feel Ron lets them down she says, yes she thinks they do, and asks Liz what she thinks. Liz changes tack. Ron, she says, is an amusing person and a great guy on an evening out, but she too is clearly not entirely happy with him as a colleague.

My impression is that Jean does not like Ron and feels some resentment towards him, John and Liz share the resentment to some extent but only with reluctance, basically they seem to like Ron, they just find him difficult to work with.

A later conversation with John reveals that he doesn't entirely share Jean's view of the current mood and state of the school. The teachers who have been there two or three years are tired (a word he uses repeatedly). Individually, teachers like Peter may be doing good things but the school as a whole has lost its momentum. He sees the critical problem for the school as how 'to salvage what is left of the original spirit and transmit it to the new, younger teacher'.

'A Stopping Place on a Journey ...'

Finally the pub closes. Jean offers to put me up for the night. A twenty minute drive cross country takes us to a modern pseudo-neo-Georgian estate laid out round an instant village green. Everyone is in bed. (All evening Jean has been saying she has to be home by 9:30 p.m.). She makes coffee and calls her husband down to meet me and to explain why she has brought me home. Maybe he has been asleep, he doesn't look happy.

December 18, 1973
Next morning Mike gets the kids' breakfast and gets them off to school before Jean appears, then he drives over to the school, dropping me off at Ron's flat.

'Position in the Social Scale, as Higher or Lower ...'

Ron asks how I got on ('I felt a bit bad about leaving you'). I tell him about the resentment the other teachers seem to feel about him and we talk about it on and off during the rest of the morning.

He denies being unreliable. He says he teaches eighteen lessons a week out of twenty, more than most teachers, and says he hasn't missed a single lesson this term. Everywhere we walk round the school pupils stop him and say, 'Hey Ron I need a report from you. Where's my report?' Ron says he doesn't understand it. He's sure he's done all the reports. He *likes* doing reports. He enjoys sitting with the kids writing them together. He's *sure* he's done some of the reports that other people say are missing. He doesn't want to suspect conspiracy, but everyone (teachers and pupils) seem to *expect* him not to have done them. . . .

As I watch him teaching it does seem to me that there is something about him that's different to other teachers, even the other jokesters like Liz. Ron doesn't seem to *represent* school like other teachers do. He gives the impression of simply being there because it's a job. In some subtle and indefinable way he conveys a kind of insolence that pupils frequently convey, but never teachers. There is something confident, arrogant and deeply irreverent about the way he acts. He seems to carry no responsibility for the ethos and culture of teaching. It's not just that he swears, most teachers in the school do and some much more. Not that he jokes, because other teachers joke. Not his dress or appearance which is conventional alongside many of the staff. It's a quality of presence, something in his total personal style.

We had also talked at that time of how Ron thought he was seen by other teachers in the school. He felt his reputation as a jokester stood in the way of any other kind of recognition, and thought perhaps some teachers saw in him a threat to their own identities in the school:

> It seems almost impossible to get it over to people that what they are actually seeing and judging you on as your whole relationship, is actually mainly your point of entry. It really annoys me because I sense that what most teachers think is that because you are a jokey sort of person with them, as well as with kids, you don't care, but are just in it for laughs. I've almost heard that said and I've certainly had teachers say, 'I don't think you care about kids as much as I do'. I suppose if I

wanted to get out on a hobby horse, what annoys me most of all is that the stereotyped teacher is an over-earnest individual. The classic phrase all the while is, 'I'm very worried about such and such', recurs all the while and you've got to *appear* to be very worried — that's what annoys me.

I'm very worried about a lot of things, I *care* about lots of things, but I don't appear to be very ulcerated about it. It seems to me that there is a very strong staff desire to have earnest teachers and for teachers to appear earnest, and that has persistently annoyed me, I have talked about it to all sorts of teachers because I suspect that what's most annoying about jokes is that teachers can use it as a way of devaluing you. They can say, 'Look at him over there, he doesn't give a bloody damn'. I'm sure that goes on. One teacher said to me, 'Ron I'm not like you, I can't joke about with kids. I *care* what happens to my kids'. I think I am subject to some paranoia on the grounds of how teachers respond to my relationships with kids — I sense that they feel threatened — jokes are a sign of intimacy and success with kids, particularly with kids who are classically hostile, who appear to be totally defused when talking to you. Now that, as you say, is partly a threat and also is an exclusive thing ... The dual threat is there in front of the teacher each time, kids are taking you, another teacher, away from them, *and* you appear to be doing quite well with them.

Watching Ron teach and listening to him talking to other teachers, they do mostly seem wary of him. It's as though he continually threatens to pull the ground from under their feet. He doesn't joke around and then get down to work. He jokes about everything continuously. Reports, worksheets, beliefs and values. Nothing is sacred. In the time I was in the school the only lull was a short conversation with a girl who was worried about her report. Just that once Ron took her to one side (most conversations with Ron are semi-public and anyone can join in). 'Don't worry', he said, 'I'll see everything is all right.'

'An Act of a Pageant ...'

Recorded while walking round the school at 4:00 p.m. Ron seems depressed. We walk into the Resource Area.

Rob: Christ this has changed!

Ron: How much has it changed?

Rob: Well, the first time I came here there was a lot of books in here, bookshelves dividing the area up. Last summer the books had gone but it seemed very active. What's new that I like are the murals. (large flowered murals on some of the walls)

Ron: Yeah, that's nice isn't it? That's an example of a creative tension between teacher desires and student desires.

Rob: Whereas that's just rubbish isn't it? (A wall covered with football players' names).

Ron: (Laughs) Well this (the central resource area) has become a football pitch now.

Rob: You mean nobody teaches in here?

Ron: Well, Dave is supposed to be teaching in here but *that's* his class (pointing to four tables — no chairs — in one corner). He's only retained about four people. The rest have either gone off into other classes or fucked off altogether. It's sad isn't it? It really eats me up now going round.

Rob: I can understand how an HMI would react coming in here.

Ron: Yeah, they came in at 11:20 a.m. and people were still playing football. The blackboards are the goals (putting on a mock official voice). 'Let me just explain the architecture of the school. The blackboards are in fact its *goals*.'

Rob: The whiteboards. Did the inspectors give any signs of what they felt?

Ron: They said there were some good things going on but what they were really offended by was the general appearance of the school and certain particular areas. Like they said the Resource Centre was a disaster and several other things were total disasters. It's always been true there's a been a lot of vandalism. It's not that the incidence of vandalism has gone up, just that its effect has finally taken its toll. If you kick a building around fairly regularly for three years in the end it begins to look suddenly kicked in.

Rob: Was there any move to jazz things up for the inspectors?

Ron: Nothing at all.

Rob: They really saw it as it is.

Ron: No effort at all, which I think says a lot for either the apathy or general honesty of the school. I think it was probably a bit of both actually.

Rob: How have the teachers reacted?

Ron: All most of them talk about to the kids is football and Pop music.

Rob: Do you see that as a sign of success?

Ron: Well, no. I think it's a sign of substantial failure actually. Most of them came in with a lot of ideas and they've just got knackered in the course of three years and abdicated. There are still good things going on but most teachers have just locked themselves in their rooms, tried to save themselves. That's the difference in the school now. People just didn't talk any more, they just go home and rest. People don't go down to the pub anymore.

Rob: They don't know each other any more?

Ron: No — new teachers who come in, know nobody except themselves, they just don't enter into any kind of community. So there's no way of selling ideas to new teachers either. For them it's just rather a shambling new school that they've rolled up in, nothing particularly exceptional about it. Nothing really exists to indoctrinate new teachers — to sell the whole ideology of the place to them.

Rob: That's what it was very good at.

Ron: Yes, superb, but you see, you can't go on doing that, it's too tiring. The excitement of the new building, the new institution obviously fades anyway doesn't it? With time, you're just repeating yourself. There's a kind of consensus in the old guard about what it's all about and that's enough to sustain us.

Rob: Do you talk about the past at all, the myth?

Ron: Oh yes there is, very much so. Not that it was necessarily better, but it was certainly bloody exciting then, if not a bit hairy — certainly it was very hairy, we took a lot more risks. Yes, there's a myth about the past. I've heard teachers say 'Oh you wouldn't know, you weren't here in the first year', definitely a lot goes on, which annoys a lot of the newer teachers. I think that's a very strong myth. It's always great being in at the beginning of something. It's been the most exciting thing I've been through in my life I think, and I only paid partial attention to it at the beginning, it never entered my consciousness in the first year or two really, I didn't feel a strong sense of commitment. I was more involved in personal affairs. I get really depressed when I think about it. It's just the way a place grows old, I suppose. It's the whole ageing process speeded up. Everything is less and less interesting as you get older and you

get more and more tired; everything tires you more and con-
sumes you more, none of the exhilaration is there. You're not
doing anything for the first time. It's the ageing process in an
institution. It's just that it takes three years in a school and
eighty years in a life time.

Rob: Do the kids talk about it at all?

Ron: Oh, that's why I wanted those kids to come today. I went
down to the launderette with Pat one Sunday afternoon, we met
a crowd of them going by on their bikes, and they saw us and
came in. One of them was that kid I did a report for ... and he
started off, ''ere, do you remember in the first year'. There was
just a long list of anecdotes, none of which I could remember
actually, that they all remembered one after the other, ''ere, do
you remember when ''e did this, and 'e did that'. Pat was just
buckled up with laughter. ''ere do you remember the day you
came in with smelly socks and you was asking everybody what
the smell was, and somebody realized it was your socks.' Oh
yeah, they thought the first year was a real bombshell. It must
have been a real amazing thing for them, to suddenly get
somebody who was so different — not just me, but teachers in
general were so different and so open and so amenable to a
laugh of any sort. Yeah, I think it's radically affected the way
they look on that first year. That was good, we talked for about
two hours about things that had happened 'do you remember
this, do you remember that', and I haven't had them for two
years.

Rob: They've left now have they?

Ron: Oh no, they're in the fourth year now. I started up with
them again, this was in the summer and I was going to start
taking them again, and I hadn't had them for two years and
that's when they started to say ''ere we're going to have you
again, ''ere do you remember'. And it was really good. There's
a terrific sort of camaraderie — I also went into a pub with Pat
about three weeks ago and there was a crowd of kids there who
had all left and all of them, every one of them came up, two of
them stood with us all evening, somebody who had just got
engaged with her boyfriend stood with us all evening and
bought us drinks and chatted to us and introduced us to people,
and generally showed us around the pub, it was quite amazing.
Literally every kid in there that I'd ever taught came up and
said something, most of them went through the motions of
buying a drink or offering a fag or some kind of money sac-

rifice. It really was strange, I felt quite tearful once or twice, it really touched me, I really was quite taken by that. I'm sure you do touch more this way, you do actually get ... they do miss you, they do identify with you, something happens, very different to what happens in a normal school. It happens with a different group of kids maybe, it happens to kids who normally are pissed off and glad to leave school and wouldn't want to say 'bum' to you if they saw you.

Rob: It's not all the ones who have gone on to a college of education?

Ron: Oh no, it's the ones that end up in the local pub, that's the group I'm talking about. It's not radically altered their lives maybe but in a way it has. When they think of school they think of an experience which was firstly happy and maybe, just perhaps, successful. It certainly wasn't a trauma, it wasn't something to pull out of you — it was something to remember and enjoy remembering, and that's bloody important I think. Even if that's all, that's for Elm Wood, at the very least it's a happy experience. I wouldn't want to make that argument about it of course, but I think it's a substantial one.

Looking Back

Rob Walker's notes on the visit: 'As I left the school I was aware that the image I had of it that time was very close to the image Ron has. I've been there several times before, once for a period of two weeks in its early days, and on previous visits I think I've left with a more objective view. Right now, I thought on the bus back to the city, the vision of the school has of itself is blinkered and fragmented and it is difficult to see it at all except filtered through one perspective. There no longer seems a strong communality amongst the teachers which overrides individual definitions of the situation. The buoyant optimism we felt on our visit last June seems to have dissolved. But perhaps I simply saw Ron on a bad day when he's had a row with his girlfriend.'

Cut to Long Shot, the Curriulum Field, the Sun Setting Over the Horizon

This account attempts to tell the story of two days in the life of Ron Fisher, my life and his. It is presented in the form it is for a number of reasons.

One is out of the belief that people in the situation know it best. Generally it is the parent who best knows the whole child, the teachers who best know the pupils, the students collectively who best know the whole school. Experts can know a lot about a little. They can bring unusual and sometimes bizarre perspectives to bear on a familiar situation. They can generalize from the instance. But the language of the expert is essentially the language of generalization and abstraction. Useful though generalization often is, we believe that there is also a need for knowledge of immediate experience. We portray Ron Fisher's world, not for the light it throws on theory but because we feel it might speak directly to other teachers in other schools without being explicitly mediated through the language of educational theory.

Second, the focus on the person, and the interrelation of personal and social identity, is intended to redress a hidden assumption in much writing in education. We talk a lot about plans, designs and theories: very little about persons. Yet in the folklore of the education system the qualities of persons loom large.

When research does consider *personality*, it considers it from the point of view of generalization and theory. When practitioners consider 'personality', they consider the unique and idiosyncratic qualities of persons. The gap between the two usages creates hidden agendas in decision-making. Curriculum development decisions may be justified in the rhetoric of theory, abstraction and design; in practice they are more often taken on the basis of judgments made about the key people involved. As Barry MacDonald and the UNCAL[2] project have pointed out, if evaluators are to portray the whole programme, they need to find ways of handling unofficial as well as official information, particularly when decision-making bodies are clearly using 'unofficial' evidence (for instance judgments about people) in making decisions (Macdonald, 1974).

Other points that emerge from the study are, in the order they come to us:

1 Some feeling for the indivisibility of curriculum and pedagogy, at least in this school.
2 How the close focus on one moment in time (like looking at a photograph) has the effect of highlighting the changes that individuals and institutions undergo seasonally and over time. Looking back we recognize both Ron and Elm Wood School in what we have written, but we also recognize that both have changed in the interim.
3 The connections between youth culture and the curriculum

reform movement of the 1960s is more complex than we first thought. For Ron Fisher there definitely is a connection, he identifies strongly with youth culture and feels that to be important in his teaching. But despite his attraction to rock music and teenage lifestyles it is the school he has become committed to, almost against his own sense of direction. Style may disguise commitment as often as it reveals it.

4 Involvement in innovation, for Ron at least, is not simply a question of technical involvement, but touches significant facets of his personal identity. This raises the question for the curriculum developer, what would a project look like if it explicitly set out to change the teachers rather than the curriculm? How would you design a project to appeal to the teacher-as-person rather than to the teacher-as-educator? What would be the effects and consequences of implementing such a design?

5 Ron works in a school that has been generally recognized as a centre of innovation. Would teachers in schools where innovation has come from outside sources balance their commitments to personal and social identity in the same way? How typical is Ron? How typical is the school?

6 In the first part of this account we described in some detail Ron's joking relationships with pupils. These are part of a general perception of *fraternization*. Ron seems quite simply to be on the side of the pupils. This is a pervasive value position which he can articulate in terms of general politics or specific curriculum ideologies. But it is a value position at odds with the conventional teacher and the conventional school. Truth may indeed reside in the margins.

Notes

1 Later a research design emerged which brought the idea of school-case study into the research program. Helen Simons, who had extensive involvement in the program has written about this elsewhere (Simons, 1988).
2 'Understanding Computer Assisted Learning'. This major evaluation of a government sponsored innovation is the project referred to at the beginning of this chapter. In the event, links did emerge between the UNCAL and SAFARI projects, the latter proving a test bed for case study methods which became more formalized and structured in the former.

Chapter 4

An Alternative Culture for Teaching

Ivor Goodson

Extracts from a Diary, 1973

For several years I have had a recurrent dream:

It was the staff party and each member of staff was asked to entertain for fifteen minutes. The contributions were predictable — shop-windowing the various talents of a professional community. The music teacher played a short piece on the cello, the English teacher read some of his own poems, a group of teachers presented a short play highlighting many staffroom jokes and rumours, the head made a short morale-boosting speech and so on — shades of my school speech day. In the middle however, the lights had gone down and a rock n' roll band started playing — heavy saxophone, subversive lyrics — some of the most troublesome pupils were playing on drums and guitar — three of the cutest girls were singing 'ooh-wahs' to the side and there singing was — oh my God — a teacher.

After two songs — one a Little Richard, one a Larry William — the curtain closes. The school staff talk in embarrassed whispers. It is as if an alien has visited; the tribe close ranks. The authenticity and excitment of an alternative culture has been glimpsed — then rapidly purged from the memory. The staff party continues.

What I encounter in schools when I am wearing my working-class culture or youth culture hats is a group of people (teachers) whose lifestyle contradicts or ignores those criteria most central to my existence.

Since beginning to join them as a group and since changing my lifestyle towards theirs, I have experienced a sense of anti-climax so monumental that it leaves me with an existence which feels hollow and worthless.

During the 1970s the sociology of education in Britain was dominated by the work of Basil Bernstein. This chapter, and the three that proceed it, were written at the time when Bernstein's interests were moving from the sociology of language (and particularly the much publicized debate over the notions of 'restricted' and 'elaborated' codes), back to his prior concerns with questions of schooling and curriculum. It is important to emphasize that, in this shift in topics and perspectives, the central ideas remained fairly constant. Essentially these relate to the connections between language use and culture, culture and identity and derive from the writings of Benjamin Whorf.

Like many others at the time we were caught up in this same set of ideas. We have shown in the first three chapters how they influenced our ideas about research, pulling us away from the conventions of the time, while we were dominated by survey research and testing, towards observational studies, portrayal and to a rediscovery of life history methods. But it is also important to show how the same ideas changed our views of teaching, both in schools and teacher education. Chapters 4 and 5 pick up these concerns.

Culture and Teaching

In this short piece I want to take as my starting point Bernstein's (1969) statement: 'If the culture of the teacher is to become part of the consciousness of the child then the culture of the child must first be in the consciousness of the teacher'. I want to describe certain aspects of my own consciousness of the child's culture derived from my experiences both as a child at school and within working class and youth culture and as a teacher in comprehensive schools where such cultures predominated among the students.

In particular I shall argue that 'alternative cultures' exist among adolescents which span a range of factors in childhood and adolescence that are unrelated to or patently divergent from most contemporary secondary school life. Perhaps 'alternative culture' is the wrong term to use, for it is an alternative that constitutes a significant, perhaps even an essential, element of the mainstream. But I have stayed with it, not least because the word 'alternative' conveys part of what it means to be inside it. It is essentially a culture of resistance. The cost of entry to this culture is most often exclusion from success at school, but once this decision is made the alternative culture offers a spectrum of opportunities to the adolescent; involving occasional actions for some through to a complete lifestyle for others. Certainly for many of the comprehensive school students I have taught the alternative culture has provided important vocabularies of motive. Once the preserve of a deviant minority for whom it provided a lifestyle, the alternative culture now forms a significant part of the 'world' of many secondary school children (Murdoch and Phelps, 1973).

The central focus of alternative culture exists at the points of intersection between working class and youth culture. It is from here that vocabularies of motives, and rhetoric of interaction are derived and in which they are situated. Two elements of alternative culture would seem particularly central and symptomatic:

1 The pursuit of 'fun', 'kicks' or 'laughs'. This is seen as an essential ingredient of all activity which must be present in the 'here and now'. Whether something is 'fun' is the means of evaluation, the yardstick by which all activity is judged. The centrality of this criteria can be illustrated in the conversation of John Lennon where all things are judged in this light: 'It's no fun being an artist', or 'Heroin? It was just not too much fun' (Wenner, 1970, p. 11).

2 The 'image' one creates is of critical importance: irreverence or rebelliousness are common elements of image. Image is, of course, clearly delineated from self and it is easy for the child to 'image' as a rebel without ever being rebellious to others who are sensitized to the demands of image. Image is extremely vulnerable to changes of fashion: it can move from being simply a pose of endless boredom ('this all bugs me') to a uniform and highly stylized complex of body movements that communicate a casual and disdainful aloofness ('looking cool') (Werthmann, 1963).

Certain elements of image however appear timeless. There are certain ways of staring, glaring, walking and talking which I experienced as a teddy boy in the 1950s that form the basis of instant recognition and acceptance among the adolescents I taught twenty years later. Clearly some of the intimate signs and symbols by which past and present participants in alternative culture recognize each other are less susceptible to fashion than others.

Alternative Culture and the School

'FUN'

Schools are not places where fun and laughter are readily accepted. In fact you could define schools as social mechanisms concerned with the replacement of fun by seriousness, and of play by work. In general the teacher is expected to project a rather grim and earnest professional image if he or she is *really* to teach: the spirit is best captured by that recurrent staff room phrase 'I'm terribly worried about so and so ...' Certainly many trainee teachers have been advised to 'never smile before Christmas' or else respect (and by implication, control) will be lost.

I would argue that exactly the converse is true. In purely educational terms, the best way to earn the respect of adolescents is to be able to handle fun and laughter in just the way one has to in life. The criterion for acceptance of the teacher at the level of alternative culture is his ability to 'take a laugh'. Students have a number of strategies for testing this ability, strategies that have received some attention from American sociologists who use the term 'sounding' to broadly describe the strategy employed by Negro students in New York's secondary schools. Once the ability to 'take a laugh' is proven the testing of the teacher abates — one of the prime tests of alternative culture has been passed.

But, while fun is a powerful educational force, attempts to mobilize it (especially in secondary schooling) run straight into those more brutal socializing functions of schooling in which control dominates learning.

The way that school acts to exclude fun and laughter is a source of alienation consistently alluded to in the internal language of alternative culture. This judgment is confirmed and perpetuated by many working-class/youth cult figures. In his pop song 'School Day' Chuck Berry caught the spirit in which alternative culture perceives school — it is the spirit in which the worker goes to the factory:

Back in the classroom open your books
Even the teacher don't know how mean she looks

or again:

Soon as 3 o'clock rolls around
You finally lay your burden down ('School Day')

The continuity is clear through to today. From Pink Floyd:

> We don't need no education,
> We don't need no thought control
> No dark sarcasms in the classroom
> Teacher leave those kids alone ('Brick in the Wall')

to Paul Simon, 'Kodachrome':

> When I look back on all the
> crap I learned in high school
> It's a wonder I can think at all

to Bruce Springsteen:

> Learn more from a 3 minute record baby,
> than I ever learnt in school. ('No Surrender')

Keith Richard of the Rolling Stones went to school in Deptford:

> I really wanted to learn when I was a kid. I really did. I mean I
> wanted to watch how things were done and try to figure it out
> and leave it at that. I was going to school to do something I
> wanted to do, and then the assholes manage to turn the whole
> thing around and make you hate 'em because they have to run
> their little Hitler numbers, and then you just hate the learning
> thing. You don't wanna learn anymore. School is just like the
> nick. (Scudato, 1974, pp. 37–38)

In his last phrase Richards anticipated the National Union of School
Students' banner which pronounced 'School is Prison'.

'IMAGE'

Image is what allows adolescents to love David Bowie and Boy George
and yet proclaim that they detest homosexuals: 'No problem, it's just
his image'. Each child negotiates her or his image within the immediate
peer group and the wider class unit: some will be 'hard', some 'way
out', some 'straight' some just plain 'bored' (or 'bugged').

In the same way as kids test the teacher over 'laughs' so the
teacher is tested for sensitivity to image. The image determines the
rules which the students want observed in their dealings with the
teacher. So, if a kid is 'bugged', one of the rules is that she or he will
not make any obvious show of being interested or enthusiastic when
the teacher talks. Once sensitized to this there should be no problem
in talking to and teaching them: without such recognition there would

rapidly be a breakdown of communication. Similarly, once recognized, it is perfectly possible to allow the 'hard' student to act out an image without there ever being a confrontation.

Recognition of the student's image normally ensures a reciprocal acceptance of the requirements of the teacher's role — I think that is one of the rules of the game. The crucial point is that image, once recognized, is divorced from actual behaviour. Recognition pre-empts the need for proof so that it becomes the opposite of the tacit accept-ance that many teachers might quite validly fear.

In this game the teacher also has to attend to her or his own image. Since the school is viewed as a prison without much credibility, teachers tend to be viewed in a similar light if they echo some of the fallacies and hypocracies that the students sense (often rightly) in the situation. Too often the teacher is simply seen as the representative of an alien lifestyle. In this situation I would argue that it is perfectly defensible for the teacher to 'image' in ways that make teaching and the student's learning more successful:

> As I watch him teaching it does seem to me there is something about him different to other teachers, even the other jokesters like Liz. Ron doesn't seem to *represent school* like other teachers do. He gives the impression of simply being there because it's a job. In some subtle and indefinable way he conveys a kind of insolence that pupils frequently convey but never teachers. There is something confident, arrogant and deeply irreverent about the way he acts. (Chapter 3)

In this situation the teacher is imaging as a 'rebel' in pursuit of a viable teacher–pupil relationship.

Conclusion

A major variable in classroom interaction, often misunderstood or ignored by teachers of education, is the teachers' consciousness of what I have called alternative culture. I am suggesting that this con-sciousness could be once-and-for-all acquisition — rather like under-standing the rules of a game.

Once grasped the rules of alternative culture transform the reality which the teacher perceives, encounters and constructs in this class-room. As Werthmann (1969) said of his pupils, who were specifically delinquent:

> When gang members are convinced that the educational enter-
> prise and its ground rules are being legitimately pursued, that a
> teacher is really interested in teaching them something, and that
> efforts to learn will be rewarded, they consistently show up on
> time, leave when the class is dismissed raise their hands before
> speaking, and stay silent and awake. (p. 8)

Given an understanding of the alternative culture this is exactly what a
teacher could expect. As Howard Becker (1952) has written:

> School teachers experience problems in working with their
> students to the degree that those students fail to exhibit in
> reality the qualities of the image of the ideal pupil that teachers
> hold. In a stratified urban society there are many groups whose
> lifestyle and culture produce children who do not meet the
> standard of this image, and who are thus impossible for
> teachers like these to work with effectively. Programs of action
> intended to increase the educational opportunities of the
> under-privileged in our society should take account of the
> manner in which teachers interpret and react to the culture
> traits of this group, and the institutional consequences of their
> behaviour. (pp. 75–80)

Becker was writing in 1952 and the emergence of youth culture since
that date has clearly complicated the process of 'mapping' the child's
culture yet his statement retains its validity. Instead of a growing
consciousness of the child's culture, the prerequisite of educational
success, we have a system in which the professionalism of the teacher
is associated with attitudes to fun, image and other central cultural
manifestations which ensure broad-based educational failure. Hence
the definition of alternative culture as deviant derives from the way
schools operate and prescribe teachers' actions. It is to this process that
the sociologist should look rather than continue the reification of
delinquescence.

Author's Note: These notes were prepared during my final year as a
comprehensive school teacher in 1975. In many ways time has not
treated them well and clearly patterns of working class and youth
culture have continued to change, giving some of the statements a rather
'faded' aura.

The optimism of changing the culture of teaching by specifying some
new ideas and guidelines reflects a historical moment of cultural

optimism in the early 1970s. Plainly one would now need to ally such arguments with a plan for contextual and structural redefinition.

With these provisos in mind I think the arguments still reasonably represent some of my views and values with regard to the culture of teaching.

Chapter 5

'Other Rooms: Other Voices' — A Dramatized Report[1]

Rob Walker, Caroline Pick and Barry MacDonald

Prologue

People who take an interest in what goes on in schools are moved by diverse concerns, and have varying purposes. Some have a commercial stake; they dress and feed the inhabitants of schools, or equip and maintain the buildings. Many have professional roles within the school system; teachers, administrators, policymakers, theorists, inspectors, developers. They create, manage and participate in the activity of schooling. Others receive, and evaluate, the service thus provided; parents and their children, taxpayers and ratepayers.

For almost all of them, in our society, schooling is, or has been, important in their own lives, influencing their life-chances and their self-perceptions. Though few of them are well-informed about what goes on in schools, none is ignorant. All have had an experience of schooling which, however idiosyncratic in its particularities of time, place, personnel and pedagogy, however 'tacitly'[2] it is stored, nourishes their assumptions about what goes on, constrains their perceptions, shapes their advocacies.

One consequence of these circumstances is that schooling is both descriptively and prescriptively controversial at every level of society. What goes on is as furiously contested as what should go on. This might be puzzling were it not for the fact that schooling, like many other social services, is secretive about its activities and processes.

Automatic access to classrooms is generally restricted to the few whose formal powers entitle them to entry; others, such as parents, researchers or journalists, must negotiate such access with the staff. Even access to teachers is mostly confined to ritual-laden occasions or special appointments. The posture of the schools is characteristically defensive, somewhat grudging, even suspicious. This is not fully explained by the undoubted need of schools to get on with the job without undue interference.

The need for information could be met by providing self-reports. This does not happen, apart from the patent cosmetics of brochures, prospectuses, conventional school reports and magazines. Such documents tell virtually nothing about what schooling is like as a process and as an experience for pupils and teachers. Much of the schools' conservatism in this area can be put down to tradition and habit. That's the way it has always been, and pressure for more information is a recent phenomenon with which they have yet to come to terms. New demands in any case are difficult to meet — there is little 'slack' in the resource system. Partly also it reflects the teaching profession's fear of 'uninformed' criticism, and partly their fear of justified criticism (House, 1974). Perhaps crucially, the education profession realizes that the distribution of information entails a risk of diminished autonomy.

The barriers which presently inhibit the flow of information, both within the community of education professionals and between it and the community outside, will doubtless yield in time to mounting social pressures. Meanwhile, researchers and evaluators have the opportunity to bridge the gap by providing accounts of school life which would extend and enrich understanding of its contemporary forms.

Curiously, the educational research community has shown little interest in the experience and processes of schooling. Only in the last few years has the study of what happens in classrooms become an established area of educational research and evaluation (Stubbs and Delamont, 1976). Educational investigators have studied other elements in the system, concentrating on measuring the charateristics of pupils, of teachers, or studying learning in relatively pure forms. In retrospect the late appearance of classroom study on the scene might seem odd. Surely what happens between teacher and pupils in the classroom is at the centre of the educational *process*? Why hasn't it been at the centre of research and evaluation?

The reasons are no doubt complex. Until ten years ago the key questions of educational policy (and politics) concerned the differential allocation of students to different types of school, rather than the nature of different forms of classroom experience. Perhaps only with curriculum reform movement have classrooms ceased to become evidently transparent and the nature of teaching and learning easily taken for granted. Previously we felt we knew what teaching and learning were like without looking carefully at what went on in schools. Educational expansion in the form of the curriculum reform movement established the necessity for examining classroom events and processes more closely, and virtually simultaneously easy access to video-tape recording and cheap audio-tape recorders opened up new research methods in a quite dramatic way.

Of course, it does not follow that this new focus upon schooling will serve the purpose of providing more information for all the people we mentioned at the beginning. Researchers have shown themselves to be eminently capable of rendering any knowledge area inaccessible to anyone but themselves. But there is a growing interest, particularly among the evaluation community, in the possibility of developing accounts of schooling which are descriptive in style, couched in language that most people can read and understand. Stake[3] has coined the word 'portrayal' to indicate the aspiration of such efforts, which attempt both a fuller and a simpler rendering of the activities and circumstances of schooling. Portrayal suggests that people need, as a basis for debate and choice, more knowledge and understanding of what goes on in schools, and that an important task for the evaluator is to display the educational process in ways which enable people to engage it with their hearts and minds.

Our experience of evaluative research into the curriculum development movement leads us to reinforce Stake's argument. Although our concern in the SAFARI project is with the structure of innovation at the system level, we have found it essential to pursue our quest for understanding into the classrooms of innovating teachers and pupils, to try to grasp and represent what the system means in their lives. In the course of our enquiry we have paid increasing attention to the perceptions, feelings and responses of those intimately involved in the process of schooling, and felt the need to portray their experience to those who debate the merits of particular forms of school provision.

But how best to convey this experience to all those 'interested' people remains a problem. Conventional frames of reporting seem poorly suited to the kind of data we present in the unusual format which follows. It seems clear that the portrayal of schooling calls for formats and skills unfamiliar to researchers and evaluators. One possibility, which we have explored here, is collaboration between researchers and those who are skilled in forms of communication which constitute a research novelty.

This script has been developed from the files of our research project; the source data concerns how teachers who were involved in Nuffield Science saw it after some years teaching it. A critical event in the acquisition of the data was a weekend conference[4] in the Summer of 1974 to which we invited twenty young teachers who had been using Nuffield Science projects to talk to us about their experience of curriculum innovation, their experience of teaching generally, and their perceptions of themselves as persons who happened to be also teachers.

In the event what emerged from the weekend were twenty professional life histories in which the teachers wrote about how they came to specialize in science, in their experiences as science undergraduates, in why they turned to teaching as a job or as a career, in their motives for becoming involved in curriculum development. The information we gained about Nuffield Science was most useful, but what impressed us most was the total picture. The way the teachers saw themselves in the schools they taught in, their memories of their own schooldays, the questions they asked themselves about the value of what they were doing. We kept up a correspondence with some of them, and other pictures emerged — the routine of the school day, the press of events in a busy school.

We recognized the authenticity of the accounts we had collected and began to think about them in relation to the pictures of science teaching that emerge from curriculum project publications. But despite the value of the information, our efforts to report it in conventional written forms left us dissatisfied. It was not until Caroline Pick of the Open University[5] responded positively to the possibility of a 'dramatized documentary' radio script that we felt we had perhaps found a format which matched the data. We gave Caroline access to the full accounts (which run to over 100,000 words) and, with Rob Walker as consultant, she produced a draft script which formed the basis of the script reproduced here. Despite severe selection and strong editing the testimony of the teachers remains in its verbatim form.

The truth status of what follows is a matter for the reader's judgment. The data are authentic. All the statements used were made by teachers in the form in which they appear. Moreover, they were made by the teachers individually and in privacy, in diaries over which they retained control. We subsequently negotiated the release of the data. The interpretation, inherent in the process of selecting, editing and sequencing the material, was the joint responsibility of Caroline Pick and Rob Walker. Selection of data was guided by (1) *Thematic relevance*. The idea was to combine an account of a routine day in the professional life of the teacher with the reflections of teachers about their roles and identities. (2) *Anecdotal vividness*. We looked for the crystallizing incidents often cited by teachers as important formative experiences. Anecdotes have a quality of undeniability that tempts us to classify them as 'hard' rather than 'soft' data. (3) *Range and varia-*

tion. The choice of data, whilst not representative in a statistical sense, was guided by the need to reflect the multiple character of the teachers' perspectives and responses. Within the compass of a brief interchange (the broadcast is limited to twenty minutes) the selection cannot span the range, but merely hint at it. Moreover, the reader should keep in mind the composition of the teacher group from which the data was elicited. All of them were young graduate science teachers who found it worthwhile to travel from different parts of the country to respond to the basic question we formulated in our letter of invitation: *'What is the relationship between the person you are, and the teacher you are?'* The question constituted a further criterion in the selection, editing and sequencing of the basic data.

Other Rooms, Other Voices

(Bell)

1	*Narrator:*	Tuesday, 10th March, 8:30 a.m. Arrive. Go straight to lab. Put preserved foetus away — out of sight. Mr Lewis always leaves it on the front bench. I can't stand it. I use transparencies of embryos instead; they look pink and healthy.

8:45 a.m. Staff Meeting. Deputy Head asks for help with system for checking lateness. Today he's in brown suit with brown shirt and white tie; looks like member of the mafia. Meeting oozes sympathy. No-one prepared to lift a finger.

8:55 a.m. School bells stopped working. Go to classroom door and gesture them in. Several 'Hello, Mr Windmills' as they file in. Registration: Paul and David just back after two weeks' suspension for stealing. They ignore me. Then — assembly.

(in hymn cross fade to playground and school and hold under)

2 *Melvyn Bloom:* When I think of my schooldays, I remember old buildings, huge partitions, out of tune

pianos, my first ink pen, listening to songs on the radio, throwing cigarette cards against the wall. Interesting teachers who did everything better than we did, who'd been in the navy, been on long train journeys. Who could take a drag on a cigarette, drink a cup of tea and then let out the smoke. I remember the mysterious vicar in black with his apparatus for communion, ancient radiators that creaked and groaned. Prayer — 'lighten our darkness on cold wet November evenings'.

3 *Susan Dale*:   Going through the education factory we took what was offer without really liking or hating any of it. Of course, we said we 'liked' the easy subjects and didn't 'like' the difficult ones. I chose science because I was good at it. And the biology master used to let me spend hours in the science lab. Anyway, physics and chemistry were subjects I wasn't allowed to do. They were 'boys' subjects'. Science meant freedom. It meant showing the school I could do what they said I couldn't.

I never wanted to be a teacher myself because all women teachers seemed sort of frumpish and fuddy-duddy and boring.

(school background into bell)

4 *Narrator*:   Bell working again. Go to junior lab. Let in second form. Teach introduction to reproduction. Paves way for fertilization and embryo on Friday. Make joke about millions of sperm swimming to their doom; class relaxes for ten minutes of questions and answers.

(Fade up playground and school and hold under)

5 *Melvyn Bloom*:   In my probationary year in teaching, I was innocent about what really went on in schools. I was totally inequipped to teach 'general science' to unacademic kids in a new comprehensive school. It was a disastrous start.

I misjudged the children — their capacities and interests. Also my ability to hold their attention. I had continual trouble with 'control' and 'discipline' and failed my probation.

6 *Susan Dale*: In my first year I had a very difficult third year class. I spent six weeks getting nowhere. We were doing chemistry. One day I had a bottle full of red lead. I stood at the front and banged the bottle to get the class to be quiet. No response. So I banged again. Again no response, I banged harder, and the bottom of the bottle fell out. Red lead from head to foot. What's more it's bright orange and I was wearing cream. There was just me and a cloud of red lead. The first time I ever got absolute silence. All the kids reacted beautifully. They howled with laughter, rushed to the front, tried to brush me down. They just brushed it in! Then I fell off the rostrum, I was laughing so much. After that no problems because the kids were impressed that I could laugh at myself.

7 *Richard Crane*: I began by teaching science in a London comprehensive which was just starting. The head seemed very intelligent, liberal and enthusiastic. He said 'There will be no corporal punishment in this school'. Applause, applause from all the staff. A few weeks later he caned the first pupil.

My favourite class was remedial biology. One day we were 'doing' earthworms. I asked the kids to write poems; one boy wrote this:

> 'Little earthworm all calm and placid
> til I shoved him in some acid....'

(School and playground into bell)

8 *Narrator*: First form. The biology of any animal of their choice. I'm bored but they enjoy it. All I can do in one lesson a week.

(Fade up playground and school and hold under)

9 *Melvyn Bloom*: I teach by instinct. If it goes well then I carry on, if it doesn't, I try and think of something better. I've never been one who analyzes what he's done.

10 *Barbara Green*: I went to a very authoritarian girls' school and I try not to be like the teachers there. But you've got to be careful it's not all you giving and them talking. When I'm tired, fed up or got a hangover, I just want to say 'You just shut up because I tell you to'. This whole authoritarian thing's very difficult. Also get a lot of trouble with fourth year boys and fifth year boys are always touching me up.

11 *Richard Crane*: When I'm teaching, if somebody mutters something funny, usually I laugh. But if it disrupts the lesson totally, I'll laugh and then tell the bloke off. OK, it was funny but it wasn't the time or place for humour. One of the things he's got to learn is there's a time and place for everything.

12 *Melvyn Bloom*: Someone said — if you can teach at this school you can teach anywhere. I almost believe it, but still there's an enormous gulf between me and the pupils. Though I've tried I can't seem to get into working-class culture at all.

(Fade school background into bell)

13 *Narrator*: 10:45 a.m. Break: Chat to John. He's spent more time with educational psychologists than anyone, but seems on good form with 'bovver' haircut and 2 inch platform-shoes. Warn him that deputy head has views. John says he'll hide his feet in public!

(Bell)

11:00 a.m. Upper Fifth. Ask whether they've been given brains since last week. Actually they're very bright.

(Fade up school and playground and hold under)

14 *Melvyn Bloom*: The head of physics makes me insecure. He's a very nasty person, calls me 'bloody Smith'. I call him 'bloody Jones'. All good-humoured, but he definitely dislikes me and what I stand for. He's two years off retirement, and has taught here ever since the war, when he got the job after two hundred others had applied for it. Then he saw himself at the top of the scale, his pay on par with the local doctor. All this has vanished ... he's not a happy man, and it's all *my* fault!

15 *Barbara Green*: Life really is difficult in this school. One week I asked leave to attend a job interview, the headmaster advised me to give up teaching, *and* I was hit over the head by a pupil with a chair. Perhaps it's my problem, a problem I have to live with, which I can't unload. But a greater sense of belonging to a department would help. At least I'd get advice then and share it with others.

(School background into bell)

16 *Narrator*: 11:45 a.m. Lower Sixth. Most finishing notes as instructed. Go through filter action of *Glomerulus* and then set homework.

(Fade up school and playground)

17 *Susan Dale*: I think too much is expected of us. For most people it's impossible to do the job even adequately. People compensate; they compromise in the way they teach, in the materials they prepare. The roles they're expected to play are too wide and there are too many different ones. They're expected to be authoritarian and to relate to children at the same time. You've got to tell them off for not wearing school uniform and have a trusting relationship with them.

18 *Richard Crane*: When the kids actually ask questions that I've not thought that they could, and when one of them goes further and expands something, and then the bell goes and they say, 'that's not the

bell, is it sir?', it's exhilarating. Mind you, it also makes me hopping mad. The bell controls their lives. Normally they pack up five minutes before it goes.

(School background into bell)

19 *Narrator:* 12:30 a.m. Lunch: Chat to two groups about 'open careers meeting' in library — a follow-on from last term. They decide to have it on Thursdays. Send note to careers master for OK. Another note back — 'yes, damn you'.

1:30 p.m. Back to lab. for own third form. Prepare demonstration of injected kidney.

(Bell)

1:50 a.m. See Blackburn. He didn't have permission to be out at lunch. Says he went to chemist to get plasters for blisters caused by new shoes, black, to replace old shoes, brown, which deputy head didn't like.

(Fade up playground and school and hold under)

20 *Susan Dale:* The best times teaching are out of school. I went for a fortnight camping with some kids once — I'd taught about thirty of them and we took ninety. They live all round the common, but never go out and look at it at all. They didn't realize you get oak trees and sycamore trees. Each was just 'a tree'. The first day we went into a wood and told them we had to be quiet and creep about and not disturb anything because they were there to observe. They'd never been in that situation before. They started creeping round but finally they were rushing up with this and that and the other and saying 'come and look'. I'd never seen them so interested. We were with them from the time they woke up until bed, getting to know them very well. You appreciated them so much more, even kids that you couldn't stand previously.

21 *Melvyn Bloom:*   The worst thing is teaching something you've taught often before. You assume the kids know something about it. You miss important points or you tend to dwell on things that came up in an earlier class. If you've not taught it before you don't know what to expect and you're much fresher. I don't like teaching the same thing on the same day, even the same thing in the same week. But, if you are doing things like Nuffield Combined Science with the apparatus and everything out, it's much more practical.

(School background into bell)

22 *Narrator:*   2:30 p.m. Free Period — in staff room. Check teaching notes for two fourth forms tomorrow.

(Fade up playground and school and hold under)

23 *Richard Crane:*   The kids are generally very sophisticated. From second form upwards, they start getting off with each other. But some classes have idiosyncracies. Like 3XY girls hate 3XY boys. It's all hell, spitfire and brimstone. Everything the boys like, the girls hate — and vice versa. In other third forms they get on very well. They don't regard girls as softies. In fact, the girls tend to be the spokesman for the class.

24 *Susan Dale:*   I taught a lesson on hormones and I was talking about adrenalin and the fact it make you blush. 'That's why you go red and pink,' I said. There were some coloured girls and one of them turned round and said 'Well, I don't go pink.' We all collapsed, me included.

(School background into bell)

25 *Narrator:*   3:10 p.m. Fifth form in other lab. 'Bracing chat' about 'O' levels, jobs and the importance of these next two terms. Then get on with lesson about Perilymph and Synosial Fluid.

(Fade up playground and school)

26 *Barbara Green*: Being a schoolteacher's a battle. It's the putting things in boxes; school hierarchy, size of classes, everything. Teaching's a terribly immoral profession. It's one of the most dangerous jobs you can do. I think school's a place where people inflict their fantasies on others. All their feelings of power and authority. The education system seems as uneducative as possible. The whole *thing* about syllabuses, exams and the contradiction of my taking an 'O' level group and not believing in it or CSE or *anything*. And having to teach kids something they don't want to know because it's boring and I think it's boring too. But I have to make sure they pass their 'O' level because of their future careers. And then what's a career doing for them? It's helping them to be even more exploited.

27 *Melvyn Bloom*: I am increasingly unclear as to what schools are for. I've got the feeling that many, perhaps most, embody values which I find alien or perverse. I'm obsessed with the way they depersonalize kids.

28 *Richard Crane*: My class were bored and did nothing. They were fed up and accepted their position as that of the damned. When *our* first assembly day loomed close, they had produced nothing. So I said, 'Know any good rock music?'. Heads turned. I said 'What makes you most fed up in the world today?' and off we went. We rifled through my stock of colour slides and put together a tape-slide sequence ending with Crosby, Stills, Nash and Young — 'Teach Your Children Well'. (fade up music).... It worked marvelously. The kids felt brave and out of line and they were first ones to have done their own kind of assembly.

There began to appear chalk on tables and blackboards all over the school '3K Rule OK'!

(Music and school background into bell)

29 *Narrator*:   3:50 p.m. Back to form room to dismiss class. Paul, David and Judson skipped off already.

3:55 p.m. Back to staff room. Tea urn packed up so no tea.

4:00 p.m. Go out to car. Find Judson, Paul and David beside workmen's shed on building site (looking very conspiratorial). Smile, say hello and ask if they'd forgotten about registration after five years at school. They move off cheerfully. If they're going to form a triple alliance my work's cut out. Must see them individually. Depressing thought. Suspension seems to have done little to influence them.

(Fade up school and playground)

30 *Melvyn Bloom*:   After years of teaching I'm becoming a little sour and uninspired. I'm depressed by lack of staff, lack of good science teaching colleagues, lack of lab. assistance and by lack of imagination by local authority. I'm a teacher still full of good ideas but less and less willing to put them into practice.

A teacher with a lot to do outside the classroom — ordering apparatus, planning courses and

(fade up music)

without time to do it.
A teacher at the cross roads.

(peak music)
(fade music and background effects)

Announcer: The script was devised by Caroline Pick in collaboration with Rob Walker.

The narrator was John Barcroft
The voices of the teachers:

Anna Barry

Norma Ronald

Geoffrey Matthews and

Peter Pacey

Script consultation was by Donald Holms
The producer was Caroline Pick

Notes

1 This script and introduction were first produced for The Open University course, E301 Curriculum, Design and Development, in 1976.
2 The concept of 'tacit knowledge' has only recently been introduced into discussions about educational research and evaluation. Tacit knowledge is the kind of everyday, subsidiary, unarticulated grasp of complex situations which forms the basis of ordinary judgments and responses to social life phenomena. Polanyi, who coined the concept, contrasts such knowledge with 'propositional' knowledge which can be verbalized and systematized. 'We know more than we can tell' is how the distinction is sometimes characterized. The relevance of the issue to educational research is clear enough: researchers and evaluators are often accused of oversimplifying and selectively representing the knowledge states of learners and teachers, and of ignoring the ways of becoming knowledgeable that their audiences prefer. The issue is most pertinent to our aspirations in this presentation, see, Polanyi (1961).
3 Stake introduced the concept of portrayal in an address to AERA in 1972. Stephen Kemmis subsequently explored and elaborated the concept (Kemmis, 1976).
4 Clem Adelman, Harold Silver and Hans Brugelmenn helped us in organizing and running the conference.
5 Caroline was, at the time, a BBC producer on attachment to the OU. She has since established herself as an independent producer and film maker.

Chapter 6

Social Research as a Deviant Activity[1]

Rob Walker

My theme is a simple one. Any discussions of deviance that look to research for evidence need to keep constantly in mind that research provides not merely information, but by implication particular, and sometimes peculiar, social values. These values emerge at a number of levels; conceptual, theoretical, philosophical, methodological, empirical; and at various stages of the research enterprise; but especially at the points of commission, omission and sale.

Many of the points of contact between the process of research and social values are well rehearsed but are generally discussed in terms of the professional research worker. Here I want to consider a wider definition of research; one that encompasses the observational activities of those with a field role in education. Research, I want to claim, is itself deviant also.

To begin with I shall describe a research project in which I was engaged on in the early 1980s. This project is not one apparently concerned with deviance, on the contrary it is concerned with the mainstream of day-to-day life in school systems. The aim is to study the roles played by teachers, pupils, parents, headteachers, advisers, inspectors, college supervisors and others who are continually involved in collecting information in, about and from schools. This process of information collection may be more or less systematic, and it may be directed to a number of ends, but if information is collected in order to aid understanding we can think of it as involving a research process.

There are many reasons to support the development of research expertise among professionals and other participants in education. There is, though, at least one reason to be cautious. Sometimes the adoption of a self-conscious 'applied research' approach is made in the form of a bid for authority, in which ownership of the research process is seen as a means to political ends. Central to the value of research in these terms is its claim to objectivity. A good reason to argue for research as a deviant activity is to undermine its authority and so to reduce its value as a political resource.

People working in the system claim to 'know' their schools, teachers, classrooms or pupils, and will frequently suggest that this knowledge is one of their most important resources in 'making the system work'. Yet we do not know of what such knowledge consists, how it is assembled, tested or used; what problems of reliability, validity or utility it poses for those who create, shape or consume it. The research problem is to understand such knowledge better, not to underwrite the claims that some might make to define it.

Set against this task my research is small in scale and narrow in scope. I have tried to devise two illustrative and critical case studies. One concerns the role of local authority advisers and inspectors, the other an attempt to document the life of a school using photographs as the main medium and teachers, pupils and parents as the primary audience.

My reason for discussing this project with you at this conference is not because the content of this study has anything to say about 'deviance', but because the way the study has been designed, and in particular the attempts have made to shift the roles of researchers, subjects and audience, does have implications for the conference theme. I will return to this point later, but first I need to tell you a little more about the project itself.

Advisers and Inspectors

The first case study has attempted to look at how advisers and inspectors look at classrooms and schools. I chose advisers and inspectors because a large part of their job is specifically observational; local authorities employ them, at least in part, to know what is going on in schools, and since the Auld Report on the handling of the William Tyndale School case, this aspect of the role has been looked at by senior administrators and local politicians rather more sharply than previously. Given my starting point, my intention was to look only at one facet of the inspectors' role, their information collecting/observational task in classrooms and in schools. Increasingly though, I have found myself drawn towards making a protrayal of the role in all its facets and complexities. Partly this was because the people I have looked at do not restrict their information collecting to clearly specified times and places; in this they act more like an ethnographic fieldworker than a measurement researcher. Many of the activities the rest of us consider recreational or personal — churchgoing, sport, shopping, parenting or gardening — carry considerable professional traffic for the adviser or inspector living in her or his own territory. There are though other reasons that quickly, but somewhat reluctantly, led me to broaden the scope of the study. In the past two years (1976–7) many people in education have been concerned with problems of change. My first contact with advisers and inspectors was with people who talked about change incessantly; most have formal responsibility for particular areas of curriculum innovation and many are people who lived through the curriculum innovations of the 1960s first hand, often being promoted out of schools on the basis of reputations earned as classroom innovators or progressive headteachers. One adviser confessed he got his job because as a primary school headteacher in the heady days of Plowden he worked hard on his classroom wall displays. Perhaps because many had this background they have seemed quick to see the implications of recent changes in the administration of schools. They have been at the centre of debates over reorganization schemes, locally administered testing programmes and the increasingly public stories of scandal and resignation. As education has seemed to become more and more politicized in recent years, advisers and inspectors have found themselves in a key position, not because they have formal power, but because, if they are effective, they have information.

In this context I found myself becoming intrigued by the fact that advisers and inspectors tend to have a high degree of institutional invisibility. It is a long standing joke in the schools that advisers and inspectors spend all their time drinking coffee in the office, going to meetings and conferences or dozing in their cars in some secluded lay-by. It is mostly assumed in the schools that, being local government officers, advisers and inspectors work closely to orders from above. In some large, bureaucratic LEAs this is probably an accurate perception, but typically the administration has just as vague an idea of their role as the schools, and the Education Committee knows even less. One chief education officer was reported in Ray Bolam's report as saying that he really had no idea what advisers in his Authority did, and recently another CEO reported asking his advisers to tell him what their diary entries were for a randomly selected week because he was curious to find out what they actually did.

This institutional invisibility is interesting because it marks a point of major structural discontinuity in the organization of education in this country. In many ways the schools and the office operate independently of each other. It does not always feel that way, especially at the present time, for those on the inside, but there is no denying that there is a major rift between these two kinds of structure.

While the system appears to have two discrete parts, the office and the schools, advisers and inspectors occupy a role that bridges the two. Not all choose to maintain this position. Some, as one chief inspector put it, 'find themselves a quiet corner of the office to file themselves away in'; others become vagrant (this seems especially true of some subject advisers — especially in art and music). Some though continue to hold the middle ground and carefully guard the space they have won for themselves. For these people 'observation' takes on an especially critical function, for they have to watch every move they make, and every move that is made around them, in order to maintain their position. Indeed they may at times find they have a vested interest in holding the worlds of schools and office apart in order to create more space in which to manoeuvre. In the context of the argument I am developing for this conference the point I want to emphasize is that 'observation' for advisers and inspectors is not a neutral activity but fits into a set of activities that relate to the way their role is constructed within the administrative and management systems within which they are located. A point I will return to in terms of academic research, for we often forget that the same can be said of us. Academic research is not a neutral activity either.

I have talked about this case study to show how an apparently straightforward research problem, studying the observational practices of inspectors and advisers, once it begins to take into account the context in which the phenomena occur, can quickly get into considerable complexities. I hope too, that it will be clear to you that I see advisers and inspectors as to some degree deviant. They do not fit easily into line management structures, often feeling misunderstood, marginal or institutionalized.

Pictures

The other case study I have been working on within the context of the project has been a collaboration with Janine Wiedel, a photojournalist and photographer. Using a combination of photographs and interviews Janine and I have begun documenting the life of a secondary school. Our main purpose in doing this has been to provide teachers with material that can be used as a basis for communication with parents. The main products of the study are not books and reports but displays; displays that go on classroom notice boards and in the halls and meeting places of the school. At the moment we are right in the middle of this study and our aspirations are still running some way ahead of our achievements, but we use the word 'display', rather than the word 'exhibition' deliberately, for our intention is that the displays act as a source of data as much as a means of dissemination.[2] When we show people the pictures we are interested in knowing their response, not just so that we can add the response to the display but because we find that in the context of the kinds of questions the research is concerned with, responses to photographs seem more revealing than responses to interview questions. If you want to know about someone's common-sense understanding of their everyday world it seems one of the most effective methods of eliciting information from them is through an acceptable device that emphasizes non-technical, shared meanings (the photograph). People talk more naturally to a photograph than they will to a tape recorder, notebook or clipboard. We say that having attempted to use more orthodox methods, and having failed.[3]

Some Methodological Issues

In the study of the role of advisers and inspectors, most of the immediate problems I face stem from the fact that I am dealing with people who stand quite high in local education systems in terms of status and influence. If you look at the history of participant observation research it is clear that the research role is one largely derived from studies of deviants and one of its invisible assumptions appears to be that the researcher operates from a higher social status than the subject. In this study this is clearly not the case and one of the effects is that we tend to get into quite complex cross-cutting relationships. One senior adviser who has given me considerable access to his work, sits on the university committee that monitors the work of the centre in which I work. Many of the students who come on our MA courses are teachers from his own area. I am supervising his part-time research degree. We both sit on various outside committees and attend meetings where our roles are formally more equal. In addition, we and our families meet socially. This particular researcher-subject relationship is unusually complex, but it illustrates the kind of contextual complexity that often surrounds research in practice. Add to this complexity the fact that the content of the research is central to the concerns of the subject and it follows that from the research point of view, everything becomes data, even personal information, for to some degree the kind of person he is is also the kind of adviser he is. It works both ways too; from his point of view every conversation with me has a professional potential. It is almost impossible to talk about schools or teachers without some movement of information between the categories of research and professional practice.

You might feel that this is bad research practice on my part and that I should act to contain the research role more strictly. In fact most of the advisers and inspectors I have worked with have been distant and it has been easier to keep the process of research pure. Having been schooled in the orthodox conventions of social science method this seems to be more satisfactory, but issues of method aside I am not sure that it *is* an advantage, either for research or for professional practice. The quality of the data is different when research keeps distant; it is easier to handle, less deeply subjective, easier to manipulate and to categorize, and on the whole less revealing, less real, thin. Given the choice between data collected from strangers during intensive, but brief periods of condensed fieldwork; and that which comes from close contact over long periods of time in cross-cutting relationships, I find I prefer to work with the latter, despite the difficulties, technical and professional, because they seem to offer greater promise of insight and understanding.

Some people might find this disturbing, arguing that the central value in research must be objectivity. It is important though that we do not confuse objectivity with detachment or non-involvement. We do not have to think of objectivity as a quality with an absolute purity acquired by scrupulous observance of specified rituals. I prefer to think of it as a variable quality that can only be won by constant and active vigilance — a view of objectivity that owes more to journalistic and documentary traditions than to science. An underlying assumption in this research is that the purpose of research is to provide a fair representation of the work of advisers and inspectors for publication.

The photographic study raises other problems with relation to audience and publication. This study is conceived around a notion of successive audiences with the research keeping control over who sees the data, while the subjects keep some control over the content. Perhaps I can explain this more clearly by giving an example. Janine and I have just been working on a study of the first term in a first year maths class. This is an interesting topic because the maths course is highly individualized and socializing pupils into the organizational and procedural demands of the course presents the teachers with something of a challenge. In many ways the topic is similar to that studied by Edwards and Furlong (1978) in their recent study of humanities teaching at the Abraham Moss Centre though they work more from a sociolinguistic perspective.

Having collected some 500 photographs taken during some three weeks of contact time with the class, we began using the photographs to ask the teacher, and then the pupils to tell us what they saw in them. This provided a basis for initial selection — frames or sequences that interested them, or puzzled us, which were printed along with comments that people had made about them. This material provided the basis for the first display, which went on the classroom wall. The next stage will be to produce a display for the maths department, which will mean collecting more material and re-editing what we have already. At a later stage we hope to make a display for the school on the basis of fourth year pupils in and out of school. These topics or headings have emerged from our observations and conversations in the school; building up fragments and by continuously circulating them back to internal audiences so as to create a confidence in the process that will encourage the school to allow outside audiences access to the material, initially perhaps the parents and the community, later more distant audiences.

Usually when we write books and reports we write to the outside world or to the research community, perhaps offering to show the book to our subjects and making some gesture of gratitude in the acknowledgments. Increasingly I have come to feel that this is not enough. Participants in the research should also be given access to the process.

Research as Deviant Behaviour

I have described these studies to you because I want to establish that the subject of research/subject/audience relationships is not simply procedural, but cuts through the practice of research at every level. The process of social research is one in which meanings are negotiated between different interest groups, and this is just as true of survey research or large scale testing programmes as it is of the kind of small scale applied research study I have been describing to you. Surveys of educational opportunity or of academic performance, or of student subject choice, for instance, can only be conceived and can only exist in the context of a widespread acceptance of shared meaning across a range of more and less powerful interest groups. Such consensus, or convergence, of meaning need not be, and scarcely ever is, passive or totally accepted. The ability of some interest groups to impose their meaning on the research process almost always lies behind the report. Surveys of academic performance are a topical case in point. A glance at the composition of the committees of the APU — Assessment of Performance Unit — reveals a confluence of disparate interests — a line-up of the teacher unions, academics and administrators whose consensus-by-committee is used to locate, establish and reinforce areas and levels of shared meaning, and so to shape and guide the process and progress for the research. The underlying principle is one of representative government, a principle which in itself cuts out some kinds of understanding and particpation.

When Barry MacDonald proposed a shift away from what he depicted as 'autocratic' and 'bureaucratic' forms of evaluation and research to a form which was labelled 'democratic', we found ourselves faced with two very different views as to what constituted democracy. On the one hand there was the view that the democratic processes necessarily involved a system of representative decision-making, that democracy and representation (in complex modern societies) were virtually synonymous. This was not what we had intended. What we meant to convey in the use of the term 'democratic' was a notion of democracy that invoked participation and engagement by those who often find themselves disenfranchized by representative systems. As we saw it, evaluation and research had been captured by officials and often used against those with limited power. Our use of the term 'democratic' was intended to be more radical than may at first seem, not out of a deliberate sense to confuse, but in an effort to hold those who use the rhetoric of democracy as a means of legitimating power to publicly examine the gaps between their rhetoric and their practice. It is a view of 'democracy' that celebrates diversity of view, rather than one that attempts to impose centralized majority rule.

Large scale research becomes the means by which the state extends its reach and tightens its grasp over the education system and the process of schooling. We need to preserve 'deviance' in this context as a source of alternative ideas, points of development for the future, and as a means of preserving pluralism.

As researchers we cannot dismiss this as being simply a question of the context in which we must work. It is not just the organization of research that is affected but the process of research and the language we use. Terms such as 'disruptive pupils' or 'deprivation' or 'achievement', do not enter the process of research free of social origins and value connotations. Such terms haunt the process of research at every turn.

The terms 'informal teaching', 'open classrooms', 'evaluation', 'curriculum reform', which appear more neutral, have appeared in the titles of research projects I have worked on and have been the major constraints in locating the application of our energies to the tasks. In research, as in much else, words provide the traffic by which power is exerted: to challenge the word is a political act. So, I believe one of the most useful ways research can begin is simply by mapping word use. Who describes whom as deviant? Who can make the label stick and by what means?

Other speakers at this conference have already crossed this ground, here I am interested in a rather different issue. What words do they use to describe us?

Recently I visited a primary school to ask the headteacher if he would give me access to his school to conduct a case study. A copy of the research proposal had been mailed to him in advance and he was not very impressed with it. As we talked he seemed a little easier, then he smiled and said, 'You know, when I first looked at the proposal I thought you were a sociologist!' Perhaps that is not the best of credentials with which to face this audience, but I think it reveals how many of the people who work in schools think about us. *We* can be very perceptive about the social constructions and ideological positions that lie behind their use of words like 'disruptive pupils', 'deprivation', 'informal teaching' and 'achievement', but we are often slow to pick up the finer points of meaning that attend the use of words like 'researcher', 'lecturer' or 'sociologist'. We apply words like 'hegemony' to others, only rarely to ourselves.

One of the aspects of the work of advisers and inspectors that has struck me most forcibly is that those I have observed are very sensitive to the effect on the schools of the way the schools see them. My initial assumption when I first began observing advisers and inspectors observing was that their major problems were likely to lie in the areas of inter-observer agreement and challenges to the validity of their observations. I felt this would be so I think because these are the main challenges met by researchers who have adopted descriptive methods of reporting classroom events. In fact I found these things offered very little difficulty to the adviser or inspector for their role and status in the system are such that they are rarely challenged directly, and when they are, they may, if they choose, ignore the challenge or make their definition of the situation stick on the basis of experience or authority.

As researchers, I don't think we are very good at seeing ourselves as the schools see us, but many of the advisers and inspectors I know are acutely conscious of how the schools see them. I think this relates to their marginality in the system. We too have escaped the classroom and the ranks have closed behind us but we can hide from the guilt we feel and the bitterness and betrayal we sometimes leave behind. We have powerful other reference groups — universities, colleges, poly-technics, committees, associations, publications, even conferences. The adviser or inspector may find him or herself an out-of-the-way office to be filed away in: we have a choice of more reputable cupboards in which to hide.

The title I have chosen ('Social Research is a Deviant Activity') sounds provocative because as a professional activity, 'research' has an establishment ring to it. At the level of publications, reports, meetings and conferences; research is institutionally established. Look at the books we write, the things we teach our students, nothing could be more conventional, in its own way more conservative. But if we look at research as a social process involving negotiations and trade-offs between researchers, sponsors, subjects and audiences, and particularly if we look at what happens before and after publication, then the enterprise begins to look a little more marginal and precarious. 'What are we doing here? Who are we working for? What do we get out of it?', are questions that are increasingly asked of us when we go into schools. I laughed when the headteacher said he thought I was a 'sociologist' because he was able to convey such a rich array of mean-ing (contempt dominating) in the way he used and said the word. Then I remembered how often I had used the word 'headteacher' in the same fashion.

Perhaps 'deviance' is the wrong word to use in this context because of the value-connotations it carries. More than most words we use it is both a description and a judgment and formally research is a mainstream, conventional activity. Research though does share charac-teristics with other activities more usually considered deviant; more people talk about it than do it (many of those who write books, teach research, head departments and direct projects rarely *do* it); no-one over 30 does research (an exaggeration but it is a phenomenon of late or delayed adolescence); it is more frequent as an obsession among those lacking stable academic employment. Finally I suppose I should confess, it provides a curious excitement and offers what to some is an attractive lifestyle. Not many social researchers wish they were doing something else for a living.

You might think these things frivolous, but to some degree the kind of researchers we are are the kind of people we are. More than advisers and inspectors, research provides an ecological niche for the last vestiges of 1960s optimism. The John Lennon and Mick Jagger hairstyles are thinning under the stress of family life, economic cutbacks and college closures, but the bookshelves and record racks reveal where the heart is, and the intellect follows close after. Research, as an occupation, provides a space where some dreams can be kept alive and perhaps that is the real source of deviance, especially when the dreams become distorted and lose some of their connection with reality.

William Labov (1973) has written perceptively on this point in an article called, 'On the linguistic consequences of being a lame'. Much of Labov's research has been on the study of the black American variety of non-standard spoken English, and one of his key groups of subjects has been adolescent male street gangs in the urban NE of the USA. In the vernacular of such groups 'lames' are marginal members of the group, often though not discernible as such to the outsider, for whom they may appear to be central members. Labov locates lames in the groups he studied by a combination of sociometric methods, fine-grained linguistic analysis and participant observation. One of the implications he draws from his study is that with participant observation alone he might not have located the lames, indeed it seems that in many respects his descriptions of them match the description that ethnographers often give of their 'reliable informants'. On a more speculative note he goes on to suggest that linguists themselves are often lames. Lacking intimate and continuous contact with the culture of the street from a point sometime in early adolescence they emerge as adults only able to act as convincing members of the vernacular culture to outsiders. Allowing for differences in culture, Labov might be describing one of Jackson and Marsden's (1962) working-class grammar school boys.

As an occupation, research provides the promise of a way back in; as Edmund Wilson said of his drinking in an otherwise sedate middle-age 'it was a way of getting back then, or re-entering youth'. A life missed can be recaptured vicariously. It is a way we can return to what we might have been, but with a safety-net. Nowhere is this more likely to be true than in the field of research on deviance.

I say this, not out of criticism or condemnation. I recognize some of my own motives in it as well as pointing to those of others. Of course any attempts to play games with the lives of others has its dangers, but we all do this and research has no more guilt to carry in this respect than administration or teaching. And some research claims to be disinterested in its subjects and protected by strong conventions of objectivity anonymity and detachment.

But I have already argued myself into a situation where such conventions stand in the way of understanding. The closer I get to the world of the advisers and inspectors (especially those who are lames)

the better my understanding, the more I take down the barriers between subject and audience in studying schools, the greater the promise and productivity of the research.

A Final Comment: On The Dangers of Methodology

Much of what I have said concerns research methodology. As sociologists we are often quick to point to processes of reification in the
thinking of others but tend not to see our own research methods in the
same light. The reification of methodology is I think an important
thing to guard against because it so rapidly and invisibly penetrates all
we say. This is especially true of large-scale research that becomes
inextricably linked to bureaucratic control.

The geographer and social scientist Gunnar Olson has made this
point most powerfully in a paper he wrote in 1974 called 'Servitude
and Inequality in Spatial Planning: Ideology and Methodology in
Conflict'. Writing about the large scale administrative use of social
science data to equalize social justice across the various regions of
Sweden, Olson points to the fact that the deep assumptions implicit in
the methods of research used led to actions which in fact conflicted
with the values to which the planners aspired. As survey data became
increasingly integral to decision-making, Olson argued, 'the initial purpose of creating a just society became altered to that of finding a set of
efficient solutions to a problem of geometric partitioning'. (Does this
remind you of comprehensive reorganization?) He goes on: 'Un-
noticed to spectators and performers, the play was changed in the
middle of the act. The *ought* of justice disappears in the wings, invisibly stabbed by the *is* of methodology. Exit man with his precious
visions, hopes and fears'.

Despite the vulnerability of the small scale interventive research I
am engaged in it seems to me that such studies do offer a medium
technology response to the demand for large-scale, bureaucratic research increasingly being commissioned in education. When Gunnar
Olson looked at spatial planning he noted that:

> If regional planning in Sweden, the Soviet Union and the
> United States have nothing in common, it is exactly this sim-
> plified and de-humanizing conception of man. Instead of creat-
> ing a world for becoming, we are creating thingified man: by
> treating the relations between people as if they obediently
> followed the multiplication table we are ridding ourselves of
> that challenging ambiguity which alone makes life worthwhile.[4]

If you share Olson's vision, then research provides a source for exposing, even for creating, ambiguity; not out of a sense of mischief or to crystallize structural conflict, but as a contribution to the quality of life. I find that an interesting and pertinent challenge for educational research for as research becomes increasingly controlled by the state it is only by deviance that we can challenge the assumptions of government. This is a particularly pressing problem in applied research where the tendency is increasingly to see research as a technology for managing means rather than a way of imagining alternative ends.

Notes

1 This paper was written as an address to The Westhill College Sociology of Education Conference.
2 A later report on this study appears in Walker and Wiedel (1985).
3 A similar point has been made by John Berger and Jean Mohr. See for instance, Berger and Mohr (1982).
4 This echoes the quote from John Berger in our introduction.

Chapter 7

Making Sense and Losing Meaning[1]

Rob Walker

The task of research is to make sense of what we know. The investigator dismantles and reassembles conventional or commonsense meanings, altering the balance between what seems strange and what is familiar, striving to find new ways of looking at the world. This paper is written from commitment to the belief that the subject being studied can impose its own authority on the sense that is made of it by the investigator. Discipline-free research is not undisciplined research. If the immediate context of the study becomes the bounded instance, rather than the theoretical problem, then the case under study will impose its own logic on the practice of the researcher. If the investigation begins with problems, issues or concerns that are endemic to the subject and pursues them within the context of bounded cases, then it is possible for discipline to stem, not from the canons of social science, but from the continuing practice of research and the authority of the subject.

Methodology: In Retrospect and Prospect

When researchers and evaluators choose to write about problems associated with design, methods or techniques, they usually do so with reference to work already accomplished. After all, who would be interested in half-formulated ideas that remain untried and untested. Inevitably, technical papers and textbooks, whether on participant observation, interviewing, questionnaire design or test construction, attempt to accumulate and condense the wisdom to be gained from past experience. In total, the picture they present is of an achieved and available critical tradition to which the beginning project can turn.

At the time of writing this paper, I am at a point where one project I have been working on is drawing to a close,[2] and where I am about to start on two related but different projects.[3] When I think about research methods in education in relation to these projects I am aware of two distinct sets of discourse. The world of 'methodology' represented by the textbooks, it seems, is primarily a world seen in retrospect. It is a world in which condensation and accumulation of knowledge are possible, where you can learn from the literature, where criticism thrives and alternative schools of thought flourish. The world of research practice on the other hand, has an oral rather than a literary tradition, and is essentially prospective. The concerns of each world are really very different (perhaps comparable to the differences between literary criticism, and setting out to write a novel). What looks like a problem when you are discussing research already accomplished, often does not look like a problem when you are doing it: and vice versa.

It appears the distinction is not confined to educational research, for Peter Medawar, an eminent biologist, has written a well known paper asking 'Is the scientific paper a fraud?'. He suggests that as a fully accurate account of the process, practice and conduct of research, the scientific paper is highly misleading, since it glosses and edits almost all you can actually need to know to replicate the process of discovery (Medawar, 1963).

In prospect the most important methodological problems are those that fall under the questions: How am I going to go about this piece of research? In what ways are decisions I make about how to do it going to determine what I find out, and what I will fail to discover? Part of the difficulty, certainly, comes in trying to move easily between retrospect and prospect. It isn't always easy learning how to learn from accumulated wisdom and past experience, for what apparently worked at one time at one place is always difficult to disentangle from its specific context. Attempting to build on past success can lead to accumulated blindness so that a central problem of method becomes, not how to apply the wisdom of the past, but how to get past accepted wisdom.

In case-study research particularly, methods and techniques have to emerge from the authority of the subject. They have to be customized to fit the exigencies of the situation. 'Discipline' derives from substantive rather than theoretical sources. The problem with past experience is that it tends to stand between the investigator and the subject of study, masking issues and distorting perceptions; not freeing action, but freezing it.

Doing Research and Reporting It

Whether the investigator is orientated to quantitative or qualitative information; to case study or to survey; once the information is collected it has to be organized, manipulated and presented in ways that make it make sense.

In the classic structure of research reporting the problem hardly exists. The final report is virtually the 'proposal with the results tables filled in' (a phrase I think I owe to Malcolm Parlett). But as Medawar has pointed out, such forms of reporting compound a fiction, for they give no clues to practice or to the actual process of discovery or to the ways conventional wisdom has had to be stretched and squeezed. The assumption is that what emerges from the case study in terms of facts, findings or information, is pre-specified in the design.

Viewed *retrospectively* the problem of making sense of the data, is seen essentially as a technical problem. The textbooks provide processes and manipulations that allow you to get from raw information to a form that can be interpreted (cooked?). They key themes in handbooks of research or evaluation methods are mostly concerned with how to collect, organize, verify and process information. Very rarely are they about how to understand it.

In prospect the route looks more daunting and fraught with unknowns. A direct comparison can be drawn with documentary film-making. In film-making a great deal of planning and selection is involved before the cameras start to roll, but it is still impossible to pre-specify the results. The most experienced and well-prepared director cannot tell quite what will happen in front of the camera; nor can the most skilled and imaginative cameraman know quite what the projected image will look like. In the spaces between planning and realization, between exposure and projection, there is always the promise of surprise and the essence of discovery. Perhaps more important there is always a dramatic loss of meaning stemming from multiple causes. Here the editor's role is critical, for the editor reassembles a semblance of reality on the basis of conventions quite different from those of the participants, the cameraman and even the director.

Perhaps in research and evaluation we should be more conscious than we usually are of our editorial role. Conventional techniques help us to make sense of the information we find, but mostly these techniques are devices for making multiple selections, compressions and juxtapositions of the information we have. As such they demand judgments about appropriateness which are not altogether technical but theoretical and moral.

Notes for a Prospectus

I want to give some illustration of four kinds of problems (all profoundly interrelated) which are essentially prospective and primarily methodological. The account that follows cannot be exhaustive. I want simply to state some obvious difficulties and illustrate each briefly. The four themes are: first, different aspects of the problem of selection; second, the problem of finding out too much; third, the problem of not finding out enough; and fourth, the problem of discovery.

Problems of Selection

How do you get from the initial idea to a working design (from the idea to a specification, to usable data)?

What do you lose in the process?

What unwanted concerns do you take on board as a result?

How to find a site which provides the best location for the design?

How to locate, identify and approach key informants?

What are the consequences of neglecting to contact or cultivate those who remain outside the scope of the study?

How they see you creates a context within which you see them. How can you handle such social complexities?

How do you record evidence? When? How much?

How do you file and categorize it?

How much time do you give to thinking and reflecting about what you are doing?

At what points do you show your subject what you are doing?

At what points do you give them control over who sees what?

Who sees the reports first?

I offer these questions as a beginning; it wouldn't be hard to extend the list considerably.

Finding Out Too Much

Only rarely can the design for an evaluation or piece of research fully contain the range and quantity of the information generated by the process of investigation. In even the most parsimonious study, the investigators learn more than they tell, or feel able to tell. Furthermore, the conventional formats of research reporting and professional contact impose recognized and characteristically 'polite fictions'.

Wastage of information is intrinsic to social research (whether qualitative or quantitative). If it were not so, research would hardly ever by embarked upon: its purpose is to make the world more answerable to understanding not merely to rehearse its complexities. As in film-making, some of the best scenes end up on the cutting room floor in the interest of the story line. Much of what the social investigator learns becomes absorbed into folklore; frequently emerging as anecdotes, jokes, professional small-talk and gossip. Very often the story the investigator wants to tell remains untold, or is told only within a small professional circle.

In social research the investigator asks questions, listens; but always hears more than they intend. You look, but see more than you expect. Contact with phenomena, however, sanitized by the technology of the research, inevitably brings about changes in the observer and in the frame of observation.

Despite the sensation of cultural shock that researchers often feel in first-hand contact with the world of their subjects, once the process of research begins, the phenomena and the observations touch, intermingle and interact. The world of research and the world of the subject may be insulated one from another, but the phenomena and the observations provide points of contact between them. In time the observations can themselves become the phenomena (which has its dangers, as well as advantages, for the investigator can come to believe that they are actually witnessing such ideal abstractions as 'learning', 'open classrooms', 'discussion' or 'discovery methods'). In short, social research is essentially a social and cultural activity which frequently has effects other than those intended, or even predicted, by those who engage in it.

Not Finding Out Enough

While it is inevitable that the investigators know more than they tell, it is equally true that they rarely find out all they need to know. Almost always the project fails in some significant way to capture all the evidence initially intended, or retrospectively considered necessary. Even in the most massive empirical enquiries only a small fraction of the possible meaning is tapped. Between the initial design and the final results, between definitions and operational categories, lie vast oceans of uncharted possibilities for intimate understanding. The obligatory disclaimer of all final reports is that 'more research is necessary'.

To some extent problems of selection of data at the presentation stage are problems of design after the event. Significance has to be won from chaotic patterns; 'meaning' does not naturally fall out of the data, sense has to be *made* of it. The process of making sense demands remedial action, meanings often being re-injected so as to approximate to the form dreamt of in the original inspiration, design or commission.

What we feel we know is always less satisfying than what we hoped to know. Like the rainbow, the promise of certainty seems to recede as we approach it. Writing the final report often functions for the investigator like exams do for the undergraduate student. Whatever the limitations of the evidence, the time comes when you have to make the best of what you know, to a particular audience and within sharp constraints of time and space.

Discovering Something

Nothing creates more problems for the straightforward reporting of research than discovering the unexpected. If the unexpected is relatively simple — one variable left uncontrolled in an experimental design for example — it can usually be accounted for. But in social research more dramatic changes can be expected during the course of the investigation. Changes in policy, fashionable concern over particular issues, organizational structure of the patterns of the culture can cause the focus of the research to move or to be displaced. Close contact with the area being studied can cause the framing of the study, and the interests and motivations of the researcher, to shift. In extreme cases, the situation under study can disappear.

One danger of discovery is that it allows hindsight to replace insight. Once a critical relationship has been identified and established it becomes relatively easy to structure the account of the investigation around it. Medawar (1976) describes how experimental biologists talk about the evidence falling into the pattern of a 'story'. In the face of mounting data: 'Does it tell a story yet?' they ask each other.

Suddenly it all seems so simple to the researcher, whose understanding is from first-hand contact. Can they communicate that understanding? That is the key theoretical issue ('It does not tell a story — the researcher does').

Ideally 'discovery' in research provides a closure. It closes the story and seals the fiction, creating a product for which a ready market exists. In this sense orthodox research procedures are designed to produce 'findings'. But genuine *discovery* in the sense of something that shakes the conceptual base of your working assumptions, can only wreck the design as originally conceived and disrupt the story.

Reformulation

Making sense is essentially a matter of constructing meaning. The problems are not peculiar to case-study research. Nor are they simply technical problems that emerge only at a certain stage of investigation, after the data have been collected and before the report is presented. Problems of making sense are continuous and continual: sometimes they lie within the investigator's control; sometimes not. For the social researcher, in whatever medium, they have to be accepted as both endemic and systemic. While we may often treat such problems as narrow and technical, and hide them from public gaze, we should recognize, perhaps more often than we do, that they invariably carry heavy traffic.

I began this paper with the idea that research could be 'naturalistic' in that it could take its authority from its subject rather that begin from theory. The consequence would appear to be to create an increased emphasis on the 'theorizing' of the researcher in the face of research problems that are conventionally thought of as methodological issues amenable to technical solution.

The emerging conclusion is that we have misplaced theorizing by locating it within established disciplines and thereby creating an image of objective research. The development of theory requires rethinking methodology and in particular re-examining the role of the researcher as subject.

Notes

1 Paper written for the second Nuffield Workshop on the use of Naturalistic Methods in Evaluation, Cambridge, 1976.
2 The Ford SAFARI Project, based at CARE.
3 The NSF funded, 'Case studies in science education' (CSSE) project. Based at CIRCE, University of Illinois. The SSRC funded, 'Classroom practice: observations and perceptions of teachers, headmasters and LEA advisers: based at CARE.

Chapter 8

History, Context and Qualitative Methods

Ivor Goodson

The preceding chapters have detailed our concern with personal values and lives, with an associated variety of methods and modalities which seek to capture these essential ingredients. The following pieces seek to pull these loose threads together in a manner which is in harmony with our shared aspirations and chosen points of focus. The concern moves towards showing how general and more theoretical patterns emerge from a concentration of what might often appear marginal minutiae or individual details or idiosyncratic interpretations.

This chapter begins from a belief in qualitative methods and argues for a broadening of those methods to rehabilitate life stories and integrate studies of historical context. In the introductory section the reasons for concentrating on life story and curriculum history data are explored by analyzing some of the inadequacies of research methods as perceived in the mid 1970s when my own work began (Goodson, 1987).

It should be noted that since then other studies have emerged which have also sought to address these inadequacies. Studies of teacher socialization have focused on teacher culture and careers (e.g., Lacey, 1977), whilst a range of 'strategies' studies have pointed to the importance of background and biography (e.g., Woods, 1982). This work has considerably extended the range and theoretical aspiration of qualitative studies but in this chapter I shall stay with the original intention of exploring the role of historical studies in redressing certain emergent tendencies within qualitative methods.

In retrospect several reasons would seem to have led me to a personal predilection for historical and biographical work when devising a research programme: —

1   It grew out of my teaching experience. Certainly after Countesthorpe (recently described as an 'unemulated educational
maverick') I was susceptible to Nisbet's arguments in *Social
Change and History*, where he argues that we are often de-
luded into thinking fundamental social change is taking place
because we do not take account of a vital distinction between:

> readjustment or individual deviance within a social
> structure (whose effects, although possibly cumulative
> are never sufficient to alter the structure or the basic
> postulates of a society or institution) and the more
> fundamental though enigmatic change of structure,
> type, pattern or paradigm. (Nisbet, 1969, quoted in
> Webster, 1971, pp. 204–5)

To pursue this distinction demands, I think, that we undertake
historical work. This holds whether we seek to understand
how change is contained, as readjustment or individual deviance
in particular schools like Countesthorpe or within curriculum
reforms in general.

2   The documents and statements of the curriculum reform
movement inaugurated in the 1960s reveal a widespread belief
that there could be a more or less complete break with past
tradition. A belief that history in general and curriculum history in particular could somehow be *transcended*. Writing in
1968 Professor Kerr asserted that 'at the practical and organizational levels, the new curricula promised to "revolutional-
ize" English schooling' (Kerr, 1971, p. 180). Retrospectively
there still seems something admirable, however misconceived,
about such belief in contemporary possiblility that history
seemed of little relevance. At a time when traditional curriculum practice was thought to be on the point of being over-
thrown it was perhaps unsurprising that so many reforms paid
scant attention to the evolution and establishment of traditional practice.

  In the event radical change did not occur. By 1975 when
my reseach programme began I was in the position of needing
to re-examine the emergence and survival of the 'traditional' as
well as the failure to generalize, institutionalize and sustain the
'innovative'.

3   But if this was a view from the curriculum chalkface it later
became clear that the *transcendent* view of curriculum change

had infected many of those involved in researching schools and curriculum. The irony is supreme but for the best of reasons. Once again it is partly explained by an historical climate of opinion where curriculum change was thought the order of the day. Parlett and Hamilton's (1972) influential paper, though claiming general application, focussed on the evaluation of innovation. They wanted 'to study the innovatory project; how it operates, how it is influenced by the various school situations in which it is applied; what those directly concerned regard as its advantages and disadvantages'. Preoccupation with 'those directly concerned', with 'what it is like to be participating' were to characterize a major school of evaluators and case-study workers. Indeed this posture characterized those researchers both most sympathetic and sensitive to the aspirations of the innovators. Above all they wanted to 'capture and portray the world as it appears to the people in it'. Some went even further 'in a sense for the case-study worker what *seems* true is more important than what is true' (Walker, 1974, p. 80).

Writing later, with a strong sense of my own delusions on curriculum reform, I saw the evaluators who had studied my school as merely confirming the participants' myopia.

> Focussing the evaluators' work on the charting of the subjective perceptions of participants is to deny much of its potential — particularly to those evaluators aspiring to 'strong action — implications'. The analysis of subjective perceptions is incomplete without analysis of the historical context in which they occur. To deprive the subject of such knowledge would be to condemn the new evaluation to the level of social control — a bizarre fate for a model aspiring to 'democratic' intentions. (Goodson, 1977, p. 160)

4   Yet if many of those employing qualitative methods in evaluation and case study took a transcendent view of history they were not alone. As was argued elsewhere by peculiar convergence many contemporary interactionist and ethnographic studies were similarly ahistorical. I noted that 'paradoxically the interactionist and ethnographic models which were conceived in reaction to this model have often focussed on situation and occasion with the result that biography and historical background have continued to be neglected' (Goodson, 1988, p. 81).

Life Stories and Curriculum History

With respect to contemporary curriculum there are three levels (though of course this is in a sense falsely separate) that are amenable to historical study and which offer escape routes from the confines of descriptive research:

1 The individual life story. The process of change is continuous throughout a person's life 'both in episodic encounters and in longer-lasting socialization processes over the life history' (Jackson, 1968, p. 72).

2 History at the group or collective level: professions, categories, subjects or disciplines, for instance, evolve as social movements over time.

3 History at the relational level, the various permutations of relations between individuals, between groups and between individuals and groups; and the way these relations change over time.

Writing a Curriculum History

Once I left teaching and began working in curriculum development and research, it seemed to me that an historical perspective was necessary and at the time of planning the book, *School Subjects and Curriculum Change*, the blending of individual history and curriculum history had been recently explored in Mary Waring's study of Nuffield Science. For Waring (1979) the understanding of curriculum innovation is simply not possible without a history of context:

> If we are to understand events, whether of thought or of action, knowledge of the background is essential. Knowledge of events is merely the raw material of history: to be an intelligible reconstruction of the past, events must be related to other events, and to the assumptions and practices of the milieu. Hence they must be made the subject of inquiry, their origins as products of particular social and historical circumstance ...

Waring's focus on individual background as well as curriculum history grew from an awareness of how the Nuffield innovations were implemented:

> Organizers of individual Nuffield projects were given con-

> siderable autonomy with regard to the interpretation and
> carrying out of their brief, and to the selection and deployment
> of their teams. As a result, these aspects reflect very clearly the
> background and personality of the men and women chosen.
> (p. 12)

This belief in the importance of individual history and personality is
confirmed in the study (although the role of ideological bias is conceded):

> The evidence in this study supports the view that, while differ-
> ences of degree no doubt existed between individuals, the
> sincerity, the commitment and the dedicated work over a long
> time on the part of the principal characters at least, and prob-
> ably of many others, dwarf and transcend whatever vested
> interest may have been operating. (p. 15)

Whilst I am unsure about the primacy of individual will over
vested interests (hardly a lesson of history!) the contention does add
force to the need to explore curriculum at both the individual and
collective level. Combining life stories with contextual history seemed
therefore a strategy for building on the wide range of case-study,
evaluative and interactionist work. In this way a methodology is established which stays with the focus on participation and eventfulness but
which allows examination of the constraints beyond, which in fact
allows us to see how *over time* individual will and fundamental vested
interests interrelate.

School Subjects and Curriculum Change

Symptomatic of the focus of research and evaluation studies on participants and events has been the absence of work on school subjects.
Young (1971) has gone so far as to speak of these as 'no more than
socio-cultural constructs of a particular time' (p. 23) but an historical
view of curriculum would attribute considerably more sigificance to
school subjects that this. In choosing to research school subjects I was
cognisant that in studies of schooling the subject provides *par excellence* a context where antecedent structures collide with contemporary
action; the school subject provides one obvious manifestation of historical legacies or as Waring puts it 'monumental accretions' with
which contemporary actors have to work. It provides a basis from

which to question what is taken for granted by many of those within the situation under study.

Williams (1965) made the case for studying the content of education over twenty years ago. He argued that:

> The cultural choices involved in the selection of content have an organic relation to the social choices involved in the practical organization. If we are to discuss education adequately, we must examine, in historical and analytic terms, this organic relation, for to be conscious of a choice made is to be conscious of further and alternative choices. (pp. 145–6)

Developing this notion of the school subject being dependent on previous choices the concern in *School Subjects and Curriculum Change* was to begin with the histories of those teachers who had played a central role in defining a school subject over the last half century. The school subject in question, Rural Studies, changed from being a deeply utilitarian subject based on gardening in the 1920s to a subject offering 'O' and 'A' levels in environmental studies in the 1970s. By collecting the life stories of key participant teachers spanning this generation it was hoped that insights might be provided not only of how the curriculum changes but of how structural constraints are evidenced in such a process. Understanding a curriculum innovation such as the launching of environmental studies required a detailed understanding of historical context and life stories provided a valuable access point to this context.

In talking to the key participants understandably a range of personal values and idiosyncracies emerged but on certain points their life stories substantially concurred. At this point, however, a number of doubts surfaced. The most significant was that in talking to the main innovators, I was clearly adopting one of the tactics for which I had indicted earlier research. The innovators represented a group who had been able to 'hijack' the subject association and thereby change the direction and definition of the subject. But they in no way represented the range of traditions and 'alternative visions' among the teachers of the subject. In fact a fascinating aspect of the testimonies of the key participants was their cognisance of 'other voices in other rooms', of the alternative traditions and choices, which were intentionally closed off in pursuit of the status and resources that would promote the subject.

At this point the research might have progressed in a number of directions. I was aware of three that seemed sustainable. (1) was to fill out the life stories of the key participants into fully-fledged life histories which would be of sufficient depth to capture and portray the main issues within this curriculum area. (2) was to collect a wider range of life stories, to try and cover the main 'traditions' and sub-groups within the subject. (3) was to develop a detailed documentary history of the subject and of the conflicts over the innovations that were generated, during a period of over half a century.

In retrospect all three of these strategies seem to offer both problems and possibilities but in the event strategy (1) was rejected. The main reason was that the focus on the innovative in-group seemed unrepresentative and in a strong sense 'against the grain' of much of the history of the subject. To be too focussed on this group opened up the problem mentioned in the introduction where historical perspective is lost by a focus on an 'innovation' which might in the longer span turn out to be merely an 'abberation'.

To seek a way of overcoming the problems of uniqueness and idiosyncracy which combine with other methodological problems in the life history method, a combination of strategies (2) and (3) were adopted. A number of additional life stories of non-innovators were collected whilst the main focus of the study turned towards documentary research of the history of the subject. Combining a group of life stories with a subject history resembles the methods adopted in range of recent 'oral histories'. Certainly the combination offered a strategy to 'triangulate' the data and thereby partially assess the reliability of the findings.

The problem addressed in this chapter is how to characterize the blend of curriculum history and life story data without involving a substantive and recapitulative account. The major intention in the next section is therefore to fill out the argument with some data which gives a 'feel' of combining life stories with historical context. Of course the account has all the normal problems of trying to evidence the general category with one very specific case. In addition, it should be remembered that in assembling final accounts not just one but a range of life stories would be presented in combination with studies of historical context.

The following section deals with certain critical episodes in one teacher's life. They are chosen because they represent a common viewpoint in the life story data collected: namely a conviction that the embrace of specialist examination subject identity was a watershed in the original educational visions of a generation of rural studies teachers. But above all the concern in the section is to provide an account of certain critical decision points in one teacher's life: critical in the sense that the teacher, who is now retired, regards these episodes as the main turning point in his professional life.

The work began with a long series of interviews with the subject teacher — covering a period of eight years up until his retirement and after. Again and again in the interviews the teacher returned to the episodes when in his terms 'the dream began to fade', 'the alternative vision died'.

Critical Episodes in a Teacher's Life

1947–1954 The Innovative Secondary Modern

The 1944 Education Act foreshadowed the tripartite system of grammar, technical and secondary modern schools. (The compulsory school leaving age was raised to 15 years in 1947.) The Act marked the beginning of the modern era of curriculum conflict because from this date onwards curriculum conflict became more visible, public and national. Glass (1971) has noted that in this respect there was no 'pre-war parallel', for there was now:

> a recognition that secondary education is a proper subject for discussion and study ... in striking contrast to the pre-war position when attempts to investigate access to the various stages of education tended to be looked at by the Government as attacks on the class structure. (p. 35)

In practice the grammar schools inherited the curriculum of the public schools, while in the emerging secondary modern schools the curriculum was initially free from the consideration of external examinations. This freedom allowed some schools, always a minority, to experiment with their curricula and to pursue vocational and child-centred objectives. Social studies and civics courses, for instance, were rapidly established in a number of the schools. Kathleen Gibberd (1962) has argued that the secondary modern school as conceived in 1944 was never intended to work to any universal syllabus to take any external examination: 'it was to be a field for experiment'. She considered that:

> Behind the official words and regulations there was a call to the teacher who believed in education for its own sake and longed for a free hand with children who were not natural learners. Many of those who responded gave an individual character to their schools. (p. 103)

However, the period during which certain secondary moderns were a 'field for experiment' with vocational, child-centred and integrated curricula was to prove very limited. This can be evidenced by following the changes in rural education in the secondary state sector.

Entering the Profession — Secondary Modern Innovations

At the time the new secondary moderns, a few embracing the integrated concept of rural education, were being launched Patrick Johnson was completing his training at Wandsworth Emergency College. His choice of subject was initially somewhat fortuitous:

> Well, I didn't really know what subject I wanted to do. In fact I really wanted to do English. But when I got home after the war I didn't feel I could be couped up inside. I moved into Kent where all my wife Jean's people were farm workers on the fruit farms ... I heard there was a thing called rural studies.

First Job: Snodland (age 27–28)

In November 1947 he got a Teacher's Certificate and then had to do a probationary year. His first year was spent teaching general subjects at a school in Kent ...

> Gardening it was really, but I taught everything. It was a secondary modern, a very early one, illiterate kids — their standard was terrible, just after the war. It was a big elementary school at a place called Snodland, with a big cement works on the Medway estuary, Rochester direction. Terrible place, the kids were very backward. I always remember the first day I arrived. The head said, 'Good God!' a teacher!' and grabbed me, shoved me inside a classroom saying 'this is your lot' and shut the door! Then I was faced by this mob who hadn't had a teacher for some years during the war. I fought a running battle with them.
>
> IG: What had they been doing, then?
> PJ: Well, they had been going into the classroom occasionally. They literally could not read or write. They were desperate kids, nice kids but they were absolutely, completely illiterate at 12 years of age. And undisciplined too.

IG: So did you just have a class?

PJ: Yes, I did everything — PE, music, everything.

IG: So you weren't a rural studies teacher in your first post.

PJ: No, there was a lesson called gardening, and I did some of that as well.

Wrotham Secondary Modern (age 28–34)

Patrick's next job for his second probationary year was a new secondary modern at Wrotham. The head, 'one of the very exceptional headmasters', had run the village school where his wife and son had attended. The head was very enthusiastic about school gardens and invited Patrick to come and teach rural science:

> So I said 'yes', I could see the opportunities ... I'd often talked with him of things I'd like to do. When he started the new school I went along to teach rural science. The new school consisted of three Nissen huts in a field. Literally, that was all. The type made of clay bricks with cinders, half way between Wrotham and Borough Green. That was the school. There wasn't a classroom. One of them, the largest, doubled for assembly and art room. One half was elementarily equipped as a lab. The others were ordinary classrooms. I had an ordinary classroom and I had fourth year class, which was then the top leaving class of the school. There were three streams and the third and fourth year classes were called 4F (farming) and 4P (practical) with extra needlework and cooking, and 4A (academic) where the kids did extra English and so on. But of course there were no examinations, so in fact A wasn't the top class, but they probably did turn out a few who could read and write. They were really equivalent and we used to sit down once a year and think out who would we get into each class. Well, 4F class, which I had ... we established a school farm. We built this up from nothing. We had one and a half acres of land along the playing fields as it was too steep for football pitches. I got that fenced off, got bits of wire so on ... as things developed I had my class for practically everything — not quite every subject, but a good deal and I developed my ideas on this form. We built bits and pieces gradually. We built a pigsty, and the 4 Practical did the actual building of that. We built a rabbit house which we built up. Eventually we kept

about two calves, about six goats, a pig and a litter; we had a poultry run and hens of course, a dairy which we fitted out, and I managed to get from Gascoynes because my father was a friend of the chairman or something, dairy equipment.

Johnson taught 4F for about two thirds of their timetable, other teachers taught science and woodwork. He was much influenced by the idea of rural education as the 'curriculum hub' which his head-teacher actively encouraged.

I taught them maths, English, history etc., all tied in completely, because, for example, maths I based as much as possible on the farm activities. In fact, I used a series of books which was popular then, called *Rural Arithmetic* — the other I can't quite remember the title of. They were all about problems of the land: e.g., if you were mixing things for the pigs, you didn't buy ready-made meal for the pigs, You calculated by the weight what meal they require, you broke this down, the various ingredients of the meal, you get them all out separately, weighted them up, mixed them up and it had to work out right fourteen rations, one for every morning and evening of the week. That was a piece of arithmetic it could take two people most of the day to do.

We were fairly poorly off for books in those days, frankly, so we read a lot of literature associated with the countryside. We didn't over do this to the extent of doing nothing else. They wrote compositions. We had an English textbook, which I at any rate, kept an eye on to make sure some sort of progression of spelling was maintained. But a lot of English was straight-forwardly connected with the farm. For example, they each had to write a diary every day and they had to write a summary at the end of the week. It was passed on to the next students who took on the animals. That was a good piece of English, and I had said that must be perfect — no spelling mistakes, no blots — nothing!

Johnson reckons that these were some of the happiest days of his teaching career. His own enthusiasm (and that of his wife) coupled with the interest of the children seem to have generated considerable motivation to learn:

IG: Did they respond pretty well?
PJ: They absolutely lapped it up, loved it. You'd never get absences unless the kid was really ill. You'd get kids ... often

at the weekends ... we had to feed them at the weekends —
there was no-one else to. I can't remember any occasion when
the kids didn't turn up at the weekend. It may have happened
but I can't remember.

IG: So you had to spend a lot of time at weekends?

PJ: Lived up there. But Joan helped a lot too. Frankly we hadn't
any money to be doing anything else in those days. Until it
reached a stage when my kids were getting a bit older and I
took a job during the holidays because I needed the money —
pay was poor. But I still did that as well.

Johnson attributed the main influences on his developing concept of
rural education to his contacts with the Kent farm workers' family
which he had married into and which he lived among:

I did a lot of walking about the orchards in Kent talking to
farm workers and I can remember lots of occasions when the
attitude of these people struck me very much. I had a strong
feeling that education wasn't just book-learning — that's an old
phrase — it involved in fact skills in the field and common-sense
applied to a problem.

Johnson feels that he dealt with many very able pupils in 4F;
partly a reflection of the social structure in Kent in the early 1950s.
The pupils were, with one exception (for whom he could not find a
job), boys, the most able of whom today would be in the sixth forms,
who went as agricultural apprentices to farms who were glad to get
them. 'Good farms, good employers!' I asked at this point if he felt
any resentment that they were forced to go on to the land:

PJ: No, first of all because I didn't know anything about 'A'
levels at my level of teaching. Grammar schools were a separate
world and while I knew my own background, I never associated these kids with it. It never occurred to me at the time that
these kids could have got into the sixth form. It didn't occur to
me at that time that they were bright.

IG: Why didn't it occur to you that these children were bright?

PJ: They were bright to me but it didn't occur to me that that
meant they should have an academic education. Because I was
meeting people throughout the war — meeting people then
whose field of work was similar to farm workers and every bit
as bright. I don't think this is true today. One of the effects of
the introuduction of the 11+ was to cream the working class of
its bright people who went into academic jobs. You constantly

hear it's happened in places like India — all being bank clerks or professionals. There were a lot of intelligent people in the working class then, who by and large are not there today. They have all been creamed off into sixth forms and professional jobs. At that time I know there were people as simple farm workers who were highly educated — not educated — but highly cultured intelligent people. I didn't find it a problem at the time, nor did the kids, it was never raised.

Secondary Modern Examinations: Towards Rural Studies Examinations

From the early 1950s more and more secondary modern schools began to focus on external examinations. This posed insuperable problems for those heads and teachers in secondary moderns who were exploring new integrated modes of curricula such as rural education. As the tripartite system of education gradually emerged in the form of new school buildings and modified curricula, it became clear that rural studies and gardening were only developing in the secondary modern schools. In a questionnaire survey of gardening and rural studies teachers in Kent produced, with three exceptions, the reply from grammar and technical schools of 'subject not taught', whilst in sixty three of the sixty five secondary modern schools the subject was given an important position in the curriculum (Kent Rural Studies Association, 1952).

Rural education having been decimated as a concept within the increasingly exam-conscious secondary moderns it now became clear that the successor subject of rural studies faced major problems. Writing in 1957 Mervyn Pritchard described the situation in this way:

There appear to be two extremes of thought in secondary modern schools — a) a concentration on external examinations b) those who won't have them at any price.

In those schools where the brighter pupils are examined it is unusual to find Rural Science as one of the subjects taken and as the pupils concentrate more and more narrowly on their examination subject it is unusual to find Rural Science used as a social subject such as craft, art or music may be.

Even where pupils are not examined there appears to be a concentration of the teaching of the subject in streams of classes of duller children. (p. 14)

The concern of rural studies teachers at the deteriorating status and position of their subject led to a variety of responses in the latter part of the 1950s. Mervyn Pritchard exhorted: 'as often as possible the Rural Studies teacher should mix with his collegues, even if he has to kick off muddy gum boots to drink his cup of tea. Much useful interchange of knowledge and information is carried out among the staffroom gossip. Informal discussion of school policy can be helped along judiciously by the Rural Science Teacher. Frequent contact can convince our colleagues of one's normality and value' (p. 5). Apart from such exhortations some teachers were concerned to develop a 'Philosophy of Rural Studies'. In 1954 Carson and Colton produced a paper which appeared in the Kent Association Journal, and later in 1957, in the Lincolnshire 'Rural Science News'. It was a systematic attempt to think through a subject philosophy, a first, embryonic attempt to define a subject, and one equipped with a contemporary rationale. They argued:

> For this study to justify its inclusion in the school curriculum it must be shown to play a vital part in developing a fully educated citizen who is aware in his heart of his kinship with the rest of life and yet realized the unique qualities of the human spirit. (Carson and Colton, 1954)

Carson and Colton were editors of the Kent Association of Teachers of Gardening and Rural Science Journal. The 'Rural Science' appendage was added at Carson's insistence when the Association was formed in 1949. The Association was predated by an ephemeral association of rural science teachers in 1925, and by a small association in Nottingham founded in 1940, and the Manchester Teachers' Gardening Circle founded in 1941. By 1954 the Kent Journal was beginning to define a philosophy for rural studies and soon after claimed, 'this Association has constantly sought parity of esteem with the rest of the curriculum for all rural studies' (Carson and Colton, 1954).

At the same time new rural studies associations were forming in other counties, normally to pursue the aims expressed in the Kent Journal. By now rural studies was a specialized subject of very low status, literally fighting for its existence in the exam-conscious secondary modern schools. In 1960 the county subject association banded together to form a National Rural Studies Association with its own journal. The 1961 Journal stated in 'The Constitution':

The aim of this association shall be 'to develop and coordinate Rural Studies'. Rural Studies includes Nature Study, Natural History pursuits of all kinds, the study of farming and the activities of the countryside, as taught in primary and secondary schools. Rural Studies should be regarded as an art, a science and a craft; a subject as well as a method of teaching. (p. 5)

The Association soon became involved in promoting examinations in rural studies. They initiated a pilot CSE project and although many practising teachers complained at the inappropriateness of written examinations a range of new CSEs in Rural Studies were duly promoted.

1954–1958 Secondary Modern Certification (age 35–38)

In 1953 the headteacher at Wrotham who had so strongly promoted rural education left; his successor was more examination conscious. Johnson began to look for a new job and in the Spring term of 1954 noticed a post at Royston in Hertfordshire where a teacher was required to start an ambitious rural studies programme. On the interviewing panel was a rural studies adviser, Geoff Whitby (he was, in fact, the first rural studies adviser and was steeped in the concept of rural education in which Herfordshire had long been a pioneer).

Whitby asked me about rural education and I described what I'd been doing in Kent, and I could see at once that I'd got the job. I should guess he's never met anyone else who had done this sort of thing. The head saw it differently. This was very interesting. He didn't see it as rural education in that sense because he was already thinking ahead to raising the standards of this school to what could eventually be CSE. None of this existed but he was thinking in terms of this. Although I understood when I got there I could have the same set up as in Kent, with three top classes and I could have anyone who wanted to volunteer for the subject, it never in fact worked out. The classes were streamed; I only ever got the lower of the three streams. While at first I could do what I liked with that bottom stream, and I did the same sort of thing as in Kent, over the next few years this was whittled away from me, and more specialism invaded the curriculum and these kids eventually spent practically no time in running the farm. Whereas in Kent they did the whole operation of running the farm in lesson time, in

Herts they had to do it before school. So it never really got going.

The problems were in fact both internal and external to the school. Inside the school there was streaming and a belief that it was vocational training for agriculture. Outside the school the community remained hostile to the whole concept, partly a result of the very different social structure of Hertfordshire compared with Kent. In Kent farm workers were better paid and treated and respected because their job was skilled.

> In Hertfordshire there was a long history of poverty on the land going back to Arthur Young's travels. If you meet any of the farm workers in this area there are tales of great poverty even in this day. So there was a feeling that going on the land here was nothing but condemnation ... nothing but ploughing and sowing, no other skills, very little mixed farming, no orchards.

But beyond the different social structure of the new locality Johnson had moved towards an awareness that 'society was changing'.

> The concern was that selection was important, children were getting into grammar schools and other people were beginning to see what was happening to them. Therefore they wanted their children to do as well academically as possible in order to get better jobs ... certainly the atmosphere was different.

Johnson's disillusionment with his new school grew as he realized he would only ever be given the problem children and those stigmatized as less able. In 1956, his third year, he had a series of interviews with the head, Mr Young:

> I had arguments with Young. I made my case and he was adamant that this was not what was required today. They gave a school leaving certificate, and they required qualifications in other things. In my opinion he never really saw what I was up to.

At the time he felt a deep sense of professional betrayal. After all in Kent he had seen a working model of rural education as an integrated 'eminently satisfactory situation of mixed ability type'. Again and again in his retirement interviews he returns to this critical point when, as he puts it, 'my dream faded', 'my vision of educating children

Biography, Identity and Schooling: Episodes in Educational Research

faltered'. However, at the time, although disappointed there were other goals:

> My ambition was to be a head, and I had long talks with Young about how I could get to be a head. It became increasingly obvious to me that as a rural studies man I wasn't going to get a look in.

1958–1979 Rural Studies and Environmental Studies Adviser (age 39–59)

In 1958 Johnson was asked by the rural studies adviser who had brought him to Hertfordshire if he would like to take over his job.

> I didn't think twice when Whitby asked. I thought an opening like this, I'll do something good in this. I started off in '58 with part-time, half my time, and he worked the other half for a year and then he retired, and I got his job. By this time I'd really given up hope of getting rural studies seen in the way I'd taught it in Kent. Then I saw it as a specialist subject which had certain weak links. For the first 2–3 years I did two things; I read all about the rural education tradition in the papers Whitby gave me on his background, etc. At the same time I was visiting the secondary school teachers and stimulated them to get themselves organized to try and get any kids other than the least able, to get them better facilities in their schools. I spent the first 3–4 years with this aim.

At this stage in his life Johnson was enthused by the prospect of using his influence as an adviser to change things. Initially this enthusiasm carried him over the loss of 'hope of getting real rural education' for by now it was clear that, whatever his preference, the specialist subject was taking over.

> IG: What kind of people were they, as you travelled round in 1958–60?
> PJ: They were pre-war teachers of gardening who'd come back, and there were people of my own generation living through the war who came into teaching. Gradually then we began to get the post-war younger teacher coming in and the colleges who specialized in rural studies from the 60s onwards. Before that they were the older chaps generally.

IG: So what did you decide would be your strategy? By then you were involved in the national association?

PJ: No, we started the national association in 1960. I called the first meeting in the name of the Herts Association. We knew there were various other groups around the country. I have no idea how we found that out.

IG: What was the thinking behind calling this meeting?

PJ: It was quite definitely to raise the standard of rural studies as a subject and the status of it because we decide that until it was raised nationally we wouldn't be able to do much in Herts. 'If you're not given a proper classroom refuse to teach this subject in any old place, and as adviser call me in', was what I told my teachers, and I will say 'this chap is entitled to a classroom just the same as anyone else'. To some heads this was a bit of a shock. They'd never been faced with this problem. If it rained they all just sat in the bicycle shed. We had Broad who was sympathetic to ideas ... we produced that report, and as a result every school from 1960 onwards where I was adviser, we got minimal provisions called the rural studies unit in Herts.

From this point on Johnson became a leading compaigner for rural studies as a subject — self-promotion and subject promotion became finally and inextricably linked. This pursuit of subject promotion over time was reflected upon in an article he wrote in 1963 for the Rural Studies Association Journal. It begins with the polarity that teachers actually have two duties 'one to their classes and one the educational climate in which they worked'. It was argued that the subject had to respond to these 'changing climates' to ensure influence and resources.

> During the next few years considerable changes are likely both in the framework of our school system and in the curricula within school if rural studies is to retain its influence, then those teachers who believe in the subject must be clear about their aims and ready to adapt their methods to new conditions. (Carson, 1963, p. 14)

He concluded:

> Thus the climate is changing continually, now perhaps more rapidly than ever before. But rural studies teachers are used to British weather. Have we not all got a lesson up our sleeves for the sudden downpour or the unexpected fine day? Within the

educational climate too, we are ready with new ideas to meet whatever the weather has in store! (p. 15)

In fact what the weather had in store at this time was the new Beloe examinations for secondary moderns. Rural studies became one of the pilot studies for the new examination and despite a range of evidence that it was ill-suited to written examination, subject opportunism demanded a positive response to the changing climate. As a result CSEs in rural studies were promoted wherever possible. This embracing of examinations was pursued obsessively when the comprehensive system was launched. Rural studies then, Johnson thought, had to 'adapt or perish'. Again the response was opportunistic. Rural studies was changed into environmental studies, and a new 'A' level in the subject was launched for as Johnson says 'this way, you got more money, better kids, better careers'.

The Alternative Vision: A Retrospect

Although during the period when he was building his career Johnson embraced the notion of his subject as an examinable specialism, in later years doubts surfaced. On his retirement he stated quite clearly that it was the embrace of the specialist subject examination that killed his educational vision. 'This was when my dream began to fade, I was not aware of it at the time.' For him now his alternative vision, his dream, is all powerful:

> My alternative vision was that in more general terms and I'm still convinced this is true, a lot of kids don't learn through paper and pencil and that we do far too much of this. A lot of kids could achieve success and use all the mental skills that we talk about in the classroom such as analyzing and comparing through physical activities. Through such things as building the school farm, looking after animals. I used to talk about the fact that the real reason for keeping the farm wasn't to teach farm work. With the farm it was a completely renewing set of problems and the fact it was a farm was incidental. You were thinking in educational terms of process with these kids. That's the sort of dream I was well aware of giving up, and talked about it a number of times. I always felt dissatisfied since and I've met many teachers who have come across the same realiza-

tion, not in quite such explicit terms as they'd never had the chance of doing it, whereas I had. I meet them now in schools ... a teacher whom I met today knew that the teaching she was doing with these less able girls was not the right way to educate these girls, but what was the right way she couldn't think. Well, I know what is the right way. The right way is the sort of thing we were doing in '47 whether it's using the farm or whatever. The attitude is that you use your hands. You don't always sit at a desk necessarily. You are facing problems of a three dimensional kind at an adult level. You use terms like man's problems; and this is no longer feasible in a school situation. I couldn't tell that girl today to do that sort of thing; she wouldn't succeed at all.

To my mind one of the tragedies of education in my life, and I would call this the secondary modern ethos, maybe it's one of many, but I don't know, was that the best thing that secondary moderns did was to promote this idea that it's just as good to be as skilled craftsman as, say, a white collar worker, and that you get as much satisfaction and challenge from it at your own level. This was what was really behind what we were doing in Kent. The fact that this is no longer recognized in schools at all is I think responsible for the problems we have in school today, both academically with the less able and with the anti-school group and the apathetic group.

Conclusion

These episodes in a subject teacher's life illustrate the way that the collection of life stories and elucidation of the historical context can combine. Above all the strength of beginning curriculum research from life story data is that *from the outset* the work is firmly focussed on the working lives of practitioners. Other researchers have commented in similar manner on the peculiar force of this kind of data as the initial strategy in a research programme:

When one conducts a life history interview the findings become alive in terms of historical processes and structural constraints. People do not wander round the world in a timeless, structureless limbo. They themselves acknowledge the importance of historical factors and structural constraints (although of course, they would not use such pompous language). The analysis of life histories actually pushes one first of all to the problems of constraints bearing down upon the construction of any one life ... (Faraday and Plummer, 1979, p. 780)

In articulation their response to historical factors and structural constraints life story tellers provide us with sensitizing devices for the analysis of these constraints and the manner in which they are experienced. We are alerted to historical legacies and structural constraints and can pursue understanding of aspects such as, in the instance given, strategies for self and subject promotion and career construction.

Certainly in the life of Patrick Johnson we gain insights into him wrestling with imperatives in the social structure. From his early professional life he develops a vision of how schools might be, this vision is challenged and defeated as subject specialism and examinations invade the early secondary modern schools; we see how self-promotion and subject promotion interrelate; and we see how one educational ideology is initially replaced by another as the teacher's career is constructed; the ideological renunciation only follows his retirement at the end of his career. Our attention is therefore left on the link between the structuring of material interests, strategies for career aggrandizement and the acceptance of particular educational ideologies.

I believe the instance gives some grounds for seeing how Bogdan's (1974) exhortation might work. He argued that the fully-researched life history should allow us to:

see an individual in relation to the history of his time, and how he is influenced by the various religious, social, psychological and economic currents present in his world. It permits us to view the intersection of the life history of men with the history of society, thereby enabling us to understand better the choices, contingencies and options open to the individual. (p. 4)

A combination of life stories and curriculum histories should then offer an antidote to the depersonalized, ahistorical accounts of schooling to which we are only too accustomed. Above all we gain insights into individuals coming to terms with imperatives in the social structure. From the collection of a range of life stories located in historical context we can discern what is general within a range of individual studies. We can thereby develop our understanding from a base that is clearly grounded within personal biography and perception.

Critical Questions

In this chapter I have taken the view that a combination of life story and curriculum history data can both broaden and deepen our accounts of schooling and curriculum. But a range of critical questions remain. Certain problems are specific to life story data, others specific to curriculum history and a further set of questions arise from the relationship between the two.

Firstly, life stories provide us with only partial accounts collected at certain stages in a life. If we seek a full retrospective life story then we come at the stage Vonnegut Glendening has described so well in his most recent novel. He argues that sociologists have ignored the fact that:

> We all see our lives as stories ... If a person survives an ordinary span of sixty years of more, there is every chance that his or her life as a shapely story has ended; and all that is to be experienced is epilogue. Life is not over, but the story is. (Glendening, 1983, p. 47)

But John Mortimer (1983) has summarized the problems of writing an autobiography at this stage. In the last paragraph he says:

> That is how it was, a part of life seen from a point of view. Much more happened that I cannot tell or remember. To others it would be, I am quite sure, a different story. (p. 256)

At root the problem is to retain and defend the authenticity of the participant's account. But to do this such problems of lapsed memory or partial or selective recall must be faced. We only get a part of the picture, to be sure a vital part, but we need to push for more of the picture, more bits of the jigsaw.

In part the problem is addressed by triangulation through collecting a range of life stories, and by developing a documentary history of the context. But the development of research which moves from a range of life stories to curriculum history concentrates the focus of the work; arguably in a way which challenges the authenticity of the accounts and certainly in ways which effect the relationship between the life story teller and the researcher. By moving from life story to curriculum history control is passing irrevocably to the researcher. In addition the life story data is being concentrated onto particular issues and themes. In this case the linkage with the history of a subject could well have led, in spite of the range of life stories gathered, to an over-concentration on the career conscious, upwardly-mobile teachers.

Once again there is the danger of an over-emphasis on the unrepresentative.

I explore later the relationship of the work to theory. But in this respect it must be noted that as with life stories, so with curriculum histories, the specificity of their focus can act against their capacity for generalization. A further question is the nature of interpretation, the role of the commentary. As Bertaux (1981) has reminded us moving from the personal life story to wider histories involves considerable questions of methodological reliability:

> What is really at stake is the relationship between the sociologist and the people who make his work possible by accepting to be interviewed on their life experiences. (p. 9)

This question is deeply significant both at the ethical and procedural level.

The ethical and procedural questions relate closely to the relationship between life story teller and researcher and the potential for mutuality. This is further related to the question of 'audience'. If the earlier contention that life story data placed in a historical context offers the opportunity for research which 'engages' teachers is correct then the prospects for mutuality are enhanced. In developing life stories teachers could be involved in work which would illuminate and feed back into the conditions and understandings of their working lives.

Chapter 9

Teachers' Lives and Educational Research

Ivor Goodson

Some time ago, I became convinced that the study of teachers' lives was central to the study of curriculum and schooling. In reflecting on the development of my conviction two episodes stand out. Were this merely a reminiscence of personal conversion it would be of little interest, but the two episodes do speak to a number of salient issues in the argument for greatly extended study of teachers' lives.

The first episode took place in the year of postgraduate certification when I was training to be a teacher. I returned to spend the day with a teacher at my secondary school who had been a major inspiration to me, a mentor. He was a radical Welshman. Academically brilliant, he had a BSc in economics and a PhD in history. He was open, humorous, engaging, stimulating — a superb and popular teacher.

But he faced me with a paradox because when the school changed from a grammar school to a comprehensive, it was he who opposed all the curriculum reforms which sought to broaden the educational appeal of the school to wider social groups. He was implacably conservative and traditionalist on this, and so far as I know only this, issue. But he, it should be remembered, was a man who had personally visited the factory to which I had gone after leaving school early at fifteen. He had implored me to return to school. He had spoken then of his commitment to public schooling as an avenue to working class emancipation. He no doubt saw me, a badly behaved working class pupil, as some sort of test case. I knew personally then that he was very deeply concerned to keep working class pupils in school. So why did he oppose all those curriculum reforms which had that objective?

During the day back visiting my old school, I continually probed him on this issue. At first he stonewalled, giving a series of essentially non-committal responses, but at the end of the day, in the pub, over a beer, he opened up. Yes, of course he was mainly concerned with disadvantaged pupils; yes, of course that's why he'd come to the factory to drag me back to school. Yes, he was politically radical and yes, he had always voted Labour. But, and here I quote:

> you don't understand my relationship to the school and to teaching. My centre of gravity is not here at all. It's in the community, in the home — that's where I exist, that's where I put my effort now. For me the school is nine to five, I go through the motions.

In short, in the school he sought to minimize his commitment, he opposed any reform which dragged him into more work. His centre of gravity was elsewhere.

The point I'm making is that to understand teacher development and curriculum development and to tailor it accordingly we need to know a great deal more about teachers' priorities. We need in short to know more about teachers' lives.

The second episode began in the late 1970s. I was interested in some work on folk music being conducted at the University of Leeds. At the same time, I was exploring some themes for an ethnography conference that was coming up at the St Hilda's in Oxford. The work of a folklorist Pegg suddenly opened up again the line of argument which I had been pondering since 1970. Pegg says,

> The right to select lies not with the folklorist ('Sorry old chap, can't have that — it's not a folk song'), but with the singer. Today's collector must have no preconceptions. His job is to record a people's music, whether it is a traditional ballad or a hymn or a musical song or last week's pop hit!

With this basic attitude comes another revelation:

> I began to realize that, for me, the people who sang the songs were more important than the songs themselves. The song is only a small part of the singer's life and the life was usually very fascinating. There was no way I felt I could understand the songs without knowing something about the life of the singer, which does not seem to apply in the case of most folklorists. They are quite happy to find material which fits into a preconceived canon and leave it at that. I had to know what people thought about the songs, what part they played in their lives and in the lives of the community. (Interview with R. Pegg 10.9.78)

A similar point is made by the folksong collector Robin Morton (1973):

> The opinion grew in me that it was *in* the singer that the song becomes relevant. Analyzing it in terms of motif, or rhyming structure, or minute variation becomes, in my view, sterile if the one who carries the particular song is forgotten. We have all met the scholar who can talk for hours in a very learned fashion about folksongs and folklore in general, without once mentioning the singer. Bad enough to forget the social context, but to ignore the individual context castrates the song. As I got to know the singers, so I got to know and understand their songs more fully.

The preoccupation with 'the singer, not the song' needs to be seriously tested in our studies of curriculum and schooling. What Pegg and Morton say about folklorists and implicitly about the way their research is received by those they research, could be said also about most educational research.

The project I am recommending is essentially one of reconceptualizing educational research so as to assure that 'the teachers' voice' is heard, heard loudly, heard articulately. In this respect the most hopeful way forward is, I think, to build upon notions of the 'self-monitoring teacher', 'the teacher as researcher', the teacher as 'extended professional'. For instance, in the early 1970s at the Centre for Applied Research in Education at the University of East Anglia in England, a good deal of work was conducted into how to operationalize this concept. Perhaps the most interesting developments were within the Ford Teaching Project conducted by John Elliott and Clem Adelman in the period 1973–5. They sought to rehabilitate the 'action-research' mode pioneered by Kurt Lewin in the post-war period. In the interim period educational action research had fallen into decline. Carr and Kemmis (1986), who have done a good deal to extend and popularize the concept, give a number of reasons for the resurgence of action research:

> First, there was the demand from within an increasingly professionalized teacher force for a research role, based on the notion of the extended professional investigating his or her own practice. Second, there was the perceived irrelevance to the concerns of these practitioners of much contemporary educational research. Third, there had been a revival of interest in 'the practical' in curriculum, following the work of Schwab

(Schwab, 1969, pp. 1–24) and others on 'practical delibera-
tion'. Fourth, action research was assisted by the rise of the
'new wave' methods in educational research and evaluation
with their emphasis on participants' perspectives and categories
in shaping educational practices and situations. These methods
place the practitioners at centre stage in the educational research process and recognize the crucial significance of actors'
understandings in shaping educational action. From the role of
critical informant helping an 'outsider' researcher, it is but a
short step for the practitioner to become a self-critical researcher into her or his own practice. Fifth, the accountability
movement galvanized and politicized practioners. In response
to the accountability movement, practitioners have adopted the
self-monitoring role as a proper means of justifying practice
and generating sensitive critiques of the working conditions in
which their practice is conducted. Sixth, there was increasing
solidarity in the teaching profession in response to the public
criticism which has accompanied the post expansion educational politics of the 1970s and 1980s; this, too, has prompted the
organization of support networks of concerned professionals
interested in the continuing developments of education even
though the expansionist tide has turned. And, finally, there is
the increased awareness of action research itself, which is perceived as providing and understandable and workable approach
to the improvement of practice through critical self-reflection.

The focus of action research has however tended to be very practice
oriented. In introducing a survey of action research for instance Carr
and Kemmis (1986) note:

> A range of practices have been studied by educational action
> researchers and some examples may suffice to show how they
> have used action research to improve their practices, their
> understandings of these practices, and the situations in which
> they work. (pp. 166–7)

Not surprisingly with the notion of an extended professional in mind
workers have 'used action research to improve their practice'. Other
developments in teacher education have similarly focussed on practice.
The work of Clandinin and of Connelly has argued in innovative and
interesting ways that we should seek to understand teachers' *personal,
practical knowledge*. The addition of the personal aspect in this for-
mulation is a welcome move forward hinting as it does at the import-

ance of biographical perspectives. But again the personal is being linked irrevocably to practice. It is as if the teacher *is* her or his practice. For teacher educators, such specificity of focus is understandable but I wish to argue that a broader perspective will achieve more: Not solely in terms of our understandings but ultimately in ways that feed back into changes in practical knowledge.

In short what I am saying is that it does not follow logically or psychologically that to *improve* practice we must initially and immediately *focus* on practice. Indeed I shall argue the opposite point of view.

Taking the 'teacher as researcher' and 'action research' as expressing defensible value positions and viable starting points, I want to argue for a broadened sense of purpose. In particular I am worried about a collaborative mode of research which seeks to give full equality and stature to the teacher but which employs as its initial and predominant focus the practice of the teacher. It is, I believe, a profoundly unpromising point of entry from which to promote a collaborative enterprise. For the university researcher, aspiring to collaborative and equalitarian partnership, it may seem quite unproblematic, for the teacher it might seem far less so. In fact it may seem to the teacher that the starting point for collaboration focusses on the maximum point of vulnerability.

We must, I think, constantly remind ourselves how deeply uncertain and anxious most of us are about our work as teachers whether in classrooms or in (far less contested) lecture halls. These are often the arenas of greatest anxiety and insecurity — as well as, occasionally, achievement.

Hence I wish to argue that to place the teachers' classroom practice at the centre of the action for action researchers is to put the most exposed and problematic aspect of the teachers' world at the centre of scrutiny and negotiation. In terms of strategy, both personally and politically, I think it is a mistake to do this. I say it is a mistake to do this — and this may seem a paradox — particularly if the wish is to ultimately seek reflection about and change in the teachers' practice.

A more valuable and less vulnerable entry point would be to examine teachers' work in the context of the teachers' lives. Much of the emerging study in this area indicates that this focus allows a rich flow of dialogue and data. Moreover, the focus may (and I stress may) allow teachers greater authority and control in collaborative research than has often appeared to be the case with practice-oriented study. What I am asserting here is that, particularly in the world of teacher development, the central ingredient so far missing is the *teacher's voice*. Primarily the focus has been on the teacher's practice, almost the teacher *as* practice. What in needed is a focus that listens above all to the person at whom 'development' is aimed. This means strategies should be developed which facilitate, maximize and in a real sense legislate the capturing of the teacher's voice.

Bringing substance and strategy together points us in a new direction for reconceptualizing educational research and development. In the first section, I provided two somewhat episodic arguments for seeking to understand teachers' lives as part of the educational research and development enterprise. In the second section, I argued that the 'teacher as researcher' and 'action research' modes were productive and generative ways forward but that the initial and immediate focus on practice was overstated and undesirable. Strategically a broader focus on life and work is hereby recommended. Hence for substantive and strategic reasons I would argue for a broadening of focus to allow detailed scrutiny of the teacher's life and work.

Broadening Our Data Base for Studying Teaching

So far I have argued in somewhat anecdotal fashion that data on teachers' lives is an important factor for our educational research studies. I have argued that *strategically* this is desirable; so as to involve teachers as researchers and to develop a collaborative mode. But there is also a *substantive* reason. The primary reason is that in my experience when talking to teachers about issues of curriculum development, subject teaching, school governance and general school organization they constantly import data on their own lives into the discussion. This I take to be *prima facie* evidence that teachers themselves judge such issues to be of major importance. One of the reasons that these data have not been much used however is that researchers edit out such data viewing it as too 'personal', 'idiosyncratic' or 'soft'. It is, in short, yet another example of the selective use of the 'teachers' voice'. The researcher only hears what she or he wants to hear and knows will sound well when replayed to the research community.

There may of course be perfectly valid reasons for not employing data on teachers' lives in our educational research studies. But this would require a sequence of reasoning to show why such data were irrelevant or of no importance. The normal research strategy is however simply to purge such data. I have not come across any accounts which give reasoned explanations as to why such data are not employed. The most commonsensical explanation seems to be that data on teachers' lives simply do not fit in with existing research paradigms. If this is the case then it is the paradigms that are at fault, not the value and quality of this kind of data.

The arguments for employing data on teachers' lives are substantial, but given the predominance of existing paradigms should be spelt out:

1   In the research on schools in which I have been involved — covering a wide range of different research foci and conceptual matrixes — the consistency of teachers talking about their own lives in the process of explaining their policy and practice has been striking. Were this only a personal observation it would be worthless but again and again in talking to other researchers they have echoed this point. To give one example: David Hargreaves in researching for *Deviance in Classrooms* noted in talking about the book that again and again teachers had imported autobiographical comments into their explanations. He was much concerned in retrospect by the speed with which such data had been excised when writing up the research. The assumption, very much the conventional wisdom, was that such data were too 'personal', too 'idiosyncratic', too 'soft' for a fully fledged piece of social science research.

     Of course in the first instance (and some cases the last instance) it is true that personal data can be irrelevant, eccentric and essentially redundant. But the point that needs to be grasped is that these features are not the inevitable corollary of that which is personal. Moreover that which is personal at the point of collection may not remain personal. After all a good deal of social science is concerned with the collection of a range of often personal insights and events and the elucidation of more collective and generalizable profferings and processes.

     The respect for the autobiographical, for 'the life', is but one side of a concern to elicit the teachers' voice. In some senses like the anthropologist this school of qualitative educational research is concerned to listen to what the teacher says, and to respect and deal seriously with that data which the teacher imports into accounts. This is to invert the balance of proof. Conventionally that data which does not service the researcher's interests and foci is junked. In this model the data the teacher provides have a more sacred property and is only dispensed with after painstaking proof of irrelevance and redundancy.

Listening to the teachers' voice should teach us that the autobiographical, 'the life', is of substantial concern when teachers talk of their work. And at a commonsensical level I find this essentially unsurprising. What I do find surprising, if not frankly unconscionable, is that for so long researchers have ruled this part of the teachers' account out as irrelevant data.

2 Life experiences and background are obviously key ingredients of the person that we are, of our sense of self. To the degree that we invest our 'self' in our teaching, experience and background therefore shape our practice.

A common feature in many teachers' accounts of their background is the appearance of a favourite teacher who substantially influenced the person as a young school pupil. They often report that 'it was this person who first sold me on teaching'; 'it was sitting in her classroom when I first decided I wanted to be a teacher'. In short such people provide a 'role model' and in addition they most probably influence the subsequent vision of desirable pedagogy as well as possibly choice of subject specialism.

Many other ingredients of background are important in the teacher's life and practice. An upbringing in a working-class environment may for instance provide valuable insights and experience when teaching pupils from a similar background. I once observed a teacher with a working-class background teach a class of comprehensive pupils in a school in the East End of London. He taught using the local cockney vernacular and his affinity was a quite startling aspect of his success as a teacher. In my interview I spoke about his affinity and he noted that it was 'coz I come from round 'ere don't I?'. Background and life experience were then a major aspect of his practice. But so they would be in the case of middle-class teachers teaching children from the working class or teachers of working-class origins teaching middle-class children. Background is an important ingredient in the dynamic of practice. (See Lortie, 1976.)

Of course class is just one aspect as are gender or ethnicity, teachers' backgrounds and life experiences are idiosyncratic and unique and must be explored therefore in their full complexity. (Treatment of gender issues has often been inadequate — see Sikes, Measor and Woods, 1985. Recent work is more encouraging — see Acker 1988.)

3 The teacher's *lifestyle* both in and outside school, her or his

latent identities and cultures, impact on views of teaching and on practice. Becker and Geer's (1971) work on latent identities and cultures provide a valuable theoretical basis (pp. 56–60). Lifestyle is of course often a characteristic element in certain cohorts; for instance, work on the generation of 1960s teachers would be of great value. In our study of one teacher focussing on his life style Walker and I stated:

> The connections between youth culture and the curriculum reform movement of the sixties is more complex than we first thought. For Ron Fisher there definitely is a connection, he identifies strongly with youth culture and feels that to be important in his teaching. But despite his attraction to rock music and teenage life styles it is the school he has become sommitted to, almost against his own sense of direction. Involvement in innovation, for Ron at least, is not simply a question of technical involvement, but touches significant facets of his personal identity. This raises the question for the curriculum developer, what would a project look like if it explicitly set out to change the teachers rather than the curriculum? How would you design a project to appeal to the teacher-as-person rather than to the teacher-as-educator? What would be the effects and consequences of implementing such a design? (See Chapter 3.)

This I think shows how work in this area begins to force a reconceptualization of models of teacher development. We move in short from the teacher-as-practice to the teacher-as-person as our starting point for development.

4 The teachers' *life cycle* is an important aspect of professional life and development. This is a unique feature of teaching. For the teacher essentially confronts 'ageless' cohorts. This intensifies the importance of the life cycle for perceptions and practices.

5 Focus on the *life cycle* will generate insights therefore into the unique elements of teaching. Indeed so unique a characteristic would seem an obvious starting point for reflection about the teachers' world. Yet our research paradigms face so firmly in other directions that there has been little work to date in this area.

Fortunately work in other areas provides a very valuable

framework. Some of Gail Sheehy's somewhat populist work in *Passages* (1976) and *Pathfinders* (1981) is I think important. So also is the research work on which some of her publications are based carried out by Levinson. His work, whilst regrettably focussed only on men does provide some very generative insights into how our perspectives at particular stages in our life crucially effect our professional work.

Take for instance the case study of John Barnes, a university biologist. Levinson (1979) is writing about his 'dream' of himself as a front-rank prize-winning biological researcher:

> Barnes's Dream assumed greater urgency as he approached 40. He believed that most creative work in science is done before then. A conversation with his father's lifelong friend around this time made a lasting impression of him. The older man confided that he had by now accepted his failure to become a 'legal star' and was content to be a competent and respected tax lawyer. He had decided that stardom is not synonymous with the good life; it was 'perfectly all right to be second best'. At the time, however, Barnes was not ready to scale down his own ambition. Instead, he decided to give up the chairmanship and devote himself fully to his research.
>
> He stepped down from the chairmanship as he approached 41, and his project moved into its final phase. This was a crucial time for him, the culmination of years of striving. For several months, one distraction after another claimed his attention and heightened the suspense. He became the father of a little boy, and that same week was offered a prestigious chair at Yale. Flattered and excited, he felt that this was his 'last chance for a big offer.' But in the end Barnes said no. He found that he could not make a change at this stage of his work. Also, their ties to family and friends, and their love of place, were now of much greater importance to him and Ann. She said: 'The kudos almost got him, but now we are both glad we stayed'. (p. 267)

This quotation I think shows how definitions of our professional location and of our career direction can best be arrived at by detailed understanding of people's lives.

6   Likewise, *career stages* and *career decisions* can be analyzed in their own right. Work on teachers' lives and careers is increasingly commanding attention in professional development workshops and courses. For instance, The Open University in England now uses *Teachers' Lives and Careers* (Ball and Goodson, 1985) as one of its course set books. This is symptomatic of important changes in the way that professional courses are being reorganized to allow concentration on the perspective of teachers' careers.

     Besides the range of career studies in *Teachers Lives and Careers* a range of new research is beginning to examine this neglected aspect of teachers' professional lives. The work of Sikes, Measor and Woods (1985) has provided valuable new insights into how teachers construct and view their careers in teaching.

7   Moreover, the new work on teachers' careers points to the fact that there are *critical incidents* in teachers' lives and specifically in their work which may crucially affect perception and practice. Certainly work on beginning teachers has pointed to the importance of certain incidents in molding teachers' styles and practices. Lacey's work (1977) has pointed to the effects on teachers' strategies and the work of Woods (1979) has further elucidated the relationship to evolving teacher strategies.

     Other work on critical incidents in teachers' lives can confront important themes contextualized within a full life perspective. For instance, Kathleen Casey (1988) has employed 'life history narratives' to understand the phenomenon of teacher dropout, specifically female and activist teacher dropout. Her work is exceptionally illuminating of this phenomenon which is currently receiving a great deal of essentially uncritical attention given the problem of teacher shortages. Yet few of the countries at the hard edge of teacher shortages have bothered to fund serious study of teachers' lives to examine and extend our understanding of the phenomenon of teacher dropouts. I would argue that only such an approach affords the possibility of extending our understanding.

     Likewise with many other major themes in teachers' work. The question of teacher stress and burn-out would, I believe, be best studied through life history perspectives. Similarly the issue of effective teaching and the question of the take-up innovations and new managerial initiatives. Above all, thus illuminating the choices, contingencies and options open to the individual. 'Life histories' of schools, subjects and the teaching profession would provide vital contextual background. The initial focus on the teachers' lives therefore would reconceptualize our studies of schooling and curriculum in quite basic ways.

Collaboration and Teacher Development

Strategically I have argued that to promote the notion of teachers as researchers and to develop an action research modality where collaboration with externally situated researchers was fostered we need to avoid an immediate and predominant focus on practice. I have further argued that this focus on practice should, at 'least partially, be replaced by a focus on the teacher's life.

What is at issue here seems to me almost anthropological: we are looking for a point for teachers (as researchers) and externally located researchers to 'trade'. Practice promises maximum vulnerability as the 'trading point'. This is a deeply unequal situation in which to begin to 'trade' — for it could be argued that the teacher may already feel vulnerable and inferior in the face of a university researcher.

Talking about her or his own life the teacher is, in this specific sense, in a less immediately exposed situation; and the 'exposure' can be more carefully, consciously and personally controlled. (This is not, it should be noted, to argue that once again 'exploitation' might not take place, nor that there are no longer major ethical questions to do with exposure.) But I think this starting point has substantive as well as strategic advantages. Some have already been listed, however, in terms of the 'trade' between teacher/researcher and external researcher, this focus seems to me to provide advantages.

Much of the work that is emerging on teachers' lives throws up structural insights which locate the teacher's life within the deeply structured and embedded environment of schooling (Goodson, 1990; Goodson, forthcoming). This provides a prime 'trading point' for the external researcher. For one of the valuable characteristics of a collaboration between teachers as researchers and external researchers is that it is a collaboration between two parties that are differentially located in structural terms. Each see the world through a different prism of practice and thought. This valuable difference may provide the external researcher with a possibility to offer back goods in 'the trade'. The teacher/researcher offers data and insights; the external researcher, in pursuing glimpses of structure in different ways, may now also bring data and insights. The terms of trade, in short, look favourable. In such conditions collaboration may at last begin.

I noted earlier that this possible route to collaboration does not suspend issues of ethics and exploitation. This is above all because the collaboration between teacher/researcher and external researcher takes place in an occupational terrain which is itself inequitably structured. In terms of power, the external researcher still holds many advantages. Moreover the conditions of university careers positively exhort researchers to exploit research data: the requirements of publications and peer reviews have their own dynamics.

So whatever the favourable aspects of a focus on teachers' lives we must remain deeply watchful. For if the teacher's practice was a vulnerable focus, the teacher's life is a deeply intimate, indeed intensive, focus. More than ever procedural guidelines are necessary over questions relating to the ownership and publication of the data. These issues themselves must be conceived of in terms of a collaboration in which each party has clear rights and in this case the teacher's power of veto should be agreed on early and implemented, where necessary, late.

Chapter 10

On Understanding Curriculum: The Alienation of Curriculum Theory

Ivor Goodson

On Understanding Curriculum: The Alienation of Theory

The present relationship between curriculum and curriculum theory, is one of profound alienation. I use the term alienation in its more traditional derivation from the adjective 'alien' which the Oxford Dictionary defines as 'not one's own; foreign, under foreign allegiance; differing in character, repugnant'.

Curriculum theory and curriculum study are closely interlinked since curriculum studies feed into theory but also, perhaps more importantly, because theoretical paradigms guide the general directions and aspirations of curriculum study. The reconceptualization which I shall later argue for will involve both the manner in which we study curriculum and also in which we develop theory. By developing historical studies of curriculum it will be contended that our theoretical focus, and therefore the general character of our studies might be refined and redefined.

The value of curriculum theory must be judged against the existing curriculum as defined and as negotiated and realized in schools. But contemporary curriculum theories do not generally seek to explain or theorize about what is evidential, what is there. They are not theories of curriculum but merely programmes. They are utopian not realist, concerned only with what should or might be, not with the art of the possible. They act not to explain but to exhort.

This alienation of theory from reality means that we encounter fundamental problems in creating educational policy in the face of a predominance of curriculum theories as *prescriptions*, (or in Reid's, 1978, words as 'idealized practice,' p. 17). The link between theory and policy is seldom perfect or direct. Wise (1979) has warned that:

No matter how educational policy is created, its purpose is to affect (presumably to improve) the practice of education. Inevitably it must be based upon some theories or hypotheses about educational practice. If these assumptions are correct the policy will have its intended consequence ... Policies based upon incorrect assumptions probably will not work and may well have unintended (possibly undesirable) consequences. (pp. 54–5)

Wise may have stepped too far in suggesting that assumptions may be 'correct' rather than appropriate or intelligent. The genesis of curriculum theory as prescription is of course related to the broader social and economic context into which schooling is placed in Western countries. Particularly under American influence (where many of the first attempts to provide theories of curriculum arose) the emphasis has been on providing *rational* and *scientific* modes of curriculum design and implementation. Operating a rational model of 'scientific management' in education demands that curriculum theorists offer maximum help in the defining of objectives and programmes.

Wirth (1983) has characterized this American model of curriculum management in the following manner arguing that 'in the 1960s and 70s we witnessed a transformation of American schooling by technocratic ideology and systems analysis techniques — the sophisticated successor to Taylorist social efficiency practices of the early twentieth century':

Believers in the new technocratic ideology hold to a faith that a systems analysis approach which produces airplanes will also produce efficient child learning, and to belief in a crude form of behaviourism which assumes that behaviours will occur if it is specified that they shall occur. They assume that the principles of a mechanical model of production and cost/benefit economic principles can be transferred to education. The intention is to conceive of a science of education analogous to the sciences of mechanical production. (p. 120)

Given the predominance of the existing political and economic order and associated ideologies it thus becomes clear in which direction curriculum theorists will be steered. The theorists' task will be to provide a range of objectives for the system to sponsor, test and achieve. In addition a 'science of education' is required to underpin scientific management of the system. The management imperative and the support it offers in maintaining the legitimacy and control of the status quo is clearly in evidence. 'To true believers in educational results by "scientific efficiency" and bureaucratic social controls, the rationalistic model of schooling, . . . , is unquestionably correct. If the schools are given clear, measurable objectives, the objectives will be met'. For Wise, the model gains its force and legitimacy from its origins in the factory. He says that the

> policy-making process has an affinity for a rationalistic concep-
> tion of teaching and the teacher. The reasons are simple: The
> will of the policy maker must be implemented; the expectations
> for what the schools are to accomplish must be translated into
> action; the workers (teachers) in the factory (school) must
> perform their assigned tasks and the bureaucracy must be peo-
> pled by bureaucrats who will implement the official goals of
> the institution. (1979, p. 94)

But there are dangers in writing with the power of hindsight from a location in Reagan's America or Thatcher's Britain. For the moment the tendency outlined may be dominant and it has always been mas-sively powerful. Yet we must remember that in the 1960s and early 1970s in Britain a range of contradictory tendencies were also evident, sometimes influentially. To explain the overwhelming influence of prescriptive curriculum theories we need also to analyze the previous responses of those educators with a more sensitive appreciation of the educational enterprise. Why was it that those who did, and do, oppose the simplifications of rationalism and scientism were either coopted to prescriptive curriculum theories or, more often, abandoned theorizing altogether?

The explanation I believe turns on a sad irony. Those educators and curriculum theorists who opposed the reductionism of scientific management counter-posed a view of education as potentially liberat-ing and exciting. They were in short concerned to build an improved world. Above all they wanted to be involved in *action* not theory. They believed their action would have fundamental and long-lasting effect. Analysis of what was already in schools was therefore mere archeology: theorizing if there was a need for it could come later, after the curriculum revolution. This response to existing practice and theory has happened in previous periods of flux in curriculum. Kliebard (1975) tells us that in the United States in the 1920s the curriculum reformers almost totally rejected earlier established pro-cedures and practices, which they generally associated with the dis-credited doctrine of mental discipline. 'The belief in change now was sufficient to argue for transcending all past notions of theory and of practice. The ambivalence to research and theory is particularly significant'.

> In the curriculum field,..., the urge to do good is so immediate, so direct, and so overwhelming that there has been virtually no toleration of the kind of long-range research that has little immediate value to practitioners in the field, but which may in the long run contribute significantly to our basic knowledge and understanding. (p. 41)

Westbury (1973) some time ago identified this *meliorist* tendency along with its implications for curriculum theorizing:

> A vision can so easily slide into meliorism and, unfortunately, the consequences of such a meliorist perspective have long beset our field: too often and for too much of our history we have not been able, because of our commitment to what should be, to look at what is. To look at what is betrays, our emphases suggest, too little passion, even perhaps a conservative willingness to accept schools as they are. Indeed, all too often our stances imply a condemnation of what schools do. (p. 99)

In later sections I develop further the argument that a major stumbling block in effecting change in the 1960s and 1970s was our arrogance in initiating change from above and beyond without assessing what was already there. But again a sense of historical period is a major part of the explanation for these failings. It is now difficult to reconstruct the optimism and commitment of curriculum debate and reform initiatives at that time. But the documents give testimony to a widespread belief that schooling was about to change in fundamental and revolutionary ways. One is reminded of Clancy Segal's (1984) description of California in the mid-1960s: 'Each moment of the present promised so much of the future that the past seemed irrelevant'. Hence the times gave support to an ahistorical view of curriculum theorizing and action, to a belief that the focus was rightly on 'what should be rather than what is'.

A further reason for the ambivalence to curriculum theory might be added. I believe that a number of the more radical theorists actively embraced Trotsky's notion of 'impossibilism'. The point was to proscribe impossible goals for teachers (and pupils) to achieve in school. That way, so the argument proceeds, they will come to embrace the real 'truth' which is that the system can never — by its very structure and intentions — meet their needs. This moves the struggle closer to the day of actual revolt. Reid (1978) has characterized the radical theorist in this manner:

> The theorist is aware of problems of 'hidden curricula' of purposes and processes that lie behind the calls for the achievement of objectives or for the extension of the claims of systems over individuals. But his response is either to remove himself to a higher moral and intellectual plane from which he can safely criticize those who actually get involved in the practical curriculum tasks, or to declare that the only way of being involved in the improvement of curricula is to work for social revolution (usually in a Marxist sense). (p. 10)

But this was only one tendency within the radical critique; as we shall see later other radical tendencies were to help in pioneering new and valuable approaches.

To summarize: the mode of curriculum theorizing which has dominated the field is rationalistic and closely aligned to modes of scientific management and analysis: curriculum theories are essentially prescriptions. Ironically those who have sought to counteract these tendencies have failed to present a coherent alternative mode of theorizing; above all they have been concerned with curriculum action. In the former case we have a logical pursuit of a political (and educational) view. In the latter case, I shall argue, the ambivalence to theorizing is a betrayal of the cause. Meliorism (and indeed impossibilism) do violence to the complexities of educational practice; sometimes for the best of reasons they have led to a simplistic and ahistorical view of process. In their different ways both the prescriptive theorists and those with an action orientation have ignored what *is* in pursuit of what *might be*. It is time both came to grips with the ongoing realities from which all sides seem to be in full flight.

Underpinning Curriculum Theory as Prescription

In analyzing what underpins prescriptive modes of theorizing there is clearly a range of locations where one might begin. In the case studies that follow I focus down on one aspect of what *is* in curriculum — the school subject. Hence in this section I want to examine the theories and definitions of objectives as they relate to school subject knowledge. By concentrating on one aspect of curriculum in this manner it may be possible to further elucidate the way in which prescriptive theory originates and operates.

Whilst psychological theory may have been a general support, particularly in the scientific management structures discussed in the first section philosophy has been of undoubted import with respect to school subjects. I do not at this point want to intrude too far on the debate between the philosophical absolutists and social relativists: plainly a dialogue of the deaf. My concern is rather to characterize the implicit *posture* of philosophy with regard to the school curriculum.

At its heart, philosophy seems to hold itself well above the fray of curriculum as existing and as currently realized. The core of this aloofness is a commitment to rational and logical pursuit. But the other side of the coin is a resistance to the force of social influence. It is as if the philosopher searches for truths *beyond* social interference. This is true of even more liberal philosophers. Take Hirst (1965), for instance, objective knowledge he says

> is a form of education knowing no limits other than those necessarily imposed by the nature of rational knowledge and thereby developing in man the final court of appeal in all human affairs. (p. 127)

or Pring (1972):

> Forms of knowledge therefore are fundamental structures picked out by characteristic concepts and characteristic tests of truth. They are not options open to us; they constitute what it *means* to think and they characterize all our particular judgments. (p. 27)

The 'philosopher king' knows only 'truth' then; there are no options for they have access to a truth beyond culture and beyond history.

At a certain level of discourse this may well be a sustainable position. But facing the process of teaching forms of knowledge are we still in a position where 'they are not options open to us': on this point some of the philosophers show signs of almost human ambivalence. Others however have the strength of their convictions. Phenix (1968) for instance deliberately equates the disciplines with teachability:

> My theme has been that the curriculum should consist entirely of knowledge which comes from the disciplines, for the reason that the disciplines reveal knowledge in its teachable forms. (p. 133)

Phenix's statement reveals I think the likely policy outcome of the more recently dominant philosophical mode of theorizing. Whatever the qualifications, whatever the studied detachment, the likely effect of the posture will be prescriptive theorizing. From a certainty that 'there are no options' it is clear that prescriptive objectives for schooling will be both the expectation and the culmination.

The extent to which philosophy has in fact contributed to prescriptive theorizing can be seen in a wide range of curriculum books from specialists of all kinds, the work of Bruner and Phenix in the United States through to Lawton and Peters in the United Kingdom. Lawton is a particularly useful example of how the curriculum specialist receives the messages of the philosopher. Lawton (1975) argues that for Hirst, 'the theory seems to me to run as follows: the first principle is that we should be clear about our educational goals. The second is that the central objectives of education are developments of the mind'. He adds later:

> I have included Hirst's viewpoint here as an example of curriculum planning which is largely 'non-cultural' in the sense of being transcultural. This is because Hirst sees the curriculum largely in terms of knowledge, and the structure and organization of knowledge is, by his analysis, universal rather than culturally based. (p. 18)

Philosophy then leads us beyond culture and above all leads to curriculum theories which allow us to 'be clear about our educational goals'.

However the believers in educational goals based on the disciplines have ultimately to face the sad truth that the world of schooling as it currently exists is played on a pitch where scoring goals is difficult and where the goalposts are not always relevant. There is a tearful little section in Lawton headed 'Disciplines but not subjects'. Here the confrontation between philosophical and prescriptive truth and curriculum reality leads to peculiar paroxysms to escape culpability for the prescription's failures. Hence Lawton writes:

> there is no reason why a curriculum based on disciplines should not be related to the children's own experience and interests. The fact that so much so-called academic teaching of subjects does tend to neglect children's everyday knowledge ... is a condemnation of traditional pedagogy or teaching-method rather than disciplines themselves as a basis of the curriculum. (p. 85)

One wonders what a philosopher would make of the logic of culpability here? (are the disciplines beyond logic as well as culture?)

But this is to do less than justice to Lawton or Hirst. Both of these writers have shown considerable sensitivity to the problems of curriculum change and implementation. I have pursued the point to show that even sophisticated theorists are on the horns of a dilemma when working within the prescriptive mode. Hirst (1974) has pronounced at length on the dilemma in his article 'The forms of knowledge revisited':

> The importance of the disciplines, in the various senses distinguished, for school education, must not be minimized. What matters in this discussion is that the logical priority of intellectual objectives be recognized even if in terms of wider human values they are sometimes judged secondary. Equally their logical structure cannot be denied if they are ever to be attained. The concerns of the universities mean that their organizations of teaching and research necessarily embody these concerns to a high degree. But schools are not universities and their teaching functions are significantly different. These need to be seen in their own right for what they are. And if once that is done then not only do the disciplines matter, but many other things matter as well, things of major psychological and social concern which must not be overlooked.

This leads to a final epilogue for the forms of knowledge as prescriptions:

> Education is a complex business and philosophical analysis can contribute to our planning of it in a limited way. What it can do is alert us to the danger of too easy decisions and the issue of the place of the disciplines in more than a philosophical affair. What more there is to it, I must however leave to others. (p. 99)

The humility of this epilogue is both appealing and a clear statement of how limited the aspirations of the philosopher have become. But several logical steps are still missing before we arrive at this denouement. It is all very well to leave it to others. But who? It is all very well to alert us to the danger of easy decision. But what if philosophy has led to the very dangers of prescriptive simplicities to which we have drawn attention? To go back even further: If schools and teaching need to be seen for what they are, why does the analysis not start there? We are left with a basic message. If curriculum theory is to be of use it must *begin* with studies which *observe* schools and teaching. Our theory must grow from a developed understanding of the curriculum as it is produced and realized and of how, over time, this has been reproduced. We need, in short, not theories of curriculum prescriptions but studies, and eventually theories, of curriculum production and realization.

The Reaction to Alienated Theory

As was noted in the first section an important counter-tendency was evident within the curriculum field in the 1960s and 1970s. There was a reaction to the simplifications, indeed abdications, of the rational, scientific school of curriculum theory, but one which was heavily laden with meliorist (or even impossibilist) tendencies.

At the centre of the reaction was the knowledge of the complexity of the educational enterprise of which Hirst wrote. This makes the pursuit of a 'science of education' utterly illusory and as Goodlad (1975) has noted this is of great significance for those pursuing scientific prescriptions:

> There is not a science of education sufficient to give credence to the scientism necessarily indicated if any model of accountability ... is to function effectively. It is an idea whose time has not yet come, whatever rhetorical and political support it is able to muster. (p. 10)

Ernest House has made a similar point in writing about 'Evaluation as Scientific Management in US School Reform':

> The systems analysis approach to evaluation promises to substitute specific techniques derived from 'science' for the knowledge of craft in teaching. It is a false promise, for such simple techniques cannot substitute for fully fledged professional knowledge, much of it tacit rather than explicit, which has been acquired over many years. Such a technological vision of knowledge rests on a confusion of tacit knowledge with generalizations and rules of procedure. In teaching as in speaking, if one relied on the formalized, externalized rules of procedure, one would be mute. The challenge for evaluation then is to arrive at approaches which are complementary to professional craft and which sharpen actual practice rather than those which threatened to replace practice. (1978, p. 400)

In the 1960s and 1970s the distinction between theory and practice often led to a reaction against theory not to a reformulation of theory.

Theory as constituted, as we have seen, merely collides with curriculum reality. The collision left the theorists fairly overtly at a loss — 'we'd better leave this to others'. But the 'others' who were more immersed in the reality of curriculum production and operation drew their own conclusions about theory. If it had so little to say about the reality of practice, if in fact it grievously misrepresented or even 'threatened to replace' practice was it not best to do without theory altogether or at least leave theorizing until later?

The response in the curriculum field strongly echoes the pendulum swings in sociology at about the same time. The preeminent positivist enterprise employed a scientific hypothetico-deductive model. The aim was to discover the social laws which underpinned everyday reality. Above all they followed a model related to the philosophy of science which had as its major objective the seeking of objective facts about the social world. The scientist seeks a knowledge of the social system separate and beyond the perceptions of the people who inhabit that system, pursuing wide-ranging laws and truth.

The reaction to this pursuit of scientific and universalistic laws came from symbolic interactionists, ethnomethodologists and sociologists of knowledge arguing for the rehabilitation of man himself and his subjective perceptions and 'constructions' of reality. Drawing on Weber and Mead we had the work of Schutz, Goffman and Berger and Luckmann. The latter were characteristic in arguing that 'common sense knowledge rather than ideas must be the central focus for the sociology of knowledge. It is precisely this knowledge that constitutes the fabric of meanings without which no society can exist' (Berger and Luckman, 1967).

The stress on subjective perceptions in sociology engendered substantial responses in the curriculum field. Ambivalence about theory, the manifest lack of fit with practice caused the pendulum to swing widly when the reaction began. One of the leaders Joseph Schwab sought to rehabilitate 'the practical' in reaction to incompetent theory. Writing in 1970 (interestingly the same year as the Centre for *Applied* Research in Education began in England) Schwab took an apocalyptic stance:

> The field of curriculum is moribund. It is unable, by its present methods and principles, to continue its work and contribute significantly to the advancement of education. It requires new principles which will generate a new view of the character and variety of its problems. It requires new methods appropriate to the new budget of problems. (1978, p. 287)

Schwab was absolutely clear why the curriculum field was moribund; his indictment is plain and powerful:

> The curriculum field has reached this unhappy state by inveterate, unexamined, and mistaken reliance on *theory*. On the one hand it has adopted theories (from outside the field of education) concerning ethics, knowledge, political and social structure, learning, mind, and personality, and has used these borrowed theories theoretically, i.e., as principles from which to 'deduce' right aims and procedures for schools and classrooms. On the other hand, it has attempted construction of educational theories, particularly theories of curriculum and instruction. (p. 287)

Schwab then lists the 'grave difficulties (incoherence of the curriculum, failure and discontinuity in actual schooling)' to which theoretic activities have led. This is because

> theoretical constructions are, in the main, ill-fitted and inappropriate to problems of actual teaching and learning. Theory, by its very character, does not and cannot take account of all the matters which are crucial to questions of what, who, and how to teach: that is, theories cannot be applied as principles to the solution of problems concerning what to do with or for real individuals, small groups, or real institutions located in time and space — the subjects and clients of schooling and schools. (p. 287)

Above all then Schwab wishes us to move away from the theoretic and to embrace the practical. In terms of subject matter he juxtaposes the two options in this way: the theoretic is always something taken to be universal or pervasive and is investigated as if it were constant from instance to instance and impervious to changing circumstance. The practical on the other hand is always something taken as concrete and particular and treated as infinitely susceptible to circumstance, and therefore highly liable to unexpected change: 'this student, in that school, on the South side of Columbus, with Principal Jones during the present mayoralty of Ed Tweed and in view of the probability of his re-election'.

In the United Kingdom the rehabilitation of the practice and process of schooling followed similar lines echoing the new trends in sociology and certain tendencies, not only Schwabian, within Amercan curriculum studies. A wide range of ethnographic and interactionist studies emerged focussing on the process of social stratification at the level of the school and the classroom. The Manchester School, in particular Hargreaves, Lacey and Lambart, adopted an approach with antecedents in anthropology. The commitment was to trying to understand how teachers and pupils 'constructed' the world of the school. Without detailed study of the school progress was impossible. While they were not primarily concerned with curriculum issues their academic leadership led to a more applied approach in curriculum research.

One centre which took a lead in applied work was The Centre for Applied Research in Education (CARE) at the University of East Anglia. CARE was founded in 1970 and embraced commitment to the teacher and her or his perceptions and constructions. The wide range of publications produced allow us to analyze the intentions and positions of those working at CARE. Whilst claims can be made for the uniqueness of CARE there is much that is symptomatic and typical of beliefs at the time. By looking in some detail at CARE it may then be possible to understand some of the reasons for the posture adopted by leading curriculum developers during this period.

In his influential book *An Introduction to Curriculum Research and Development* Lawrence Stenhouse (1975) stated that it is the thesis of this book that

> curriculum development must rest on teacher development and that it should promote it and hence the professionalism of the teacher. Curriculum development translates ideas into classroom practicalities and thereby helps the teacher to strengthen his practice by systematically and thoughtfully testing ideas. (pp. 24–5)

The stress on classroom practicalities echoes Schwab and became a strongly held value position at CARE. Working as a teacher at the time in contact with a number of CARE personnel including Stenhouse, MacDonald and Walker, I was a beneficiary of their commitment and quite literally, care. Walker, put the posture with regard to curriculum studies in this way. The work he argued

> would start with, and remain close to, the common-sense knowledge of the practitioner, and the constraints within which he works. It would aim to systematize and to build on practitioners' lore rather than supplant it. (1974, p. 22)

Barton and Lawn (1980) have commented that:

> In separating 'pure' from 'applied' research, Walker feels he has
> successfully rid himself of a theoretical stance and, moreover,
> reduced the isolation of the researcher. What now counts for
> him is not a theoretical understanding of any particular situa-
> tion but the understanding and self-recognition he can give his
> subjects. (p. 4)

On the latter point I can certainly testify but the points on the
aversion to theory are I think substantial and the authors go on to
claim that 'CARE's aversion to theory and to theorizing is consistent
throughout its membership ... the question often appears to be a
choice between theory and truth'.

Of course from the critique presented herein of curriculum theory
the latter point is well taken. The danger however is that the reaction
to prescriptive theory had led to a full flight from theory *per se*. There
is substantial evidence of this happening at CARE.

The significance of the CARE position, in articulating this strong
'action' and practice position, is that it was symptomatic of a major
counter-tendency in the curriculum field at the time — spreading
throughout the new 'applied research' to 'action research' and pervad-
ing case study, ethnography, interactionist studies, of classrooms and
evaluation. Macdonald, the *eminence grise* of British evaluation, once
broke cover to explain why his view of evaluation was thus, above all
it was in reaction to controlling theories of 'cost benefit' and 'management by objectives':

> The tendency of language like this is to suggest that the pro-
> duction of educated people is much like the production of
> anything else, a technological problem of specification and
> manufacture. (1976, p. 89)

The reasons for the reaction to theory are then clear but it was, one
must remember, a reaction to a particular kind of prescriptive theory
suiting the ideological and economic context in which it was produced.
The pendulum swing produced a full scale flight to the arena of action,
of practice, the classroom, the practitioner, the practical. We stand
witness to a celebration of the practical, a revolt against the abstract.
We are back with Rousseau and Emile.

The problem of the hasty embrace of action and practice was
compounded by the kind of action embraced. To the problems of the
methodology of action and practical specificity must be added the
problem of *focus*. Not surprisingly those with a strong belief in practice and action sought ways of becoming involved. Curriculum pro-

jects offered a way into curriculum action: the ethos of CARE developed from the involvement of the key personnel in the preceding Humanities Curriculum Project. The particular view of professionalism and politics developed on HCP was later transferred over to become a position about curriculum research in general.

In the 1960s and the early part of the 1970s a wide range of curriculum research studies and papers discussed the issue of curriculum change. It was always dealt with as synonymous with *innovation*. Eric Hoyle's (1969) *How Does the Curriculum Change: A Proposal for Inquiries* is a good example. In addition innovation and curriculum projects were viewed as synonymous. To confirm the point it is worth re-reading Parlett and Hamilton's (1972) important paper on *Evaluation as Illumination*. The specificity of focus for those seeking to change the school curriculum is clear. The illuminative evaluator was characteristically concerned with 'what is happening'. They wanted therefore to:

> Study the innovatory project: how it operates, how it is influenced by the various school situations in which it is applied; what those directly concerned regard as its advantages and disadvantages and how students' intellectual tasks and academic experiences are more affected.

The illuminative evaluator then

> aims to discover and document what it is like to be participating in the scheme, whether as a teacher or pupil; and in addition, to discern and discuss the innovation's most significant features, recurring concomitants and critical processes. (Parlett and Hamilton, 1972)

So a major milieu for those reacting to the rational/scientific school of prescriptive theorizing, given the terrain of the 1960s and 1970s curriculum field, was the innovative curriculum project. Those projects in a sense offered a perfect milieu for those with an ambivalence or antipathy to theory and a wish to be immersed in the day-to-day realities of practice and action. The problem however was not that it offered immersion in the milieu of action but that it was immersion in very *specific* milieu of action. This allowed project staff to initially have it both ways. There was no need for the generalizability of theories or programmes for the project normally centred on a limited number of chosen 'pilot' schools. The need for theory could be easily and justifiably suspended.

The problems began when projects sought to generalize their

work: the move if you like from the pilot stage towards new main-stream structures. Here though beginning from the opposite starting point, the projects often responded with the very prescriptions and programmes they had reacted against. There were prescriptions of idealized practice like the 'neutral chairman'; modules and courses, like 'Man a Course of Study'; and new materials and curriculum packages. The prescriptions were buttressed with more theoretical pronounce-ments, with stark similarity to the prescriptive theories they had reacted against. There were now RDD models (research, development, dissemination) or KPU models (knowledge, production and utiliza-tion).

The sad truth was that starting from utterly different points pre-scriptive theory and immersion in practice led to the same collision point: everyday classroom life and existing syllabuses, exams, subject structures and subject communities. Again the posture ended up as exhortation, or 'we must leave this to others'. Take my comments some time ago on the History 13–16 Project, one of the better pro-jects:

> History 13–16 has a very impressive record; large numbers of guides and materials have been produced and meetings and conferences held. The thorny problems of examination and pedagogic style have been consistently confronted. Significant numbers of schools are now teaching the new history syllabus. In a real sense the project has done all that could have been expected of it.

> The major weakness of the project is one common to most curriculum reform movements and projects, namely, the strategies for achieving basic change in classroom pedagogy. Such change has proved enormously difficult to encourage because of the range of constraints which persuade teachers to transmit factual knowledge to more or less passive students. 'Active learning situations', where the teacher ceases being merely a transmitter of facts, are certainly far more elusive than the implementing strategies drawn up by the project ever hint at.

> The project hardly offers a coherent scheme at this level; more a mixture of laissez-faire and hope. The former is illustrated by comments about how to deal with third-form history: 'It is a problem which most teachers must work out for themselves, in

the light of the differing circumstances in which they are placed'.

Hope is evident in a range of statements. The strategy for getting teachers to use more evidence was described in this way: 'The project hopes to give teachers a rationale for making evidence central to history teaching and also give to them, by the production of materials, some of the tools for the job'.

Fundamentally the project's hopes seem to have been for a change in pedagogy through *exhortation*. This is well illustrated by the attempts to get teachers to use discussion methods: 'Teachers will need to be willing to discuss with pupils their own reasons for teaching history and for seeing it as useful education for adolescents'. (Sylvester 1973, p. 144)

In seeking to change classroom pedagogy a curriculum project is approaching one of the vested traditions within teaching and one supported by a huge range of rational and irrational arguments. Traditional teaching patterns have not and will not be changed by exhortation or by *new* materials that can be readily put to use in teaching with the *old* method. (Goodson, 1980, p. 187)

The comments are so reminiscent of the impotence of prescriptive curriculum theory; instead of problems 'to be left to others' we have problems 'teachers must work out for themselves, in the light of the differing circumstances in which they are placed'.

The point of previous abdication it now should be clear must become our starting point. Curriculum research and theory must begin by investigating how the curriculum is currently produced by teachers in the 'differing circumstances in which they are placed'. Moreover our theory needs to move towards how those circumstances are not just 'placed' but systematically constructed. For the persistence of styles of practice is in part the result of the construction of persistent circumstances.

We need to begin by understanding how curriculum is currently produced and why matters operate in the way they do. In short we need a theory of context which underpins action. In such a manner a new curriculum initiative or project would pilot not so much materials as policy. The negotiation of new 'circumstances' for practice, of new structures would be part of the task in both theory and action.

As with industrial innovations and practices new initiatives in other countries often prove the best places to learn the lessons from previous waves of activity. For instance some of the new projects in Eire have drawn lessons from American and British undertakings. Firstly they critically scrutinize previous curriculum models:

> The RDD and KPU model, looked at from the perspective of a number of systems and agencies, is no longer sustainable. Over the past few decades, such approaches have been seen not to work, except in most exceptional circumstances. A set of educational ideas cannot be developed and packaged for use at will. (Curriculum Development Unit, 1982, p. 71)

The need that is identified comes close to a theory of context. In the section on the Early School Leavers Project on organization for change we learn

> It is good to see that organizational implications and consequences are of central concern to the Early School Leavers Project. General ideas are not enough: we must move towards an organizational framework to carry those ideas. However — and this is a serious problem — the structure that seems to be emerging — and has certainly emerged in England — is of a three-tiered kind, where the brightest, those geared for Higher Education are in the top tier, while the potential dropouts are in the bottom. Is that really what we want? Do we want to see the alienated, the dispossessed on the bottom tier of such a structure? If we do not want it, can we nevertheless avoid it? Does consideration of the particular needs of a specific group — however large and politically ominous — necessarily commit us to a kind of educational and social stratification which many of us have been trying for years to scale down if not eliminate? Will our strategies at the stage of generalization of these pilot studies take account of the consequences for school and society of this underlying trend? (Curriculum Development Unit, 1982, p. 74)

The essential point about these comments on context and structure is that they focus on the aspects which are least developed in both prescriptive theory and the reaction to it. The prescriptive mode assumes, and has assumed, that bureaucratic accountability and power can ensure implementation: the reaction has assumed that growth, optimism and ameliorism would complete the task. Neither was correct. Both modes abandoned the middle ground: existing and continuing practice and structure. Both modes shared a belief in transcending existing practice and structure. Both modes were quintessentially, sometimes explicitly, ahistorical.

This brings us back to a point made by Westbury: 'In all cases the curriculum can be seen as an *idea* that becomes a thing, an entity that has institutional and technical form' (McKinney and Westbury, 1975, p. 6). Taking these in turn: institutional form means curriculum is mediated by antecedent structures of status, syllabuses and subjects, by the professional groups and sub-groups who inhabit existing curriculum territory. Technical form — curriculum has to be translated from an idea into a technical specification, a teachable subject and an examinable syllabus. The achievement of high-status technical form will then relate to institutional form and the status attributed and resources distributed to the practitioner of curriculum.

We are left requiring theories which pursue systematic investigation of how existing curricula originates, is reproduced, metamorphoses and responds to new prescriptions. A theory in short of how people involved in the ongoing production and reproduction of curriculum act, react and interact. Put in this way it seems a tall order but there is important work already undertaken on which to build. The initial focus of future work has to be on the interest groups and structures which currently operate and frame curriculum. These are located in the middle ground between scientific/rational theories and Schwab's concrete and particular 'this student, in that school, on the South side of Columbus'. It is to this middle ground that we must now focus our attention.

Note

An earlier version of this chapter appeared in *Curriculum Perspectives*, vol. 7, No. 2, October 1987.

Chapter 11

Studying Curriculum:
A Social Constructionist Perspective

Ivor Goodson

One of the perennial problems of studying curriculum is that it is a multifaceted concept, constructed, negotiated and renegotiated at a variety of levels and in a variety of arenas. This elusiveness has no doubt contributed to the rise of theoretical and overarching perspectives — psychological, philosophical and sociological — as well as more technical or scientific perspectives. But these perspectives have been criticized recurrently because they do violence to the practical essentials of curriculum as conceived of and realized.

In this paper, I shall argue that we need to move firmly and sharply away from decontextualized and disembodied modes of analysis whether they be philosophical, psychological or sociological; away from technical, rational or scientific management models — away from the 'objectives game'. Above all, we need to move away from a singular focus on curriculum as prescription. This means that we must embrace fully the notion of *curriculum as social construction*, firstly at the level of prescription itself, but also at the levels of process and practice.

Curriculum as Prescription

The primacy of the ideology of curriculum as prescription (CAP) can be evidenced in even a cursory glimpse at the curriculum literature. This view of curriculum develops from a belief that we can dispassionately define the main ingredients of the course of study and then proceed to teach the various segments and sequences in systematic turn. Despite the obvious simplicity, not to say crudity of this view, the 'objectives game' is still, if not the only game in town, certainly the

main game. There may be many reasons for this continuing predominance, but explanatory potential is not, I think, one of the factors.

Curriculum as prescription supports important mystiques about
state schooling and society. Most notably CAP supports the mystique
that expertise and control reside within central governments, educational bureaucracies or the university community. Providing nobody
exposes this mystique, the two worlds of 'prescriptive rhetoric' and
'schooling as practice' can co-exist. Both sides benefit from such
peaceful co-existence. The agencies of CAP are seen to be 'in control'
and the schools are seen to be 'delivering' (and can carve out a good
degree of autonomy if they accept the rules). Curriculum prescriptions
thereby set certain parameters — although transgression and occasional
transcendence are permissible as long as the rhetoric of prescription
and management is not challenged.

Of course there are costs of complicity in accepting the myth of
prescription: above all these involve, in various ways, acceptance of
established modes of power relations. Perhaps most importantly the
people intimately connected with the day-to-day social construction of
curriculum and schooling — teachers — are thereby effectively disenfranchized in the 'discourse of schooling'. To continue to exist,
teachers' day-to-day power must remain unspoken and unrecorded.
This is one price of complicity: day-to-day power and autonomy for
schools and for teachers are dependent on continuing to accept the
fundamental lie.

With regard to curriculum studies the costs of complicity are
ultimately catastrophic. For the historic compromise we have described has led to the displacement of a whole field of study. It has led
to the directing of scholarship into fields which service the mystique of
central and/or bureaucratic control. For scholars who benefit from
maintaining this mystique — in the universities particularly — this
complicity is, to say the least, self-serving.

The Devil's Bargain: Critiques and Counters

I do not wish however to mount a substantial critique of CAP in this
paper. That has already been done — with conclusive success in my
view — in many other places. My intention is to repeat briefly that
critique and then explore the new directions in which we might move
if we are to provide a valid counterculture for curriculum research.

In terms of the diagnosis of the problem I am at one with Schwab
(1978). Let me briefly repeat his words:

The field of curriculum is moribund. It is unable, by its present methods and principles, to continue its work and contribute significantly to the advancement of education. It requires new principles which will generate a new view of the character and variety of its problems. It requires new methods appropriate to the new budget of problems. (p. 287)

Schwab's diagnosis should be read alongside Veblen's and Clifford and Guthries' strictures about the relationships between university schools of education and schooling. Veblen (1962) said

the difference between the modern university and the lower schools is broad and simple; not so much a difference of degree as of kind. (p. 15)

This distinctiveness of purpose and mission

unavoidably leads them to court a spacious appearance of scholarship and so to invest their technological discipline with a degree of pedantry and sophistication whereby it is hoped to give these schools and their work some scientific and scholarly prestige. (p. 23)

The resonance of Veblen's strictures has been confirmed in Clifford and Guthries' recent work:

Our thesis is that schools of education, particularly those located on the campuses of prestigious research universities, have become ensnared improvidently in the academic and political cultures of their institutions and have neglected their professional allegiances. They are like marginal men, aliens in their own worlds. They have seldom succeeded in satisfying the scholarly norms of their campus letters and science colleagues, and they are simultaneously estranged from their practicing professional peers. The more forcefully they have rowed toward the shores of scholarly research, the more distant they have become from the public schools they are duty bound to serve. Conversely, systematic efforts at addressing the applied problems of public schools have placed schools of education at risk on their own campuses. (1988, pp. 3–4)

In short, the schools of education entered into a devil's bargain when they entered the university milieu. The result was their mission changed from being primarily concerned with matters central to the practice of schooling towards issues of status passage through more conventional university scholarship. The resulting dominance of conventional 'disciplinary' modes has had disastrous impact on educational theory in general and curriculum study in particular.

The devil's bargain on the part of education was an especially pernicious form of a more general displacement of discourse and debate which surrounded the evolution of university knowledge production. University knowledge evolved as separate and distinct from public knowledge for as Mills noted:

> Men of knowledge do not orient themselves exclusively toward the total society, but to special segments of that society with special demands, criteria of validity, of significant knowledge, of pertinent problems, etc. It is through integration of these demands and expectations of particular audiences which can be effectively located in the social structure, that men of knowledge organize their own work, define their data, seize upon their problems.

In Mill's view, such a structural location of 'men of knowledge' (sic) in the university could have profound implications for public discourse and debate. Mills believed this would happen if the knowledge produced in this way did not have public relevance, particularly if it was not related to public and practical concerns:

> Only where publics and leaders are responsive and responsible, are human affairs in democratic order, and only when knowledge has public relevance is this order possible. Only when mind has an autonomous basis, independent of power, but powerfully related to it, can it exert its force in the shaping of human affairs. Such a position is democratically possible only when there exists a free and knowledgeable public, to which men of knowledge may address themselves, and to which men of power are truly responsible. Such a public and such men — either of power or of knowledge, do not now prevail, and accordingly, knowledge does not now have democratic relevance in America. (1979, p. 613)

The dilemma facing men of knowledge which Mills describes is acute when that knowledge relates to schooling. In the schools knowledge is transmitted to future generations. If our knowledge of such knowledge transmission is flawed, we are doubly imperilled: schooling is so intimately related to the social order that if either our knowledge of schooling is inadequate or it has no public relevance, then major aspects of social and political life are obscured.

Hence the question 'whither educational or curriculum research' is one of great importance. Mills, I think, comes close to the nature of our dilemma and spells out the implications of the devil's bargain when he talks of the way 'men of knowledge' orient themselves to 'special segments of society'. This has been the fate of much educational and curriculum theory and the effect has been that, as Mills put it, different groups 'talk past each other'. With few exceptions I would argue this is precisely the relationship between curriculum scholars and school practitioners: they constitute a model of how to talk past each other. It is to the resolution of this problem that I now turn.

Towards a Social Constructionist Perspective: From Diagnosis to Solution

CAP, and the major reaction to CAP, both share one characteristic, namely a concern to develop models of 'idealized practice' (Reid, 1978, p. 17). Both models are concerned with what *ought* to be happening in schools, 'our commitment to what should be', as Westbury (1973) argues, this can lead to 'meliorism':

A vision can so easily slide into meliorism and, unfortunately, the consequences of such a meliorist perspective have long beset our field: too often and for too much of our history we have not been able, because of our commitment to what should be, to look at what is. To look at what is betrays, our emphases suggest, too little passion, even perhaps a conservative willingness to accept schools as they are. Indeed, all too often our stances imply a condemnation of what schools do. (p. 99)

It is thus important to restate the problems of CAP; not only that the focus is solely on prescription but that the kind of focus is *disembodied* and *decontextualized*. We need an understanding of how curriculum prescriptions are in fact socially constructed for use in schools: studies of the actual development of courses of study, of national curriculum plans, of subject syllabuses and so on. Thus the problem, as we restate it, is not the *fact* of the focus on prescription, but the *singular* nature of that focus and the *kind* of focus. What we require is a combined approach — a focus on the construction of prescriptive curricula and policy coupled with an analysis of the negotiations and realization of that prescribed curriculum focussing on the essentially dialectical relationship of the two.

We want, in short, the story of action within a theory of context — to move a step back towards the centre following the moves of Schwab and some curriculum reformers to embrace the 'practical' terrain. Their reaction, I have argued, was too extreme a reaction, albeit understandable at the time. Since prescription continues (and given the current centralist thrust in, for example the UK, will strengthen) we need to understand social construction of curricula at the levels of prescription *and* process *and* practice. What is required is indeed to understand the practical but to locate this understanding within a further exploration of the contextual parameters of practice.

In curriculum research there are a range of foci that are amenable to social constructionist study, for instance:

—The *individual*: life history and career.
—The *group or collective*: professions, categories, subjects and disciplines, for instance, evolve rather as social movements over time. Likewise schools and classrooms develop patterns of stability and change.
—The *relational*: the various permutations of relations between individuals, between groups and collectivities and between individuals, group and collectivities; and the way these relations change over time.

Of course the relationship between individual and collective (as between action and structure) is perennially elusive. But our studies may, as has largely been the case in the past, accept or exacerbate fragmentation or alternatively, as should be our intention in the future, seek integration. Let us consider some examples.

In examining individual teachers' lives the *life history* method might be usefully rehabilitated. The genesis of life histories can be located in anthropological work at the beginning of this century; the main take-up by sociologists occurred later in a series of urban and social studies at the University of Chicago. For a number of reasons this work became less and less of a priority in the Chicago studies of the city, and as a result, the method fell into neglect until recently (Goodson, 1988). In its more contemporary usage life history work has focussed mainly on studies of deviance, crime and urban ethnography. The methodology of life history is still relatively undeveloped in the study of schooling, and its use here is only just beginning.

An exhortation to re-embrace life history as a method for the study of schooling was first presented in 1981 (Goodson, 1981, pp. 62–76). The approach was subsequently taken up in a study of teachers' careers undertaken by Sikes, Measor and Woods (1985). They were from the beginning aware of the substantial problems and commended that 'life histories do not present themselves as a fully-fledged method ready to use. There is, as yet, no substantial body of methodological literature to support life history studies' (Sikes *et al.*, 1985, p. 14). Nevertheless, their work in *Teachers' Careers: Crises and Continuities* does provide us with important insights on teachers' lives and careers. Other work such as Bertaux's (1981) collection *Biography and Society* and Ken Plummer's (1983) excellent *Documents of Life* begin the rehabilitation of life history method and the exploration of the substantial methodological and ethical problems that such work entails.

Beyond the problems intrinsic to the life history methods, there are problems of their relationship to foci and modes of analysis and investigation. As Mannheim warned in 1936: 'Preoccupation with the purely individual life history and its analysis is not sufficient' (Mannheim, 1972, p. 24). Above all, and rightly, Mannheim is railing against individualism — the fiction of the isolated and self-sufficient individual. Given the powerful legacy of individualism and of the individualist assumptions present in so many epistemologies this danger must be continually scrutinized with regard to life history work. As Mannnheim (1972) says:

> The genetic method of explanation, if it goes deep enough, cannot in the long run limit itself to the individual life history and the more inclusive group situation. For the individual life history is only a component in a series of mutually intertwined life histories ... it was the merit of the sociological point of view that it set alongside the individual genesis of meaning the genesis from the context of group life. (p. 25)

Life history study pursued alongside the study of collective groupings and milieux might promote better integration in a study of differing foci. The problem of integration is of course partly a problem of dealing with modes and levels of consciousness. The life history penetrates the individual subject's consciousness and attempts to map the changes in that consciousness over the life cycle. But at the individual level, as at other levels, change is structured — and structures change. The relationship between the individual and wider structures is central but it is through historical studies that such investigations can be profitably pursued:

> Our chance to understand how smaller milieux and larger structures interact, and our chance to understand the larger causes at work in these limited milieux, thus require us to deal with historical materials. (Wright Mills, 1970, p. 165)

Ultimately we are back with the integrative focus suggested by C. Wright Mills as essential for all good social science.

> Social science deals with problems of biography of history and of their intersections within social structures. That these three — biography, history, society, are the coordinate points of the proper study of man has been a major platform on which I have stood when criticizing several current schools of sociology whose practitioners have abandoned this classic tradition. (1970, p. 159)

In curriculum study the relationship between the individual teacher's life and the preactive and interactive curriculum will allow insights into structuration as well as action. As Esland (1971) has argued:

> Trying to focus the individual biography in its socio-historical context is in a very real sense attempting to penetrate the symbolic drift of school knowledge, and the consequences for the individuals who are caught up in it and attempting to construct their reality through it. (p. 111)

What is needed is to build on studies of participants immersed in immediate process, to build on studies of historical events and periods, and to develop a cumulative understanding of the historical contexts in which the contemporary curriculum is embedded. The experience of the past decades has shown the painful limitations of a historical or transcendent approaches at the level of both curriculum reform and study. By developing our analysis from further back we should be able to throw more light on the present and afford insights into the constraints immanent in transmitted circumstance.

However, studies with an action orientation have too often been confined to the view of participants at a moment in time, to the here and now events. The essential omission is data on the *constraints beyond* the event, the school, the classroom and the participant. What above all is needed, therefore, is a method that stays with the participants, with the complexity of the social process, but catches some understanding of the constraints beyond. The human process by which men make their own history does not take place in circumstances of their own choosing, so too do the potentialities for negotiating reality. Historical study seeks to understand how thought and action have developed in past social circumstances. Following this development through time to the present affords insights into how those circumstances we experience as contemporary 'reality' have been negotiated, constructed and reconstructed over time. Stenhouse (1977) saw this need for history to provide an authenticated context for hypothetical actions. His concern was also with:

> what might be termed the contextual inertia within which events are embedded. It is here that history generalizes and becomes theoretical. It is, as it were, the story of action within a theory of context. (p. 7)

The historical context of course reflects previous patterns of conflict and power. It is not sufficient to develop a static notion of the historical contexts and constraints inherited *in toto* from the past. These contexts and constraints need to be examined in relationship to contemporary action. We need a dynamic model of how syllabuses, pedagogy, finance, resources, selection, the economy and all the like *all* interrelate. We cannot, in short, view the curriculum (and its associated historical contexts and constraints) as a bounded system. Williamson (1974) has reflected on the fact 'that it is not sufficient to be aware only of the fact that the principles governing the selection of transmittable knowledge reflect structures of power. It is essential to move beyond such suspicions to work out the precise connections' (p. 10). This, he argues, predicates historical study of curriculum 'if the aim is to understand power in education'. Above all we need to develop cognitive maps of curriculum influence and curriculum constraints for, as he says:

> What is provided in schools and what is taught in those schools can only be understood historically. Earlier educational attitudes of dominant groups in society still carry historical weight. (pp. 10–11)

A Programme of Work

Social constructionist perspectives seek a reintegrated focus for studies of curriculum by moving away from singular focus, whether on ideal-ized practice or actual practice, towards developing data on social construction at both preactive and interactive levels. At this point in time the most significant lacuna for such a reconceptualized program-me of study is historical study of the social construction of school curricula. We know very little about how the subjects and themes pre-scribed in schools originate, how they are promoted and redefined, and how they metamorphose.

Work on the history of the social construction of school curricula is therefore a vital prerequisite for reconceptualized curriculum study. Fortunately, a good deal of work has been undertaken in the last decade which is coming to fruition. The series *Studies in Curriculum History* now comprises a range of volumes which provide a wide range of different studies of the social construction of school curricula. (Goodson, see notes on series in bibliography) Other work, especially in North America, complements this initiative and develops our understanding of the contestation which has surrounded the develop-ment of prescriptive curricula (Kliebard, 1975).

In *The Making of Curriculum* (Goodson, 1988) I have worked with and across the range of foci from the individual to the group and the collective. In particular I have sought to examine individual life histories and how these allow us to develop themes and frameworks for viewing structures and organizations. Some of the individual testi-monies provided in this book show how teachers come to understand and reflect upon the broader contexts in which their professional lives are embedded.

Likewise in *School Subjects and Curriculum Change* (Goodson, 1987) I have tried to develop the group or collective focus by studying school subjects in historical evolution. Here I contended that

> Historical case studies of school subjects provide the 'local detail' of curriculum change and conflict. The identification of individuals and sub-groups actively at work within curriculum interest groups allows some examination and assessment of intention and motivation. Thereby sociological theories which attribute power over the curriculum to dominant interest groups can be scrutinised for their empirical potential.

> To concentrate attention at the micro level of individual school subject groups is not to deny the crucial importance of macro level economic changes or changes in intellectual ideas, dominant values or educational systems. But it is asserted that such macro level changes may be actively reinterpreted at the micro level. Changes at macro level are viewed as presenting a range of new choices to subject factions, associations and communities. To understand how subjects change over time, as well as histories of intellectual ideas, we need to understand how subject groups are all-powerful in engineering curriculum change but that their responses are a very important, and as yet somewhat neglected, part of the overall picture. (Goodson, 1987, pp. 3–4)

More recently in *Subjects and Schooling — The Social Construction of Curriculum* (Goodson, forthcoming) I have been wrestling with how to integrate different foci and levels of analysis. In developing an integrated social constructionist perspective this work pursues the promise that the theoretic and the practical, or structure and agency, might be reconnected in our vision of curriculum scholarship. Were this to come about we might be saved from the recurrent 'flight to theory' followed by the counter-balancing 'flight to practice' (and the occasional intervening 'flight to the personal'). Our scholarship would thereby be encompassing in integrated manner the complexity of levels of analysis which reflects the reality of curriculum.

To begin any analysis of schooling by accepting without question a form and content of curriculum that was fought for and achieved at a particular historical point on the basis of certain social and political priorities, to take that curriculum as a given, is to forego a whole range of understandings and insights into features of the control and operation of the school and the classroom. It is to take over the mystifications of previous episodes of governance as unchallengeable givens. We are, social production and reproduction — the school curriculum — where political and social priorities are paramount. Histories of other aspects of social life have begun to systematically scrutinize this process. Hobsbawn argues that the term 'invented tradition';

> includes both traditions actually invented, constructed and formally instituted and those emerging in a less traceable manner within a brief and dateable period — a matter of a few years perhaps — and establishing themselves with great rapidity.

Hobsbawm defines the matter this way:

> Invented tradition is taken to mean a set of practices, normally governed by overtly or tacitly accepted rules and of a ritual or symbolic nature which seek to circulate certain values and norms of behaviour by repetition, which automatically implies continuity with the past. In fact, where possible, they normally attempt to establish continuity with a suitable historic past. (Hobsbawm and Ranger, 1985, p. 1)

In this sense the making of curriculum can be seen as a process of inventing tradition. In fact this language is often used when the 'traditional disciplines' or 'traditional subjects' are juxtaposed against some new-fangled innovation of integrated or child-centred topics. The point, however, is that the written curriculum, whether as courses of study, syllabuses, guidelines or textbooks, is a supreme example of the invention of tradition; but as with all tradition it is not a once-and-for all given, it is a given which has to be defended, where the mystifications have to be constructed and reconstructed over time. Plainly, if curriculum theorists substantially ignore the history and social construction of curriculum, such mystification and reproduction of 'traditional' curriculum form and content becomes easier.

An important stage, then, in the development of a social constructionist perspective is the production of a wide series of studies on the social construction of the prescriptive curriculum. But this is only a part of the story as the advocates of 'practice' have long and correctly maintained. What is prescribed is not necessarily what is undertaken, and what is planned is not necessarily what happens. But, as we have argued, this should not imply that we abandon our studies of prescription as social construction and embrace, in singular form, the practical. We should instead seek to study the social construction of curriculum at both the levels of prescription and interaction.

The challenge is to develop new, substantive and methodological foci which integrate studies at the preactive and the interactive levels. The linkage and integration of these studies is the major problem, for we are dealing with different levels and arenas of social construction. This difference of levels and arenas has often led to the argument that there is a complete break between preactive and interactive and that the latter is to all intents and purposes autonomous. This of course leads us back to the argument that 'practice is all that matters' and hence that we should focus our studies solely on practice.

The focus of recent curriculum study on projects and innovation (noted earlier) is partly responsible for this belief in autonomy. Two observations from *Inside a Curriculum Project* illustrate this tendency:

> The project team had to explain what it was going to do before it could do it. The teachers started by doing it and only then looked for an explanation of why they were doing it that way.

But what was the 'it' the teachers were doing and how and where was it socially constructed. Likewise

> the end product of the project was determined in the field, in contract with the school, not on the drawing board...in the end it was what worked that survived. (Shipman, Bolam and Jenkins, 1974)

Both these observations celebrate the autonomy of the school and of practice. But both of them are likely to lead to our missing the point. For only what is prepared on the drawing board goes into the school and therefore *has a chance* to be interpreted and to survive. Of course if this is so for the notoriously unloved curriculum project it is even more the case for the traditional (and less scrutinized and contested) school subject. With the latter clear parameters to practice are socially constructed at the preactive level. Practice in short is socially constructed at the preactive *and* interactive levels: it is a combination of both and our curriculum study should acknowledge this combination.

And if the questions of the form and scale of 'parameters' remain elusive, it is above all for this reason that we need to link our work on social construction at the preactive and interactive levels. At one level this will mean urging a closer connection between studies of school process and practice as currently constituted and studies of social construction at the preactive level. A culminating stage in developing a social constructionist perspective would be to develop studies which themselves integrate studies of social construction at *both* preactive *and* interactive levels. We shall need to explore and develop integrative foci for social constructionist study and in this respect exploring the relational level would provide a strategy for strengthening and bringing together studies of action and of context in meaningful ways. Above all social constructionist perspectives would improve our understanding of the politics of curriculum and in doing so would provide valuable 'cognitive maps' for teachers seeking to understand and locate the parameters to their practice.

Note

This paper was written as the invited Keynote Address to the Fifth International Congress of the Nordic Educational Research Association held at the University of Uppsala in March 1989. It was published in the *Journal of Curriculum Studies* (1990).

Chapter 12

Theorizing a Curriculum

Rob Walker and Saville Kushner

This chapter consists of an extract from a book length research report which has been adapted to the present context. *Bread and Dreams* reports on a case study of the Rafael Hernandez School, a bilingual Elementary School in Boston, Mass. The study was commissioned by the Ford Foundation on the suggestion of people in the Boston bilingual education community at a time (1979) when the State law was due for review.

The book is divided into four sections. In the first section, Barry MacDonald writes about the context of bilingual schooling drawing on interviews with officials and administrators and with prominent figures in Boston civil rights and bilingual education networks. This part of the account is in narrative form, telling the story that is both historical and personal. The second section of the book consists of a case study of the Rafael Hernandez School, an 'exemplary' school — a community school for Hispanics around which much of the story unfolds. The case study attempts to portray the curriculum and the school as it was at the time of the study. A third section of the book looks at bilingual programs elsewhere in the city, where programs are mostly attached to existing schools as marginal and low status activities. The fourth section draws on the previous (largely empirical sections) to produce summary statements under a number of headings.

Our statement in the fourth section is a statement about curriculum which attempts both to conceptualize and to summarize what could be learnt from the case study of the school. The reader will discover distinct parallels with earlier chapters in this book for the Hernandez school is a school that has been, and been seen as, an exemplary innovating school from which others might learn, and which could form the basis for extending innovative practice throughout the system.

This chapter is included here as it picks up on the arguments of the previous chapter, confronting 'theory/practice' dilemmas in a particular context. It proved a difficult section to write, in part because it directly confronts the relationship of case study to theory, but also because it was around 'curriculum' that most confusion arose between the school and the researchers. We noted in the previous chapter that there are significant differences in language use between theorists, educators and policy makers around the term 'curriculum'. In this study we encountered these differences in an acute form.

Taken as a whole, the report meets the requirements set by Ivor Goodson in the previous chapter. It is concerned with the history of bilingual education in Boston (though this history does not figure in this excerpt, it was a significant element in the study as a whole). It deals with the specifics of the case, and it provides space for biography and personal determination. The difficulties we had in writing it reflect the difficulties inherent in holding together 'curriculum theory', school practice and the kind of middle level theory Ivor Goodson proposes, and to do so in a way that respects the significance of the classroom.

Curriculum Reunification

The purpose of this chapter is to provide comments on the needs and resources for the development of bilingual curriculum in Boston at the present time.[1] Our efforts concentrate on the experience of the Rafael Hernandez School. First we need a definition of 'curriculum' because in our discussions with the school this has been the term that has caused the most difficulty and confusion.

The staff of the Hernandez School spoke of curriculum in much the same terms as we are accustomed to talking of as 'syllabus'. The 'reading curriculum' like the 'social studies curriculum' was depicted as a series of events through which each student had to pass in order to reach particular levels of achievement. The content defined the experience and was for the most part unquestioned.

For the school to write a new reading curriculum initially involved examining statments of educational aims and objectives. Curriculum development was seen as a periodic renewal, an updating of texts, punctuating a stable and preordained sequence of curriculum events. Of course experimentation existed in between whiles — as we mention later — but this appeared limited to individual classrooms and was bounded by the overriding sequence of the whole curriculum. This in turn was locked into the textbooks and materials in use in the school.

We found this conception of curriculum inadequate, narrow and frustrating. Our own bias aligns itself with some of the views of Lawrence Stenhouse. Stenhouse (1980) offers an alternative perspective on curriculum which is less concerned with texts and has cultural 'feel' to it. In order to clarify the discussion it is worth quoting at length:

> What is a curriculum as we now understand the word? It has changed its meaning as a result of the curriculum movement. It is not a syllabus — a mere list of content to be covered — nor is it even what German speakers would call a Lehrplan — a prescription of aims and methods and content. Nor is it in our understanding a list of objectives.
>
> Let me claim that it is a symbolic or meaningful object, like Shakespeare's first folio, not like a lawnmower; like the pieces and board of chess, not like an apple tree. It has a physical existence but also a meaning incarnate in words or pictures or sound or games or whatever.
>
> In our imagination let us bring it into this room. The doors open and it enters on a porter's barrow, since it is too heavy to carry. Two large boxes are full of books for pupils to use in the classroom. A third contains educational games and simulations and a fourth, posters, slides, film strips and overhead projector transparencies. The big box over there is the film set — or is this the video-tape version — and the smaller one beside it contains audio-tape and gramophone records. The seventh, and in this case the last, box holds the teachers' books and materials.
>
> Who made it? Well, perhaps a curriculum research and development group funded by Nuffield or the Schools Council or the American National Science Foundation or Stiftung Volkswagenwerk. Or perhaps a group of teachers from various parts of the country working under an editor for a publisher. Or perhaps a teachers' centre group. Or a school — Abraham Moss or Stantonbury or some less fabled place.
>
> So there it stands, a palpable educational artefact. But what use is it to a student or a teacher? Often apparently, not much. Like some wedding presents it is in a month or two more likely to be found in the attic than in the living room. But that analogy is not quite right. A better one is the affluent outhouse containing the unused golf-clubs, canoe, sailing dinghy, skis,

ice skates and glider. All the possessions which implied not simply ownership but learning, the development of new skills, on the part of the owner. Mr Toad's curriculum of derelict skiffs and canary-coloured caravan. Material objects cast aside because the teacher was not prepared to face the role of learner they faced upon him.

'No curriculum development without teacher development', reads one of the poker-work mottoes we hung on our wall during the Humanities Project and haven't taken down. But that does not mean, as it often seems to be interpreted to mean, that we must train teachers in order to produce a world fit for curricula to live in. It means that by virtue of their meaningfulness curricula are not simply instructional means to improve teaching but are expressions of ideas to improve teachers. Of course, they have a day-to-day instructional utility: cathedrals must keep the rain out. But the students benefit from curricula not so much because they change day-to-day instruction as because they improve teachers.

In this view the package, or the text, is still artefactual, tangible. What changes is the nature of the relationship between teachers and curriculum. Here curriculum becomes an aspiration rather than necessarily an achievement. It is seen not as extraneous but as a living thing embodying critical processes: the teacher is the practitioner of curriculum, not simply the agent of delivery. Aspects of curriculum including sequencing, teaching style, assessment, previously depicted as static frame factors, become variable with the experience of managing them. The classroom, in this view, is seen less as the unit of cultural reproduction, and more as the laboratory for change.

We can move a stage further. We can consider the 'symbolism' and the 'meaning' of curriculum to reside in the perception of students as well as their teachers. Curriculum becomes broadened yet further. We can exemplify this by looking specifically at the Hernandez School.

The outside doors of the school are locked and secure. Students are escorted through them and onto the school bus — or out to chaperoned recreation in the playground. On one occasion, let us imagine a group of students filing in from play. The doors are locked behind them and they move into a social studies lesson where the topic is the American constitution: democracy, liberty. The students may consciously or unconsciously make associations between the rhetoric of democratic freedom and the reality of the locked and guarded doors. Having made such an association the student will have learned something (the world will have changed ineffably). The locked door — or more generally the whole environment — has been part of the curriculum for that day, and if that is true for the school doors then it will be true for the way teachers of varying ethnicity relate to each other — frequently under the observation of students; of the architecture of the building; of the experience of school picnics.

In part all this relates to what we have come to know as the 'hidden curriculum', a somewhat imprecise but evocative term which attempts to capture the fact students never only learn one thing at a time, that the whole curriculum is never fully under the control of either the teacher or the school, and the context in which curriculum messages are transmitted may override its content. While the hidden curriculum is a useful notion, and one we have used extensively by implication in this study, there are some problems associated with the use of the concept. To what extent does what is 'hidden' remain beyond the consciousness of those involved? (How 'hidden' is it?) And if it can be comprehended and articulated — revealed — can it be modified? Can we 'develop' the hidden curriculum?

Bernstein (1969) seems to take a strong position. In this critique of the notion of compensatory education, he makes the often quoted remark that: 'If the culture of the teacher is to become part of the consciousness of the child, the culture of the child must first be in the consciousness of the teacher'. Such a claim requires that teachers reveal the subtleties of learning processes and cultural meanings. This is clearly a task that is difficult, and ultimately perhaps impossible, for it requires teachers to grasp the significance of any material or phenomena that are available for students as substrates for learning. Nevertheless, this is the kind of effort required by the view of curriculum we propose, one consequence of which is that the whole curriculum has, first, to enter the consciousness of the teacher, before it can become part of the culture of the child.

We have presented this alternative view of curriculum — one that underlays much of what we say in this concluding piece but it does not account for the view the Hernandez staff hold of curriculum. They strike a clear division between teaching and learning within purposeful, pedagogical interactions (usually in class), and activities shared with their students at other times (and at other places). We will acknowledge that division by calling the former the 'formal' curriculum and the latter the 'informal' curriculum.

One of our working hypotheses in the study was that the notion of a 'bicultural' school was unrealizable — by definition, we argued, schools are monocultural and essentially bureaucratic. Given the assumption that cultures are essentially defined by alternative values there is inevitably a disjunction between the idea of biculturalism and the nature of the school. In order to test this idea we constantly looked to refute it. At one point in the study, one of the teachers, Wendy, told us that we were looking for evidence of cultural responsiveness in the wrong place. As she saw it, we listened only to the 'teachers words' and looked only at what was 'written on the blackboard'. Her view, as we interpret it, was that we should be looking at the 'informal' curriculum rather than the 'formal' curriculum. This would mean looking separately at 'formal' and 'informal' curricula but as we see it, both elements — formal and informal — are integral to the operation of the Hernandez programme. Only the two together can be regarded as the Curriculum of the Hernandez School — essentially because the division between what is formal and what is informal is something that students do not recognize.

Strategies for Curriculum Change

Among curriculum theorists and planners, current wisdom is that the large scale, centralized development projects which characterized the 1960s and early 1970s, are better replaced by smaller scale, local initiatives carried out with some central support. Large scale national developments, it is often argued, are too difficult to implement, become diluted and softened in the successive negotiations that are needed to implant them in classrooms, and are too readily prone to asset-stripping by academic 'experts' who may have little understanding of classroom realities. Thus Atkin and House (1981) have advocated: 'modest initiatives illuminated by evolutionary imagery', seeing these as 'more effective in a large and complex system than strategies that are directly interventionist'.

While Atkin and House present an alternative model for curriculum development, the present study provides an informative case study of how such a model might be realized in practice: the Rafael Hernandez School developed from a local initiative taken by the Hispanic community in Boston, when they established their own school in Dennison House. On the one hand, in drawing this community initiative into the public school system (as a magnet school), the Boston School Committee provided the kind of support that Atkin and House argue is the best strategy that central institutions can take if they are to stimulate curriculum change. At the same time the introduction of special programmes (for students needing different levels of instruction across grade levels) created a level of bureaucratic imposition which ran counter to the ethos of community control.

The result of this conflation is that while much about the school has changed, the classroom curriculum tends, for the most part, to be static, conservative, English and reading dominated, and most frequently transmitted via an instructional, didactic pedagogy. Yet while they dominate the scene, these characteristics live side by side with more experimental and innovative activities. We will look more closely at this juxtaposition.

The school was established in response to the immediate needs of a newly arrived, poor, Spanish-speaking minority community, but its development has been marked by its progress as a colony of the Boston School system rather than in response to its community and constituency. The School and the Hispanic Community has had to cede control over much of the formal curriculum in the face of the transition[2] mandate.

The first threat to the school's autonomy, however, came from the same desegregation movement that had originally given hope of change,[3] for in order to maintain its existence in the face of the desegregation threat it had to accept magnet status, this being the only way of moderating the requirements of 'racial balance'.[4] Even so, the school was forced to look beyond its immediate community for student recruits.

The second challenge to its autonomy came when, having achieved formal recognition, and having won tenured principal-status for its teacher-in-charge, the school found it could no longer retain its leading teacher who now lacked the credentials for the job. The present principal, Maria Kline, arrived in the school as the principal representing, in the eyes of many, the middle-class professionals in the downtown office; every inch a competent professional, but also the harbinger of change. Maria was a middle-class professional. A Cuban in a school whose clientele was predominantly working class and Puerto Rican, but Maria brought to the school skills which were essential to the continued survival of the Hernandez programme in the face of the rigorous demands of the public school system.

What we see in the case study is a school that has had to respond to changing conditions by emphasizing curriculum management rather than curriculum change. But there remains a tension between the two. The major innovation that the school points to with pride is the levelling system, a system that allows the incorporation of a range of special programmes — Title 1, the Resource Rooms and Special Education, within the bilingual curriculum. Levelling individualizes the route taken through the formal curriculum, while the curriculum itself tends to remain intact. Problems come to be interpreted as problems of individual performance against set standards rather than as feedback data on the impact of the curriculum. And always the special programmes sit clumsily astride the mainstream curriculum, ever hungry for time and imposing a demanding set of, mainly behaviourist, learning assumptions derived from the requirements of Title 1[5] and Chapter 766[6] programmes. Management learns and adapts — curriculum becomes fossilized.

Here the analysis provided by Atkin and House is accurate. Federal and state programmes like Title 1 and Chapter 766 require the school to act in response to problem definitions that are over-simplified in the arenas of political discourse. Common solutions cannot easily account for local variation, but local contexts do create spaces and gaps within which initiative can thrive, so adapting the programme to local circumstance. The school's highly idiosyncratic but selective exploitation of 'pairing'[7] arrangements is a good example, as is the variety of ways in which aides participate in classrooms.

A tension develops as those in schools strive to adapt central initiatives while those in central positions (perhaps seeing such practices as their ultimate target for change) find themselves tightening their grip, building-in evaluation requirements, more detailed specifications and forms of accountability. This tends to encourage the development of a formal curriculum that becomes honed down to what can be delivered, and to what can be assessed, which in turn tends to focus on narrow conceptions of learning frequently defined in terms of gains on achievement test scores. The result is a system in which teachers and students are rewarded for performance, not for compliance; for achievement, but not for wisdom or for their understanding; and in which experience is devalued in favour of 'headway'. In the Hernandez School, transition requirements and special programmes dominate — though the school shifts its efforts to areas where Federal and State accountants cannot reach.

We are left with a paradox. Central initiatives taken with the best intentions, and often motivated by liberal values, become frustrated by the difficulties of implementation in massive and diffuse systems like education. In order to maintain the priority of their intent, central agencies respond by tightening control, an action which triggers consequences that may well conflict with those liberal values that first gave them impetus.

The scenario for policy options is looking complex. If we want to introduce change to schools from the outside and maintain standardization of both treatment and outcome as a central criterion, then we run the risk of loss of teacher autonomy. This tends to devalue the experience of the teaching force and may — as in the case of the Hernandez — force educational practice back onto conservative coping strategies. The consequence is that central authorities gain a greater capacity to predict (and thereby control) what happens in the classroom. Alternatively, if we seek to retain autonomy at the periphery of systems then we have to accept that the innovations that may emerge are likely to be idiosyncratic, contingent upon local contexts and beyond the immediate apprehension of central authority.

A good example of the first option can be seen in the Boston School Committee's proposed Lau[8] Implementation Plan — not yet adopted at the time we left Boston. The Plan was, again, a case of attempting to inject liberal values into a system dominated by conservative practice through the careful use of legal instruments.

The main body of the Lau Implementation Plan bases provision upon a mastery learning programme comprising a sequence of language achievement levels through which minority language speakers have to pass before they gain access to the mainstream curriculum. Only such close specification, its advocates argue, prevents unwitting or intransigent schools from exploiting loopholes in the letter of the law. The resource and support implications of taking students to the levels define the character and extent of bilingual programmes to be supplied by the School Committee. While creating legal space for (transitional) bilingual programmes to evolve, such requirements, paradoxically, and by the necessity of their own logic, deny access to the mainstream for any but competent English speakers — once again introducing a tendency for curriculum fossilization. A substantial part of the report, futhermore, proposes a comprehensive bureaucratic infrastructure to implement and develop these programmes.

In their urgency to protect the programmes the authors of the report demonstrate a greater confidence in gate-keepers than they do in the practitioners. The 'job goal' of the proposed 'Senior Curriculum Adviser: Bilingual Education' is typical, and includes:

— Develop with (other officers) integrated curriculum standards that respond to specific bilingual programmatic needs and which maintain grade-level consistency.
— Initiate, modify, adjust, revise and terminate all efforts to develop bilingual curricula in collaboration with (other officers). (Boston Public Schools, 1979, p. 66)

The adviser is to be further asked to review and evaluate, to prepare packages, to resource in-service courses and to feed research findings into innovation plans. It typifies the approach of top-down management, assuming that innovation can best be effected by reducing the autonomy of teachers and increasing the influence of experts placed in positions of bureaucratic power. There is no recognition that 'the system' can learn from the variegations of practice — that advisers can transmit messages 'up' the hierarchy — that overviews may also atrophy for lack of innovation.

What we can also see in the Lau proposals is evidence of the third stage of the response by government to control voluntary social movements outlined by MacDonald in the first section to this report. To recap, MacDonald saw three such stages — investment, containment and finally co-option. Co-option is characterized by 'an extension of the policy-making and administrative franchise to those individuals and groups demanding recognition and participation'. Opening up the 'fold' carries dangers, of course, but, MacDonald goes on: 'These are minimized ... by the bonding effect of an increasingly shared perception of the problems of delivering effective services'.

The Lau proposals are a clear manifestion of a problem defined in bureaucratic terms consonant with an establishment, dominant-culture view. The Hernandez School — under pressure to demonstrate its performance at the forefront of bilingual development — saw itself in compliance with the Lau proposals before they were published and anticipated no change in their operation were the Plan to be adopted. One teacher went further: 'Perhaps we're different because we try to do a little more than just what the policy-makers require'.

Lau aside, the other policy option, of attempting to build on the autonomy inherent in school and classroom practice rather than to remove it, is the key to Atkin and House's (1981) vision of 'modest initiatives illuminated by evolutionary imagery'. In the light of the present study, however, their model would seem to fall foul of the fact that such strategies become caught up in processes of political control and organizational self-maintenance. The model takes good account of the failures of central initiatives to sustain innovation at the periphery, but fails to allow for its own vulnerability as yet another variant of the centre-periphery model. It seeks to capitalize on the innovative energy that can be generated in local circumstances, but seems to fail to realize that the autonomy such energy requires to develop productively cannot easily be granted by the centre. We have seen in the Hernandez School that the biography of the school staff (in one sense, the aggregate of all the individual biographies but, as importantly, the circumstances which brought them all together in this time and place) is a critical variable. Autonomy does not encourage spontaneous experiment. It is the mix between autonomy and proaction. Freedom cannot be *given* to peripheral agencies: it can only be taken (and taken away).

Teacher Autonomy, or a Learning Community

We have noted the tension between management and curriculum — partly, at least, attributable to the juxtaposition of bureaucratic intervention and local autonomy. We have suggested that this tension tends to resolve in favour of management, emphasizing the need to survive above the urge to learn and to develop. But what happens to curriculum initiatives in such a milieu?

The staff of the Hernandez have ceded control over much of the curriculum — though that accession is largely and distinctively confined to the classroom — to what we call the 'formal curriculum'. Outside the classroom — at the picnic, on school visits, at parties — lies a more 'informal' curriculum where the staff have been able to experiment with more innovative pedagogies, built upon relationships which allow teachers and students to compete, and the teachers to lose; which allow for the hegemony of the students' minority culture over the teachers.

This takes place in those few havens within the school as yet uncolonized by the transition mandate. Here is curriculum development in retreat across the boundaries of the classroom. Inside the classroom we tend to see pedagogies appropriate to transition; outside, we tend to see pedagogies more appropriate to cultural maintenance.

The more complex view we proposed earlier exposes a need to integrate the two — to reunite language arts and school picnics. In the end it is the student who is currently left to make sense of the fragments — to integrate what professionals outside school have disintegrated and what professionals inside school are prevented from fully grasping.

There are alternatives being tried in the classrooms nonetheless. We saw Susan's combined ESL/SSL class[9] — an experiment in bilingual pedagogy whose potential the whole school was prevented from exploring because of the 'huge scheduling problem' it would create. Sheila talked of a purposeful (though again not fully articulated) model for bilingual teaching but, once more, her experience has been confined to her own classroom.

A more generalized innovation within the school is the highly developed participation of teaching aides which, in the degrees of responsibility sought and permitted and in the strength and nature of their relationships with teachers is immensely productive — whilst contravening many of the more recent regulations for the deployment of aides — regulations which are designed to clarify the role of aides. Then there is the close relationship between the school and the Aquarium which brings into the school a discovery-learning/approach to science. This only succeeds because the Aquarium team have been able to establish an identity and an expertise which does not compete with the teachers' sense of boundary in relation to their own area of professional competence. Indeed, the Aquarium approach to teaching and learning is typical of the kindergarten, which both Janice and Hilary as well as the teachers in the school saw as distinct from the curriculum through the grades. However, the kindergarten curriculum, in spite of its range and freedom of expression for both teacher and student, will soon submit to the disciplinary jacket of the district-wide reading curriculum.

It is these few sparks that would need to be nurtured and fanned to ignite the process of local curriculum development but, in our view, an important constraint prevents spontaneous curriculum development. For, in order to retain control of the whole curriculum, the school would need the support to learn corporately from its own experience. It would need the space to become more self-reflective, and to institute mechanisms for accumulating institutional learning. Teachers would need to be legitimated as their own researchers — rediscovering the 'whole' curriculum. At present the school's experience is fragmented, individualized and privatized. In terms of what it knows and understands about its own curriculum, the sum of individual experience and personal wisdom vastly exceeds what the school as a whole can claim to know and to use.

It is easy to see why this should be so, for the school is staffed by teachers who have drawn on their own backgrounds and experience to sustain their professional autonomy as the school has progressively come under control of the school system. A major consequence for the school has been that each classroom strives to develop its own distinctive and self-sufficient learning economy. Another consequence of staffing the school with experienced and committed teachers has been to reduce their dependence on each other, and so to reduce the power of the faculty as a learning (as opposed to a teaching) community.

This is a point that has significant implications for teacher education, for predominantly we train teachers to survive in the system as individuals, yet the major problems they will face will be the problems of organizations and collectivities. In one sense the case study may be read as a study of the consequences of what happens when an individualized approach to teacher education come home to roost. While the staff of the Hernandez School are competent, experienced professionals they have few ways of sharing their experience. It is difficult for them to act cooperatively in curriculum planning, and when drawn out of the school they tend to act as advocates, either through allegiance with the community (Wendy's involvement in drafting the Lau Compliance Plan, for example), or out of a sense of loyalty to the school. The main exception is in teacher–aide cooperation, and it is a significant exception, but one contained by the 'economy' of individual classrooms. The school even has difficulty in mounting its own internal in-service training meetings. Precious time available for staff meetings tends to be gobbled up by scheduling arrangements and by the need to consider closely each individual child's progress. Perhaps, the very prominence and visibility of the school tends to push those teachers who put their heads outside the classroom door towards defensiveness or towards advocacy. As a general rule, lighthouse schools do not encourage internal reflection.

Several people have asked us why we made so much, in the case study, of teacher biographies, and so little of bilingual education models. Perhaps now the reason is clear, for the fact that the school is staffed by experienced and professional teachers means that we can learn more of the programme by looking at their qualities and skills than at abstractly formulated models of pedagogy, and we can see now that this has important consequences.

The implications of the staffing model spread beyond the confines of the school. We have already said that it is difficult for the teachers to share their experience with those outside, but it is difficult too for outside agencies seeking to support the school in developing its curriculum. The strength of the school remains in the experience and competence of the teachers rather than in the host of extra programmes available. The teachers are demanding of relations with outside agents, denying the Bilingual District Coordinator; skeptical of the Boston University link; certain that *they* are best qualified to engage in development — so long as they have time. The prominent exception (in the course of the case study) was in the Aquarium link. The teachers were more than tolerant of those outsiders — partly, they say, because the Aquarium staff made no claims to their territory — in fact they claimed at the outset to be incompetent. Similarly, the Plymouth Plantation visit was welcomed with no sense of defense. Again there was not conceivable territorial threat, unlike the rather awkward exchanges with Boston University.

We see curriculum development in the school caught in the space between teacher autonomy and a shared pressure simply to manage the curriculum. Part of the problem is in locating the best forum for discussion, and, in the end, it seems that much latent curriculum development exists in the school but cannot find appropriate forms for its release. Some of this we have mentioned already. Some is repressed consciously — Emilio's[10] radical views of Hispanic cultural history, for example, which the administration finds difficult to handle and the community (as represented by the other aides) find antithetical.

It is hard to imagine any significant curriculum development appropriate to bilingual/bicultural settings without a fundamental challenge to curriculum and curriculum organization as currently conceived. Both the case study and the complementary studies illustrate curricula that are 'proof' against the individuality of the child, and against feedback that might be critical of the curriculum. One consequence of the fossilization of the mainstream curriculum is the assumption that flaws in standards of achievement and discrepancies between students' performance and their natural grade 'level' are attributable to student rather than curriculum deficit.

We have seen, however, that the Hernandez tends to encourage experimentation — if only in terms of institutional variety and within programmatic parameters. Within the experience of the school there would seem to be sufficient knowledge of the range of pedagogical options to begin to develop models grounded in knowledge of effects and outcomes. Existing organizational arrangements — particularly those which force the teachers to defend their boundaries — prevent the proper articulation of that experience. The rigidly hierarchical and componentized role structure proposed in the Lau Compliance Plan could only compound the effect. The structure is devised to pass dictum and sanction from the top down; whilst exacting commitments and accountability from the bottom up.

The assumption is that current practice is transparent, obvious, not in need of careful study. And yet we opened this section with the assertion of teacher development and curriculum development going hand in hand. The way to foster both lies through agencies and arrangements which relieve teachers of duties to confirm their practice (through having to account for it) and which, instead, create the protection needed for those teachers to question their practice. Advisers and coordinators might (as they have been in some instances in Britain) be the promoters and guardians of curriculum research in the school — rather than the accountants and supernumeraries they are increasingly likely to become. Currently, pragmatism rules as the

Hernandez School gives to the School Committee all that belongs to the School Committee: literacy, basic skills and all that is assessed by the testing programme. Autonomy is preserved in expressive areas — in the picnic and the fiesta, and to a degree in the homeroom (albeit under siege from the levelling system and special programmes). Here the teachers and the students (and to some degree the community) come into their own, the curriculum breathes life and becomes 'cultural' in the full sense of the word. But privately — and in a secret garden.

In a more purposeful scheme, in a system more attuned to the overlapping needs of teachers and students to share rich and productive learning experiences, the garden that is tended in secret would be nurtured in public.

Notes

1   We have retained the present tense for stylistic reasons. The 'time' in question is 1980.
2   A key conceptual division exists in bilingual education between the notion of 'transition', i.e., moving students into mainstream, English medium classrooms as fast as possible and 'maintenance' in the sense of using first languages to maintain minority or migrant cultures.
3   The bilingual education movement in Boston (as elsewhere) was to a considerable degree stimulated by the successes of civil rights campaigns in the black community.
4   During the mid-1970s, when Boston schools were racially desegregated by court order, no school was permitted to exceed fixed proportions of the various racial groupings on its roll. The exceptions were 'magnet schools'; schools that were given some leeway on racial mix, and were given a mandate to foster 'excellence' in their field.
5   Title 1 provides special (Federal) funds for disadvantaged children.
6   Chapter 766 is the State special education law defining the conditions for mainstreaming children with handicaps and disabilities.
7   'Pairing' in Boston schools means the direct linking of disadvantaged schools with cultural institutions (museums, universities, etc.). The school consistently made strong and well articulated demands on its 'paired' institutions, exerting a price for the easing of Anglo middle-class guilt.
8   The 'Lau case' was a Supreme Court ruling which in effect requires States to provide bilingual education programs for students whose first language is other than English.
9   This class cut across the assumptions of the school's complicated levelling and grading system by mixing students who were learning English as a second language, with those learning Spanish as a second language.
10 One of the teaching aides.

Conclusion

The Development of Educational Research

Ivor Goodson and Rob Walker

In this book we have traversed a variety of topics and themes, issues and concerns. We began from the study of classrooms and classroom interactions between teachers and students. The discovery that such research was feasible was a breakthrough in the late 1960s and early 1970s which came about at a point of conjuction between technical advances (the availability of small, audio cassette recorders particularly), the rediscovery of forms of qualitative analysis (notably in sociology and in sociolinguistics) and the emergence of new questions about teaching as a result of attempts at curriculum reform.

We began with an exercise (perhaps a pastiche) of late 1960s symbolic interactionist classroom research as a point of departure for re-examining curriculum issues because, twenty years ago, this represented a significant frontier of research. In the chapters that follow we assume that the work described in Chapter 1 represents a model and we proceed by trying to trace the strengths and weaknesses of this model (the much used term 'paradigm' seems a little excessive) by testing its limits and capabilities.

One clear weakness of the model, as a device for studying 'curriculum' issues, was its relative inattention to curriculum content; another was its denial of history; another its neglect of teachers' biography; another its silence about schools. In the various chapters of this book we have attempted to address each of these points and to develop research strategies for adapting the model to different purposes.

At this point we have the uneasy feeling that, while we may have succeeded to some degree in developing the model, we ourselves have been overtaken by the events of history. In Britain, increasingly in Australia, and to some degree in North America, curriculum issues have become politicized in the narrow sense that they have become a

central theme in party politics and the politics of government. Minis-
ters of State tend to dismiss the curriculum reforms of the 1960s and
1970s as minor (perhaps ineffectual) tinkering and to look to national
curriculum guidelines and more invasive and powerful forms of testing
to give shape to school systems. The ground of the debate has shifted,
and shifted quite dramatically.

Behind these changes lies another theme — the rise and demise of
the sociology of education in Britain in the post-war period. We began
this book at the point when the sociology of reconstruction was
entering a new phase. The achievement of comprehensive secondary
schooling in the 1960s marked a point when sociology had to find
ways of understanding the processes of schooling, particularly curriculum and teaching, if it was to sustain its mission to monitor class
difference and discrimination. How to engage social interaction and
social experience at a level of complexity, subtlety and paradox, while
retaining a grip on questions of social justice has provided the main
challenge to sociology in the past two decades.

The questions are only methodological to those taking a narrow
view. More importantly, they require rethinking basic concepts. Some
have raised the question as to whether gender and race are more
significant issues than class. Assumptions about the nature of democracy have come under attack. The role of bureaucracy has changed,
capturing much of the language of the social science and of sociology
in particular. The role of the press, and more so of television has
changed. The political agenda has moved to the right.

Despite growing centralization and a new technology of control
we do not believe that the issues we have raised have been by-passed.
Schooling remains a large, complex enterprise which resists surveil-
lance. Classrooms, as we have seen, are places where events resist
predictability; and teaching is an activity which inevitably generates
unexpected learning. There is no doubt that important, even historic,
changes are occuring in education, but we should not judge them too
soon on their rhetoric alone.

Implications for Theory

One of the challenges created by current educational change is the
challenge to educational theory. Present theories, we believe, do not
cope well with understanding current events. Curriculum theories in
particular are too ready to offer judgment, too quick to evaluate, too

glib to hold up to the evidence that is available. In this book we have tried to address this question but the form of the book requires some explanation. We have made the argument by exemplar and illustration rather than by the use of polemic or rhetoric, and we have done so in order to maintain a degree of consistency with the stance we have taken. A central problem we have addressed, albeit only indirectly, is what role theory should have in educational research. We do not believe that theory and description should be rendered too easily separable, nor that theory and practice should be treated as belonging to different realms of action or discourse. At the same time, we are less comfortable with a purely empirical position than some commentators might imagine. We have accepted the label of 'grounded theory', but hesitantly, for it is a label that is frequently misapplied. (Often there is the implication that 'grounded' theory is much like any other kind of theory, but arrived at by a different route. We believe this not to be so.) We believe that the kinds of theories we are working towards here are different in many respects to other forms of theory; there may well be overlaps, similarities and points of contact, but the differences remain.

In the previous chapter, we moved from descriptive accounts to 'middle order theories', grounded in the terms Schwab defined as 'this student, in that school on the south side of Columbus at a particular historical point in time.' Our claim is that this kind of theorizing has a distinctive character. In one sense, because of the high value it places on description, it is inherently conservative. It is also conservative in that it is located in the existing defined 'middle ground' and therefore more concerned with what is, rather than with what might be. In the case of the Hernandez School the power of the status quo appears in 'the mainstream curriculum' which is 'static, conservative, English and reading dominated, and most frequently transmitted via an instructional didactic pedagogy'. However whilst such curricula 'dominate the scene, these characteristics live side by side with experimental and innovative activities' leading to a view of the classroom 'less as a limit of culture reproduction and more as a laboratory for change'. Structure then confronts agency and we are once again reminded of the undeniable truth that:

> men make their own history, but not in any way they please; they make it under circumstances not chosen by themselves but directly encountered, given and transmitted from the past. The tradition of dead generations weighs like a nightmare on the

> brain of the living. Just when they seem to be revolutionizing themselves and things, creating something unprecedented ... they nervously conjure up the spirits of the past. (Marx, 1969)

Past and present collide, agendas and parameters are thereby set through which contemporary purpose is pursued.

This then is why this book has travelled the route it has: from a detailed interest in specific incidents, individuals and instances towards attempts to define a modality for examining and generalizing from the specific. This movement from specific cases to generalizable insights is of course not new. Freud for instance confronted the 'spirits of the past' in analyzing nightmares but the influence of his work derives from general principles rather than directly from case studies or from self-analysis.

In recent years the influence of Karl Popper among others has led us to be suspicious of what looks to be a naively inductive approach. 'Naked empiricism' is seen to be flawed and theoretical speculation has assumed primacy in the thinking of many academic researchers: of course it has also been in the interests of academic researchers to do so. The pursuit of theory is to some extent an element in the pursuit of self-interest by academic writers, a key process in the accumulation of intellectual capital. In this book, we have attempted to take a step in a somewhat different direction: moving away from the idea of objectivity based on scientific detachment to an acceptance of the fact that in social research personal concerns and experiences are integral to the modality of enquiry whether our focus is on content, method or theorizing. (This could, of course, be seen as equally motivated by self-interest!) Given this view, the tensions between immediate questions about self, biography and identity and more general questions about the nature of social and cultural legacies stand at the centre of the research process. The changes this creates include breaking the ground for the growth of self-indulgence and cultivating images of the researcher as hero/heroine.

It follows that managing research tasks is not simply a technical process, it requires some sensitivity and a delicate balance. Dollard (1949), for instance, has written that in life history research:

> we must constantly keep in mind the situation both as defined by others and by the subject, such a history will not only define both versions but let us see clearly the pressure of the formal situation and the force of the inner private definition of the situation. (p. 32)

For this reason we have approached our subject obliquely, adopting a range of investigative methods in an attempt to elucidate relationships between the formal situation, the social structure and the individual; 'the inner private definition of the situation'. Each person then confronts the 'spirits of the past' and our methods must investigate the outcomes of this confrontation. Such work should allow us to view the individual in relation to the history of his time, and how he is influenced by the various religious, social, psychological and economic phenomenon present in the world. It lets us see the interaction of the life history of men with the history of society, thereby enabling us to understand better the choices, and contingencies open to each individual.

More recently Giddens (1976) has argued that '... the proper locus for the study of social reproduction is in the *immediate process of the constituting of interaction*...., just as every sentence in English expresses within itself the totality which is the "language" as a whole, so every interaction bears the imprint of the global "society": this is why there is definite point to the analysis of "everyday life" as a phenomenon of the totality' (p. 122).

In the previous chapters we feel we have demonstrated a degree of integration between theory and description, agency and structure, and to a lesser degree between theory and practice. But some readers will find the 'theory' that emerges eclectic and diffuse. We draw at various times on bits and pieces from sociolinguistics, symbolic interaction, history, social psychology and linguistic philosophy. Always we have sought to give primacy to the authority of the evidence, albeit in a methodological context where questions of selection and emphasis remain partially hidden.

In the last four chapters we have made the ground a little clearer. Our concern is with educational research of a particular kind, with *curriculum* research. We believe this to be a field which lacks convincing and coherent theories of a general kind. The field has been characterized less by theoretical presumptions than by issues. In curriculum, issues are powerful in generalizing from instance to instance and place to place, more powerful than available statements of theory. In the preceding chapters we have picked up a number of such issues and looked at them in context, for instance:

— In attempting to change curriculum, is pedagogy more significant than content?
— What happens to school subjects when curricula become integrated?

— What does teaching do to teachers?
— How do curriculum plans interact with the policies and the organizational imperatives of schooling and school systems?

In giving 'theoretical' discussion a lower profile than is customary in academic discourse our intention is not to create atheoretical debates, but to integrate theoretical discussion with discussions of policy and practice — to create the basis for a common language.

One reason for attempting to do this stems from self-reflection, for when we look at the way in which academics have become marginalized in both professional and political circles (particularly in the UK), part of the blame at least is ours. For two decades we have been in retreat. We have over-valued the accolades of the invisible college, and under-valued the worlds of policy and practice. We have invented and sustained self-indulgent and often arrogant realms of discourse. The need for new forms of theory is not simply a need for theory *per se*, but a need to rethink the purpose and functions of theory, and this in turn we believe calls for a reworking of the boundaries between theory, policy and practice.

Having achieved popular education, we face many of its consequences, one of which is the need for popular research. Near universal literacy is of little use if research responds by retreating to the margins, covering its trail with abstraction and retreating to an inaccessible language. Another problem is a division of labour which confines analysis to the work of academics, teaching to teachers and system-maintenance to those in policy positions. Research has promise only if we can prise it out of the grip of institutions, for as long as it remains institutionalized, its capacity for emancipation remains restricted.

Recently Wilf Carr and Stephen Kemmis (1986), in setting an agenda for 'critical action research', have made significant progress in this direction, but they have done so, perhaps necessarily, from a foothold within established academic language and convention. Important as this work is, the danger is that action research itself may become a way of redrawing familiar lines, successively allowing some capture of practice by theory, and some capture of theory by policy. Paradoxically, what was set out as a radical agenda may be used for conservative purposes.

The 'museum of virtue' identified by Waller in the 1920s now looks to be a means of preserving the romantic educational visions and values of the 1960s. The message is in danger of becoming corrupted by the medium.

In this book we have begun to develop an alternative line of

The Development of Educational Research

attack, one that begins with questions about the medium, about research methodology, with those questions many action researchers would label as 'technicist'. We have compromised some of the presumptions of action research, in particular we have retained a significant autocratic role for the researcher in order to retain a bridging role between practice on the one hand and policy on the other. We believe that it is necessary to constrain the outside researcher by contracts which specify the content, process and use of research reports. Nevertheless, many of the 'cases' we have included in this book have required a wider latitude of researcher judgment than an action research approach would allow. In part this reflects changes in the organization and administration of school systems. It has become increasingly difficult to keep the world of the classroom separate from other facets of the system, a development that often requires the researcher to take the initiative, perhaps standing between the teacher and the system, in a way that the action researcher may find difficult to manage, particularly if she, or he, is an employee of the system.

Perhaps the term 'theory' is an inappropriate work to use in this context, but we have chosen to use it deliberately. Some of the work of the sort we are recommending has been judged as quite simply 'atheoretical' '... doomed to be little more than a series of one-off self-contained reports, all of which return to "square-one", conceptually speaking' (Atkinson and Delamont, 1986, pp. 250–1). This view ignores the question-marks we have sought to place over the conceptualization and ownership of the term 'theory'. What some specifically claim as theory may be seen by others as mainly the academic colonization of professional practice.

This position may have been tenable when academics were able to operate from the basis of 'scientific' authority, buttressed by conventions of objectivity and method. But such conventions (in the social sciences, at least) are in disarray. We believe in such period of paradigmatic confusion we can no longer lean solely or even mainly on the authority that 'objective' methodologies once gave to educational research. In this new era what constitutes theory is contested, just as what constituted 'research' once was. The academic community can no longer lay sole claim to theory and to theorizing. The sociologically sophisticated policymaker is, to some degree at least, our creation we cannot now disown her (or him).

This kind of research and associated theory we are searching for would not be the sole prerogative of the university scholar. Our educational study would be more collaborative, more broad-based, publically available. But it should be possible too for us to make it interesting, critical, vital and useful. One role that remains for academic research is that of test-flying ideas, testing to the brink of failure ideas disconnected from contexts where not to do so might cause harm. Another, key role, is the monitoring of events in order to attempt to place them in a broader context. Perhaps most important is finding ways of closing the gaps between analysis and action which take full account of the sophistication which sociology has given us. If we lose our credibility to do so, we have little left of a significant role. We need to be ahead of the game, to be able to see it from outside its own terms of reference and yet play a part within it.

Bibliogaphy

ACKER, S. (Ed.) (1988) *Teachers, Gender and Careers*, Lewes, Falmer Press.
ADELMAN, C., JENKINS, D. and KEMMIS, S. (1976) 'Rethinking Case Study: Notes from the Second Cambridge Conference, *Cambridge Journal of Education*, 6, (3).
ADELMAN, C. and WALKER, R. (1975) *A Guide to Classroom Observation*, London, Methuen.
ADELMAN, C. and WALKER, R. (1974) 'Stop-frame cinematography with synchronized sound: A technique for recording in school classrooms' *Journal of the Society of Motion Picture and Television Engineers*, 83, (3).
ATKIN, J.M. and HOUSE, E.R. (1981) 'The federal role in curriculum development, 1950–1980', *Educational Evaluation and Policy Analysis*, 3, (5).
ATKINSON, P. and DELAMONT, S. (1986) 'Bread and circuses', in HAMMERSLEY, M. (Ed.) *Case Studies in Classroom Research: A reader*, Milton Keynes, Open University Press.
BALL, S.J. and GOODSON, I. (1985) *Teachers' Lives and Careers*, London, New York, and Philadelphia, Falmer Press, (Open University Set Book).
BARTON, L. and LAWN, M. (1980) 'Back inside the whale; A curriculum case study', *Interchange, II* (4).
BECKER, H.S. (1963) *Outsiders: Studies in the sociology of deviance*, New York, Free Press.
BECKER, H.S. (1952) 'The career of the Chicago public schoolteacher', *American Journal of Sociology*, 57, pp. 470–7; also in HAMMERSLEY, M. and WOODS, P. *The Process of Schooling: A Sociological Reader*, The Open University Press, Routledge and Kegan Paul.
BECKER, H.S. and GEER, B. (1971) 'Latent Culture: A note on the theory of latent social roles', in COSIN, B.R. *et al.*, *School and Society: A Sociological Reader*, London, Routledge and Kegan Paul.
BENNETT, N. *et al.* (1976) *Teaching Styles and Pupil Progress*, London, Open Books.
BERGER, J. and MOHR, J. (1982) *Another Way of Telling*, London, Writers and Readers.
BERGER, P.L. and LUCKMAN, T. (1967) *The Social Construction of Reality*, Harmondsworth, Allen Lane.

Bibliography

BERNSTEIN, B. (1974) 'Sociology and the Sociology of Education: a brief account', in REX, J. (Ed.) *Approaches to Sociology*, London, Routledge and Kegan Paul.

BERNSTEIN, B. (1969) 'A Critique of the Concept of "Compensatory Education"', in RUBINSTEIN, D. and STONEMAN, C. (Eds) *Education for Democracy*, Harmondsworth, Penguin.

BERTAUX, D. (Ed.) (1981) *Biography and Sciety: The Life History Approach in the Social Sciences*, London, Sage.

BIOTT, C. (1981) 'Evaluator, researcher, participant: Role boundaries in a long term study of innovation', in SMETHERHAM, D. (Ed.) *Rethinking Evaluation*, Driffield, Nafferton Books.

BIRDWHISTELL, R. (1971) *Kinesics and Context*, Harmondsworth, Allen Lane.

BOGDAN, R. (1974) *Begin Different: The Autobiography of Jane Fry*, New York, Wiley.

BOSTON PUBLIC SCHOOLS (1979) *Lau Implementation Plan*, Boston School Committee.

CARR, W. and KEMMIS, S. (1986) *Becoming Critical: Education Knowledge and Action Research*, London, New York and Philadelphia, Falmer Press.

CARSON, S. (1963) 'The Changing Climate' *National Rural Studies Association Journal*.

CARSON, S. and COLTON, R. (Ed.) (1954) *Lincolnshire 'Rural Science News'*.

CARSON, S. and COLTON, R. (Ed.) (1954) *Kent Association of Teachers of Gardening and Rural Science Journal* (4).

CARSON, S. and COLTON, R. (Ed.) (1957) *Rural Science News*, 10 (1).

CASEY, K. (1988) 'Teacher as author: Life history narratives of contemporary women teachers working for social change' PhD dissertation, Madison, University of Wisconsin; CASEY, K. and APPLE, M.W. (1989) 'Gender and the conditions of teachers' work: The development of understanding in America' in ACKER, S. (Ed.) *Teachers, Gender and Careers*, London, New York and Philadelphia, Falmer Press.

CLIFFORD, G.J. and GUTHRIE, J.W. (1988) *Ed. School: A Brief for Professional Education*, Chicago, The University of Chicago Press.

COSER, R. (1960) 'Laughter among colleagues: A study of social functions of humour among the staff of a medical hospital', *Psychiatry*, 23.

CURRICULUM DEVELOPMENT UNIT (1982) *Educational Achievement and Youth Development*, Dublin, Trinity College.

DANZIGER and CONRAD (1977) *Interviews with Master Photographers*, New York, Paddington Press.

DOLLARD, J. (1949) *Criteria for the Life History*, New Haven, Yale University Press.

DOLLARD, J. (1939) *Caste and Class in Southern Town*, New York, Anchor.

DOUGLAS, D. (1973) 'Pit talk in County Durham', *History Workshop Pamphlet No. 10* Reprinted in *Language and Social Class 1*, University of London, Institute of Education.

EDWARDS, A.E. and FURLONG, V.J. (1978) *The Language of Teaching*, London, Heinemann.

ESLAND, G.M. (1971) 'Teaching and learning as the organization of knowledge', in YOUNG, M.F.D. (Ed.) *Knowledge and Control: New Directions for the Sociology of Education*, London, Collier-MacMillan.

FARADAY, A. and PLUMMER, K. (1979) 'Doing life histories', *Sociological Review*, 27 (4).

FENSHAM, P. and INGVARSON, L. (1977) 'Case study research in science classrooms' Paper given to the Australia Association for Research in Education Conference, Canberra.

FLETCHER, C. (1975) *The Person in the Sight of Sociology*, London, Routledge and Kegan Paul.

GIBBERD, K. (1962) *No Place Like School*, London, Michael Joseph.

GIDDENS, A. (1976) *New Rules of Sociology Enquiry: A Positive Critique in Interpretative Sociology*, London, Hutchinson.

GLASS, D.V. (1971) 'Education and social change in Modern England', in HOOPER, R. (Ed.) *The Curriculum: Context, Design, and Development*, Edinburgh, Oliver, and Boyd.

GLENDENING, V. (1983) 'Slaughterhouse Epilogue', *Sunday Times*, 20 February, London.

GOODENOUGH, W. (1965) 'Rethinking "Status" and "Role": Toward a general model of the cultural organization of social relationships', GLUCKMAN, M. and EGGAN, F. (Eds) *ASA Monographs No. 1 The Relevance of Models for Social Anthropology*, London, Tavistock.

GOODLAD, J. (1975) 'A Perspective on Accountability', *Phi Delta Kappa*, 57 (2), October.

GOODSON, I.F. (1977) 'Evaluation and Evolution', in NORRIS, N. (Ed.) (1977) *Theory in Practice*, SAFARI Project, Centre for Applied Research in Education, Norwich, University of East Anglia.

GOODSON, I.F. (1980) 'History 13–16', in STENHOUSE, L. (Ed.) *Curriculum Research and Development in Action*, London, Heinemann.

GOODSON, I.F. (1981) 'Life History and the Study of Schooling', *Interchange*, 11 (4).

GOODSON, I.F. (1982) 'Life Histories and the Study of Teaching', in HAMMERSLEY, M. (Ed.) *The Ethnography of Schooling*, Duffield, Yorkshire, Nafferton.

GOODSON, I.F. (1983) *School Subjects and Curriculum Change: Case Studies in the Social History of Curriculum*, London, Croom Helm.

GOODSON, I.F. (1987) *School Subjects and Curriculum Change*, 2nd Edition, London, New York and Philadelphia, Falmer Press.

GOODSON, I.F. (1988) *The Making of Curriculum: Collected Essays*, London, New York and Philadelphia, Falmer Press.

GOODSON, I.F. (Ed.) (1990) *Studying Teachers' Lives*, London, Routledge.

GOODSON, I.F. (forthcoming) *The Teacher's Life and Work*, London, New York and Philadelphia, Falmer Press.

GOODSON, I.F. (forthcoming) *Subjects and Schooling: The Social Construction of Curriculum*, London, Routledge.

GOODSON, I.F. (Ed.) *Studies in Curriculum History Series*, London, New York, Philadelphia, Falmer Press. Series comprises:

1 GOODSON, I.F. (Ed.) (1985) *Social Histories of the Secondary Curriculum: Subjects for Study*.

2 McCulloch, G., Jenkins, E. and Layton, D. (1985) *Technological Revolution? The Politics of School Science and Technology in England and Wales Since 1945.*
3 Cooper, B. (1985) *Renegotiating Secondary School Mathematics: A Study of Curriculum Change and Stability.*
4 Franklin, B. (1986) *Building the American Community: Social Control and Curriculum.*
5 Moon, B. (1986) *The 'New Maths' Curriculum Controversy: An International Story.*
6 Goodson, I.F. (1987) *School Subjects and Curriculum Change.*
7 Popkewitz, T.S. (Ed.) (1987) *The Formation of School Subjects: The Struggle for Creating an American Institution.*
8 Woolnough, B.E. (1988) *Physics Teaching in Schools 1960–85: Of People, Policy and Power.*
9 Goodson, I.F. (1988) *The Making of Curriculum: Collected Essays.*
10 Cunningham, P. (1988) *Curriculum Change in the Primary School Since 1945: Dissemination of the Progressive Ideal.*
11 Musgrave, P.W. (1988) *Whose Knowledge? A Case Study of the Victorian Universities Schools Examinations Board 1964–1979.*
12 Finkelstein, B. (1989) *Governing the Young: Teacher Behavior in Popular Primary Schools in Nineteenth Century United States.*
13 McCulloch, G. (1990) *The Secondary Technical School: A Usable Past?*

Hammersley, M. and Woods, P. (Eds) (1976) *School Experience*, London, Routledge and Kegan Paul.
Henry, J. (1960) 'A cross-cultural outline of education', *Current Anthropology*, 1 (4).
Hirst, P.M. (1965) 'Liberal education and the nature of knowledge', in Archambault, R.D. (Ed.) *Philosophical Analysis and Education*, London, Routledge and Kegan Paul.
Hirst, P.M. (1974) *Knowledge and the Curriculum*, London, Routledge and Kegan Paul.
Hobsbawm, E. and Ranger, T. (Ed.) (1985) *The Invention of Tradition*, Cambridge, Cambridge University Press.
House, E. (1978) 'Evaluation as scientific management in US school reform', *Comparative Education Review*, 22 (3), October.
House, E. (1974) 'The conscience of educational evaluation', in House, E. (Ed.) *School Evaluation: The Politics and Process*, Berkeley, McCutchan.
Hoyle, E. (1969) 'How does the curriculum change? A proposal for inquiries', *Journal of Curriculum Studies*, 1 (2).
Jackson, B. and Marsden, D. (1962) *Education and the Working Class*, London, Routledge and Kegan Paul.
Jackson, P.W. (1968) *Life in Classrooms*, New York, Holt Rinehart Winston.
Jenkins, D. (1977) 'Saved by the bell', in Hamilton, D. *et al. Beyond the Numbers Game*, London, Collier-MacMillan.
Kemmis, S. (1976) ' "Telling it like it is": The problem of making a portrayal of an educational program', in Rubin, L. (Ed.) *Handbook of Curriculum*, Boston, Allyn & Bacon.

Bibliography

KENT RURAL STUDIES ASSOCIATION (1952).
KERR, J. (1971) 'The problem of curriculum reform', in HOOPER, R. (Ed.) *The Curriculum: Context, Design and Development*, Edinburgh, Oliver and Boyd.
KLIEBARD, H.M. (1988) 'Persistent curriculum issues in historical perspective', in GOODSON, I.F. (Ed.) *The Making of Curriculum*, London, New York and Philadelphia, Falmer Press.
LABOV, W. (1973) 'On the linguistic consequences of being a lame', *Language and Society*, 2.
LACEY, C. (1977) *The Socialization of Teachers*, London, Methuen.
LAVE, JEAN (1988) *Cognition in Practice: Mind, Mathematics, and Culture in Everyday Life*, Cambridge, Cambridge University Press.
LAWTON, D. (1975) *Class, Culture and the Curriculum*, London, Routledge and Kegan Paul.
LEVINSON, D.J. (1979) *The Seasons of a Man's Life*, New York, Ballantine Books.
LORTIE, D. (1975) *Schoolteacher*, Chicago, University of Chicago Press.
MACDONALD, B. (1975) 'Evaluation and the control of education' in MACDONALD, B. and WALKER, R. (Eds) *Changing the Curriculum*, London, Open Books.
MACDONALD, B. (1976) 'Who's afraid of evaluation?', *Education 3–13*, 14 (2).
MACDONALD, B. and WALKER, R. (Eds) (1975) *Changing the Curriculum*, London, Open Books.
MACDONALD, B. and WALKER, R. (Eds) (1974) *Innovation, Evaluation, Research and the Problem of Control: Some Interim Papers*, SAFARI Project, Centre for Applied Research in Education, Norwich, University of East Anglia.
MANNHEIM, K. (1972) *Ideology and Utopia: An Introduction of the Sociology of Knowledge*, London, Routledge and Kegan Paul.
MARX, K. (1969) 'The eighteenth brumaire of Louis Napoleon' in MARX, K. and ENGELS, F. *Selected Works* Vol. (Moscow Progress Publishers, p. 369).
MCCRAE, D. (1988) *Teachers, Schools and Change*, Sydney, Heinemann Educational Australia.
MCKINNEY, W.L. and WESTBURY, I. (1975) 'Stability and change: The public school of Gary, Indianna, 1940–70', in REID, W.A. and WALKER, D.F. *Case Studies in Curriculum Change*, London, Routledge and Kegan Paul.
MEDAWAR, P.B. (1967) *The Art of the Soluble*, London, Methuen.
MEDAWAR, P.B. (1963) 'Is the Scientific Paper a Fraud' *Listener* 70 Sept.
MORTIMER, J. (1983) *Clinging to the Wreckage*, London, Penguin.
MORTON, R. (1973) *Come day, Go day, God send Sunday*, London, Routledge and Kegan Paul.
MURDOCH, G. and PHELPS, G. (1973) *Mass Media and the Secondary School*, London, Collier-MacMillan.
MUSGROVE, F. (1971) *Patterns of Power and Authority in English Education*, London, Methuen.
NATIONAL RURAL STUDIES ASSOCIATION JOURNAL (1961).
NESBIT, R.A. (1969) 'Social change and history', quoted in WEBSTER, J.R.

(1971) *Curriculum change and crisis: British Journal of Educational Studies*, 3.

OBRDLIK, A. (1942) 'Gallows humour: A sociological phenomenon', *American Journal of Sociology*, 47.

OLSON, G. (1974) 'Servitude and inequality in spatial planning; Ideology and methodology in conflict', *Antipode*, 6 (1).

PARLETT, M. and HAMILTON, D. (1972) 'Evaluation as illumination: A new approach to the study of innovatory programs', *Occasional Paper 9*, Edinburgh, Centre for Research in Educational Sciences.

PEGG, R., Interview, 78.10.9.

PHENIX, P.M. (1968) 'The disciplines as curriculum content', in SHORT, E.C. and MARCONNIT, G.D. (Eds) *Contemporary Thought on Public School Curriculum: Readings*, IOWA, W.C. Brown Co..

PLUMMER, K. (1983) *Documents of Life: An Introduction to the Problems and Literature of the Humanistic Method*, London, George Allen and Unwin.

POLANYI, M. (1962) *Personal Knowledge: Towards a Post-Critical Philosophy*, London, Routledge and Kegan Paul.

POLSKY, N. (1971) *Hustlers, Beats and Others*, Harmondsworth, Penguin.

PRING, R. (1972) 'Forms of Knowledge and General Education', *General Education*, (19).

PRITCHARD, M. (1957) 'The rural science teacher in the school society', *Journal of the Hertfordshire Association of Gardening and Rural Subjects*, (2), September.

RADCLIFFE-BROWN, A.R. (1953) *African Systems of Kinship and Marriage*, London, New York, Oxford, Oxford University Press.

REID, I. (Ed.) (1987) *The Place of Genre in Learning: Current Debates*, Deakin University Victoria, Typereader Publications, (1).

REID, W.A. (1978) *Thinking About the Curriculum*, London, Routledge and Kegan Paul.

SCHWAB, J.L. (1978) *Science, Curriculum and Liberal Education* in WESTBURY, I. and WILKOF, N., Chicago, The University of Chicago Press.

SCHWAB, J.L. (1969) 'The practical: A language for curriculum', *School Review*, Vol. 78.

SCUDATO, A. (1974) *Mick Jagger*, London, WH Allen.

SEGAL, C. (1984) *The Observer*, 17 June, London.

SHEEHY, G. (1981) *Pathfinders*, London, Sidgwick and Jackson.

SHEEHY, G. (1976) *Passages: Predictable Crises of Adult Life*, New York, Dutton.

SHIPMAN, M.D., BOLAM, D. and JENKINS, D. (1974) *Inside a Curriculum Project: A Case Study in the Process of Curriculum Change*, London, Methuen.

SIKES, P.J., MEASOR, L. and WOODS, P. (1985) *Teacher Careers: Crises and Continuities*, Lewes, Falmer Press.

SIMONS, H. (Ed.) (1980) *Towards a Science of the Singular*, Norwich, University of East Anglia, CARE Occasional publications No. 10.

SIMONS, H. (1987) *Getting to Know Schools in a Democracy*, Lewes, Falmer Press.

SMITH, L.M. and GEOFFREY, W. (1968) *Complexities of an Urban Classroom*,

New York, Holt, Rinehart and Winston.

SMITH, L.M., GABRIEL, R., SCHOTT, J. and PADIA, W.L. (1976) 'Evaluating the Effectiveness of Outward Bound' in CLASS, G.V. (Ed.) *Evaluation Studies Review Annual*, 2, Beverley Hills, Sage.

STAKE, R.E. (1972) *An Approach to the Evaluation of Instructional Programs: Program Portrayal vs. Analysis*, AERA Annual Conference, Chicago.

STENHOUSE, L.A. (1975) *An Introduction to Curriculum Research and Development*, London, Heinemann.

STENHOUSE, L.A. (1977) *Case Study as a Basis for Research in a Theoretical Contemporary History of Education*, Centre for Applied Research in Education, Norwich, University of East Anglia.

STENHOUSE, L.A. (1980).

STUBBS, M. and DELAMONT, S. (1976) *Explorations in Classroom Research*, London, Wiley.

SUGGETT, D. (1986) 'Curriculum 85: The conference of the Australian Curriculum Studies Association', *Journal of Curriculum Studies*, 18 (2).

SYLVESTER, D. (1973) *History 13–16*, London Schools Council.

TERSON, P. (1970) *Zigger, Zagger: Mooney and his Caravans: Two Plays*, Harmondsworth, Penguin.

VEBLEN, T. (1962) *The Higher Learning in America* (reprint of 1918 edition), New York City, Hill and Wang.

WALKER, R. (1974) 'Classroom research: The view from SAFARI', in MACDONALD, B. and WALKER, R. (Eds) *Innovation, Evaluation, Research and the Problem of Control*, Norwich, University of East Anglia.

WALKER, R. (1971) *The Social Setting of the Classroom: A Review of Observational Studies and Research*, University of London, Unpublished MPhil thesis.

WALKER, R. (1973) *The Nuffield Approach*, Mimeograph, Ford SAFARI Project, CARE, Norwich, University of East Anglia.

WALKER, R. (1974) 'The Conduct of Educational Case Study', in MACDONALD, B. and WALKER, R. (Eds) *Innovation, Evaluation, Research and the Problem of Control: Some Interim Papers*, SAFARI Project, Centre for Applied Research in Education, Norwich, University of East Anglia.

WALKER, R. and ADELMAN, C. (1972) 'An alternative to television', *The Times Educational Supplement* 19 May.

WALKER, R. and ADELMAN, C. (1975) *A Guide to Classroom Observation*, London, Methuen.

WALKER, R. and WIEDEL, J. (1985) 'Using pictures in a discipline of words', in BURGESS, R. (Ed.) *Field Methods in the Study of Education*, Lewes, Falmer Press.

WALLER, W. (1932) *The Sociology of Teaching*, Dover Books.

WARING, M. (1979) *Social Pressures and Curriculum Innovation: A Study of the Nuffield Foundation Science Teaching Project*, London, Methuen.

WEBSTER, J.R. (1971) 'Curriculum change and "crisis"', *British Journal of Educational Studies*, vol xxiv, No. 3.

WENNER, J. (1970) *Lennon Remembers*, Harmondsworth, Penguin.

WESKER, J.R. (1971) 'Curriculum Change' and 'Crisis', *British Journal of Educational Studies*, 3.

WESTBURY, I. (1973) 'Conventional Classrooms, "Open" Classrooms and the

Technology of Teaching' *Journal of Curriculum Studies*, Vol. 5 (2).

WERTHMANN, C. (1963) 'Delinquents in School', *Berkeley Journal of Sociology*.

WHYTE, W.F. (1955) *Street Corner Society: The Social Structure of an Italian Slum*, 2nd edition, Chicago, The University of Chicago Press.

WILLIAMS R. (1965) *The Long Revolution,*, Harmondsworth, Pelican Books.

WILLIAMSON, B. (1974) 'Continuities and discontinuities in the sociology of education', in FLUDE, M. and AHIER, J. (Eds) *Educability, Schools and Ideology*, London, Croom Helm.

WILLIS, P.E. (1977) *Learning to Labour: How Working Class Kids Get Working Class Jobs*, Farnborough, Saxon House.

WIRTH, A.G. (1983) *Productive Work in Industry and Schools*, New York, University Press of America.

WISE, A.E. (1979) *Legislated Learning: The Bureaucratization of the American Classroom*, Berkeley, University of California Press.

WITHALL, J. (1956) 'An objective measure of a teacher's classroom interactions', *Journal of Educational Psychology*, 47.

WOODS, P. (1982) Ethnography and Theory Construction, Paper given at a conference on The Ethnography of Educational Settings, Whitelands College, London.

WOODS, P. (1979) *The Divided School*, London, Routledge and Kegan Paul.

WRIGHT MILLS, C. (1970) *The Sociological Imagination*, London, Penguin.

WRIGHT MILLS, C. (1979) *Power, Politics and People*, London, New York and Oxford, Oxford University Press.

YOUNG, M.F.D. (1971) 'Curriculum as Socially Organized Knowledge' in YOUNG, M.F.D. (Ed.) *Knowledge and Control: New Directions in the Sociology of Education*, London, Collier-MacMillan.

Index

Abraham Moss Centre, 100
academics, viii, 200–4
Acker, S., 144
action research, 44, 139–41, 148, 162, 202
Adelman, Clem, 4, 5, 139
advisers, 95–7, 102–3
alienation: of curriculum theory, 150–67; in learning situation, 53, 55, 75
applied research, 94–5, 106, 162
APU (Assessment of Performance Unit), 101
Atkin, J.M., 187, 191
Atkinson, P., 203
Auld Report, 95
autobiography, 135, 143–4

Ball, S.J., *Teachers Lives and Careers*, 146–7
Barnes, John, 146
Barton, L., 161–2
Becker, Howard, 5, 78, 145
Beloe examinations for secondary modern schools, 132
Bennett, Neville, 9
Berger, John, 1, 106, 159
Bernstein, Basil, xi, xiv, 4, 15, 25, 73, 186
Bertaux, D., *Biography and Society*, 136, 174
bilingual schooling, 182–3

biography, 116–7: and intersection with social structures, 174–5
Birdwhistell, Ray, 34
black Americans: humour, 34–5; study of non-standard spoken English, 104
Bloom, Melvyn, 84–5, 85–6, 87, 88, 90, 91, 92
Bolam, Ray, 96, 181
Boston schools, 182–96
boundaries, 17, 33, 36
Brugelman, Hans, 5
Bruner, J.S., 156

capitalism, 2
career stages amd decisions, 146–7
Carr, Wilf, 139–40, 202
Carson, S., 127, 131
Casey, Kathleen, 147
Centre for Applied Research in Education (CARE), University of East Anglia, 113, 139, 161
chief education officers, 96
Clandinin, 140
classroom: communication structures, 22, 27:-and use of humour, 28–43; experience as research subject, 81–93; identities, 7–27; organizational elements, 25, 29; *see also* formal classroom situation; informal classroom situation

Index

subcultures, and humour, 33
subject, authority of the, 108
subjectivity, 159
Sylvester, D., 165
symbolic interactionism, xii, 159, 197
systems analysis, 151, 158

'tacit' knowledge, 80, 93, 158
teacher: as-person, and -as-educator,
  52, 70–1, 83, 84–93, 145;
  classroom identities of, 21–2,
  70–1; dual allegiance, 41; as role
  models, 144; use of humour, 28–43
teacher autonomy, 81, 179–80, 192–6
teacher development, collaboration
  and, 148–9
teacher dropout, 147
teacher education, and autonomy,
  193–4
teacher shortages, 147
teacher socialization, 114
teacher stress, 67, 81, 147
teacher-pupil relationships, 11–15
teachers' lives, 141–2, 144–5, 148–9:
  critical incidents in, 44–71,
  121–32, 147; and educational
  research, 70, 137–49; factors
  supporting study of, 143–8
teaching: alternative culture for,
  72–9; broadening the data base for
  studying, 142–8; relationships and
  curriculum content, 54, 185;
  solidarity in profession, 140;
  unique elements of, 145–6
theory: 'grounded', 199; implications
  of, 198–204; and practice, 158–9,
  198
tradition, invented, 179–80
tripartite system, 121
'trivium', 1
Trotsky, Leon, 153

UNCAL (Understanding Computer
  Assisted Learning), 70, 71

universities, 149, 157, 169, 171–2

values: connotations in research, 97,
  100–2, 136; inversion of, 43;
  social, 94
Veblen, T., 170
video-tape recorders, 82
vocationalism, xii-xiii
vulnerability, 141, 148

Walker, Rob, 5, 7–27, 28–43, 44–71,
  80–93, 94–106, 107–13, 161,
  182–96, 197–204; School Subjects
  and Curriculum Change, 117, 119
Waller, Willard, viii, 202
Wandsworth Emergency College,
  122
Waring, Mary, 117, 118
Weber, M., 159
Webster, J.R., 115
Wenner, J., 45, 74
Werthmann, C., 74, 77–8
Westbury, I., 153, 167, 172
Whitby, Geoff, 128
Whorf, Benjamin, 73
Wiedel, Janine, 97
William Tyndale School case, 95
Williams, R., 119
Williamson, B., 176
Wilson, Edmund, 104
Wirth, A.G., 151
Wise, A.E., 150–1, 152
Withall, John, 22, 23–4
Woods, P., 114, 144, 147, 173
working class culture, 74
working class pupils: alienation from
  learning, 53, 55–6; and self-
  motivating teaching methods, 57
Wright Mills, C., 175
Wrotham Secondary Modern School,
  123–6

Young, M.F.D., 118
youth culture, 48, 70, 74, 145